Praise for *Lighting Up*

"Great voice ... fascinating ... [her] voice [is] compelling—hectoring, insinuating, insistent.... In the end, you can't help liking her, and waiting eagerly for the next installment of her memoirs." —*Newsday*

"This fascinating memoir takes readers along Shapiro's insightful and vulnerable journey through talk therapy to achieve her goal of smoke-free living ... raw and relatable.... Recovering from the patient's perspective is less common and far more powerful." —*Cleveland Plain Dealer*

"Shapiro proves her mettle as the grand dame of deprivation.... belongs at the top of the must-read column ... of resolutions for the new year ... [An] inspirational and often hilarious portrait of a woman who boldly clears the smoke from her head once and for all." —*Newark (NJ) Star-Ledger*

"Shapiro manages to keep the format fresh.... Three stars." —*New York Post*

"The truth, the whole truth, and nothing but the truth about substance abuse ... a wickedly funny memoir of how we love our addictions and how difficult it is to bid them adieu." —*Illinois Times*

"Warning: This book invites serious overidentification.... Not only do I feel like I've known this woman since birth, I'm starting to think maybe I *am* her.... In the sharpest and funniest scene in a book full of them, Shapiro grills Winters about his own life." —nerve.com

"A keen, revved-up account of dropping addictions ... Her razor-sharp sense of humor provides balance and perspective. The manic energy Shapiro brings to her life instills her memoir with a theatrical freshness." —*Kirkus Reviews*

"Shapiro's wit and honesty elevate the work, and her sessions with her cool, intelligent psychologist capture all that's both absurd and mundane about such encounters." —*Publishers Weekly*

"This is no cringe-inducing self-help book.... Four stars." —*Jane*

"Shapiro hilariously nixes ciggies, only to pick up other no-nos.... Laughing with a sister quitter could help you stay on track." —*Self*

"An exuberant, self-deprecating wit."

—The Book Babes, goodhousekeeping.com

"[Shapiro] confesses details of her battle to stem substance abuse, and she does so with wit, sophisticated insight, and candor."

—*Style Magazine*

"Part of Shapiro's charm is her unflinching honesty and humor."

—*New York Press*

"In the greatest comedy tradition, her pain equals genius, and manages to capture the hard truth.... This is neurotic gonzo journalism at its finest." —*North Bay Bohemian*

"[Shapiro] takes her readers on a hilarious tour through her neuroses."

—*Gothamist*

"*Lighting Up* is a memoir to make you laugh, cry, and identify—and it just may motivate you to tackle addictions and self-defeating bad habits with renewed, even fiery determination." —*am New York*

Praise for *Five Men Who Broke My Heart*

"A sly, candid memoir ... A disarmingly frank account of what happens to [Shapiro's] present when she decides to revisit the past in the form of five ex-lovers. What is best about this memoir is Shapiro's desire to tell the whole truth about her delusions and obsessions, as well as her break-throughs and triumphs." —Pam Houston, *O, The Oprah Magazine*

"Playful ... entertaining." —*New York Times Book Review*

"Shapiro is bitingly funny and revealing." —*USA Today*

"Susan Shapiro's voice is so passionate and honest, it's bewitching."

—Erica Jong

"Sly, funny, on the money." —Rita Mae Brown

"A *Bridget Jones's Diary* for the married set...."

—*Washington Post Book World*

"Susan Shapiro's promiscuously readable guilty pleasure of a memoir has a caustic, urbane feel ... a Seinfeldian quest to settle accounts with five exes ... a comedy of manners." —*Elle*

"Witty, canny, ballsy." —salon.com

"Shapiro's often funny and always heartfelt recollections of past relationships are so entertaining, it's a shame she doesn't have an endless supply of material.... A delightfully kaleidoscopic authobiography of an impulsive and passionate woman who comes of age with style."
—*Publishers Weekly*

"Susan Shapiro is a funny and original writer, with a soulfulness beneath the humor that makes it moving as well. She's one of the funniest writers about love and marriage and family that I know of today."
—Ian Frazier

"This is an engaging, amazing, extremely emotional memoir. Susan Shapiro writes so well about love gone wrong that *Five Men Who Broke My Heart* broke my heart too."
—Molly Jong-Fast, author of *The Sex Doctors in the Basement*

"Deft, diverting, and laugh-out-loud funny." —*Forward*

"*Five Men Who Broke My Heart* is like slipping into a warm, inviting bath. It's easy to take to, relaxing, and a pleasant diversion from the reader's everyday headaches.... Shapiro reveals all, slicing her life to the bone and summing up her lovers in wry sentences ... a fast and funny read that pulls us forward, curious to discover how and why relationships with five interesting, intelligent men imploded."
—*Milwaukee Journal Sentinel*

Also by Susan Shapiro

Five Men Who Broke My Heart

Food For the Soul (co-editor)

LIGHTING UP:

How I Stopped Smoking, Drinking and

Everything Else I Loved in Life

Except Sex

SUSAN SHAPIRO

Delta Trade Paperbacks

LIGHTING UP
A Delta Book

PUBLISHING HISTORY
Delacorte Press hardcover edition published January 2005
Delta trade paperback edition / January 2006

Published by Bantam Dell
A Division of Random House, Inc.
New York, New York

Book design by Carol Malcolm Russo

Three short sections of this book have appeared, in slightly different form,
in the *New York Times Magazine, New York Observer,* and the *Forward.*

Library of Congress Catalog Card Number: 2004052663

Delta is a registered trademark of Random House, Inc., and
the colophon is a trademark of Random House, Inc.

ISBN-10: 0-385-33834-1
ISBN-13: 978-0-385-33834-9

Published simultaneously in Canada

www.bantamdell.com

146742244

For my beloved father,
who passed on his dark hair, olive skin,
stubborn streak, and passion for
books and cigarettes

AUTHOR'S NOTE

Names and identifying characteristics
of some people portrayed
in this book have been changed
to protect privacy.

Part One

Chapter 1

OCTOBER 1996

"**A**aron wants you to know that he misses you and can't live without you," Dr. Winters said, looking right in my eyes and smiling.

I turned to Aaron, my cute, curly-haired, six-foot-four ex-boyfriend, whom I'd broken up with six weeks before. His face was expressionless. It felt awkward to be sitting so close to him on the couch without touching. For three years I'd begged him to accompany me to my therapist, Dr. Goode. He refused, insisting that emotional insight would destroy his career as a TV comedy writer.

"He's very happy you could make it here today," Dr. Winters continued.

"Who are you?" I asked. "Cyrano de Bergerac?"

The scene was even more bizarre because, as I'd told Aaron, our exhausting, turbulent, three-year bicoastal affair was seriously over. He agreed, but begged me to try one couples' session with his new psychoanalyst, just for closure. I agreed, just for closure, but made it very clear that I'd already fallen, head over spiky black high heels, for another man.

"Aaron said you were dating someone new," Dr. Winters said.

I nodded, feeling claustrophobic. In the past I had only bared my soul to female shrinks. The male head doctors I'd met were old Jewish guys in gray tweeds who smoked pipes; I could never talk about oral sex with anybody who resembled my grandfather. I admit I was intrigued when Aaron warned me, just before we'd walked in, that Dr. Winters was young, unconventional, and wildly provocative. With an office two blocks away from my West Village one-bedroom, I imagined angry art therapy, or complicated, cryptic Jungian dream analysis. I wasn't expecting a short-haired, clean-cut, smiley WASP, let alone one who looked like the actor Pierce Brosnan. I pondered how Aaron, the least emotionally adventurous man I'd ever met, had stumbled onto the James Bond of psychotherapy.

"So, when are you getting rid of the other guy?" asked Winters, still smiling.

"The other guy, Joshua, is deeply in love with me," I said. "What a pleasure to be with a man who has room for a woman in his life."

"You can't be serious," Winters said.

"I'm always serious," said I.

No wonder Aaron called him young. He looked forty-five; they were probably the same age. Though he was seated, Winters appeared shorter, about six feet tall. He had a slighter build than Aaron, who was the nerdy Jewish bear type I usually went for. Aaron and I were dressed the same, in black jeans, sweaters, and leather jackets, rebels without a cause. Dr. Winters dressed like an adult: navy wool slacks, white shirt, classy red and blue tie, beige blazer. Was it cashmere? His outfit was calculated, colorless enough to project anything onto. He could have been a lawyer, book editor, international spy.

"Why can't I be serious about Joshua?"

"Because you're so happy to be sitting here next to Aaron," Dr. Winters said. He was trying to brainwash me.

"I'm just here out of morbid fascination," I said, looking around his small, dusty office. There was only room enough for the couch, leather chair, French country desk, and Oriental rug. Too many miniature embroidered pillows for a middle-aged straight guy. One sensed Dr. Winters was married with kids, a model citizen. But I imagined a grisly past filled with illicit sex and rage and turmoil.

"Just morbid fascination?" He looked hurt. "Aaron makes it sound like love."

Who did he think he was sweet-talking—a dumb thirteen-year-old girl? "Look, buddy," I said, "your patient can't even commit to living in sin."

"What kind of inanity has he been feeding you?" Dr. Winters switched to a warm conspiratorial tone, as if he were now my closest girlfriend, completely on my side. "What did he tell you?"

"After three years, he refused to see me on weekdays. He'd only go out on weekends. So I said, 'Fine, let's go in.' Then Spider-Man here decides we can't have dinner—or sex—during the week. Which is why I found an easier guy who's not strangling his own dick with this boring fear of intimacy shit."

Winters looked at Aaron and said, "She does have a point."

Aaron, who hadn't yet said a word, sat up tall and finally said: "I like Batman better."

"Because Batman is upper class," I told Winters. "And lives in a cave with a cool black sports car."

"No," Aaron said. "Because Batman is the only one without superpowers."

The heterosexual men I'd known in the Midwest were sports freaks. Aaron's pseudointellectual crowd of East Coast TV comedy writers, whom he'd first met working at the *National Lampoon,* got off on deconstructing the myths of superheroes.

"The other heroes all have special powers?" Winters seemed fascinated.

Aaron nodded, lowering his voice, as if he were sharing state secrets. "Spider-Man was bitten by a radioactive spider. Green Lantern got his power ring from an alien. The Flash got his super speed from a lab accident."

"Superman left Krypton and landed in a yellow sun system," said Winters, getting into the act.

"But Batman was just an ordinary guy who studied hard," Aaron said. "He gave himself power."

"To avenge his parents' murder by killing all bad guys in the world," I threw in.

"You're a true Freudian?" Winters asked me.

"Can you see why I fell for a shrink?" I asked him.

"I don't think she should be going out with a shrink," added Aaron.

"Your ex-fiancée, Lori, was a shrink," I argued. "You went out with her for ten years." Underneath his black sweater, I could see he'd worn the light-green Gap T-shirt I'd given him last Hanukkah. He knew I thought he looked good in light green.

"Lori wasn't a shrink when I met her," he argued back.

"I know. You drove her to it."

"She was the one who recommended Dr. Winters," Aaron let slip.

"Lori knows him?" This fifty minutes was getting stranger by the second.

"He's her thesis adviser in the psychology program at Columbia," Aaron said.

"Lori's your protégée?" I asked Winters, who shrugged.

"You're bringing your latest ex-girlfriend to see the mentor of your former fiancée?" I asked Aaron, who shrugged too.

It was so idiotic, it had to be true. Aaron was a procrastinating hermit incapable of throwing away any book, article, or piece of clothing, but he never lied. I needed a cigarette. Did Dr. Winters let patients smoke during sessions? At first Dr. Goode had let me smoke but then she'd banned it, afraid that I was inhaling my hurt instead of expressing it, getting further away.

"What can we do to get you back?" Dr. Winters asked, his smile mischievous and engaging.

"Nothing." He seemed annoyingly pleased with himself, having too much fun juggling other people's lives and hearts and psyches.

"What if he stayed over weekends, Tuesdays, and Thursdays, and he proposed?" Dr. Winters threw out.

"Impossible." I shook my head. I was almost over the breakup. Trusting either of them was completely out of the question. "Aaron made it clear that he doesn't want to live together, get married, or have children. Which is why we're broken up."

Dr. Winters looked at him and said, "She thinks you can't do it."

"I can do it," said Aaron. "Just not yet."

"He's forty-five and never been married," I said. "What's he waiting for—Social Security?"

"He could do it faster if you dumped whatshisname," Dr. Winters reprimanded.

"His name is Joshua, and he's a great guy." I left out that Joshua was long-distance, bipolar, too skinny, and in the middle of an acrimonious divorce and custody battle for his two kids. "Joshua's not afraid of marriage," I taunted. "He got married when he was twenty-two."

"You're going out with a MARRIED shrink?" asked Aaron.

"He's getting divorced, but he's not afraid to remarry," I shared. "He already brought it up."

"Joshua mentions marriage after a few weeks and you're not running in the other direction?" Dr. Winters asked me.

"Is taking ten years to propose our control group?" I asked him.

I was a thirty-five-year-old writer, freelancing for the best publications in the country, for God sakes, not to mention a popular journalism teacher. I was not going to sit home, waiting for a man to call. Joshua called twice a day, like clockwork. I could get my work done. Who needed drama and headaches? I was tired. What time was it? I'd forgotten my watch, the silver one Aaron gave me in L.A. for my last birthday. I'd twisted the gift into hopeful metaphors: He was putting me on his time frame. He was giving me eternity. It wasn't too late. I was mad at myself for misreading everything.

Until Aaron turned to me and said, "Ten years is too long."

He had curly, lopsided salt-and-pepper hair I missed running my fingers through. I inched closer, accidentally brushed my arm against his big thigh. Joshua was shorter and smaller. I didn't want to pledge my life to a man who had thinner thighs than I did. He was still married, anyway; his divorce could take years. Did Aaron really make it sound like love?

"She is finished waiting and wants to know when," Dr. Winters said, opening his date book and taking a pen from his pocket. "Today's October sixth. Can we say by Halloween?"

"How about November twenty-second?" Aaron threw out, the negotiation now between the two of them.

"Why the twenty-second?" Winters asked.

"The day Kennedy was shot," I explained.

While Aaron wrote Dr. Winters a check and made another appointment, I sat in the book-filled waiting room, dying for a cigarette. I inspected the rows of antique clocks on the wall, all telling different times. I felt disoriented, as if I'd taken a spin in a time machine and wasn't sure where I was. There was a brochure on the table. Along with being a psychoanalyst and Columbia professor, Dr. Daniel Winters was also a certified practitioner in treating substance abuse and addiction. I'd never thought of myself as an addict, although after a dozen years with Dr. Goode, I was clearly addicted to therapy.

Finally James Bond and Batman emerged from the inner sanctum. When I said goodbye, Dr. Winters held out his hand and slipped me his business card, which I put in my pocket.

"Winters is an addiction specialist?" I asked, confused because Aaron wasn't an addict. I followed him down two flights of creaky stairs in the prewar building. I pulled my pack of Capri Menthol Lights from my pocket, slipped a slender white cigarette to my lips, but didn't light it until we reached the first floor. "I thought he was a couples' therapist."

"He sees all kinds of patients, but his specialty is substance abuse," Aaron said. "Love is an addiction. We'll get the love patch." He opened the door for me. "Want some coffee?"

"Sure," I said, though neither of us drank coffee. Inhaling and letting smoke out several times, I felt calmer. I loved cigarettes; I'd been smoking since I was thirteen years old. Since it was impossible for me to stop, I'd quit trying. "How long have you been seeing Winters?"

"For six weeks," Aaron said. "He wanted to meet you after our first session but I wasn't sure if I was going to like him."

"Do you?" I asked, as we crossed Greenwich Avenue.

"First book I saw on his shelf was *The Great Gatsby,* the best novel ever written. I started to reread it. Before every session, I read more. I told Winters that when Gatsby's dead in the swimming pool, I'll be cured."

"What did he say?"

"He asked the right question. What page was I on?"

"You talked about me in your first session?" I asked.

"Just to tell him what a stupid bitch you are."

"You're using present tense?" I stubbed out the cigarette on the sidewalk in front of my favorite diner, the Village Den. "A beautiful stupid bitch," he said, leaving out the verb altogether, as we crawled into a booth in the smoking section. I ordered a large diet soda. Aaron ordered chicken soup. It was a telling choice, as if today's level of intimacy had made him ill; he needed Jewish medicine. He was too quiet. I feared the promise of marriage was a mirage, that he couldn't even say the word without Winters as his front man. Then he put his hand on mine. I took it back to light another cigarette, which I vaguely knew was my self-medication. Along with the caffeine-laden diet soda I constantly sipped.

"I wonder if Winters helps nicotine addicts."

"I don't think he discriminates," he said. "Why? Do you want to quit smoking?"

"No." I hoped Aaron didn't think I was willing to stop anything to get back together with him, 'cause I wasn't. "I have to go soon," I said. "I'm on deadline. I need a quote for this article I'm working on. 'Ways New Yorkers Kick the Habit.' I bet he'd be good. He's funny."

"Ha-ha funny or hard joke funny?" inquired Aaron.

"He's just witty. You're gut-wrenchingly hysterical," I reassured. "Much funnier than Winters."

Outside my red brick apartment building, Aaron stopped and kissed me on the cheek. I waited for him to say, "Let's finish this conversation," or "Let's have dinner later," but he didn't. Unsure whether everything or nothing had changed, I gave him a quick hug but didn't invite him to come upstairs. Inside I hung up my black leather jacket and reached for my pack of cigarettes. Dr. Winters' business card tumbled out of my pocket. I noticed the note he'd written on the back. His words, in black Flair pen, read: "Listen slower for quiet love." A mini shrink haiku. I thought it was sweet and picked up the phone to call Dr. Winters. Not about Aaron, about my article.

He agreed to give me ten minutes on the phone and answered my questions quickly. He said he had smoked a pack a day for twenty years himself, and had a rough time quitting. I didn't believe him; he seemed the type who'd bum two cigarettes at a bar every other Saturday night. I'd already interviewed an acupuncturist, a hypnotherapist, a psychopharmacologist, and two SmokEnders leaders who'd said it was easy to nix nicotine when one was ready. Dr. Winters disagreed with all my other experts. "When you stop smoking, you're not going to feel better. You're going to feel like hell for a year," he said. "You can't successfully treat an addiction without confronting the deep psychic issues behind it. If you don't, the addiction returns."

I liked that he'd said "you," as if he were talking directly to me. Was he? After twelve years of therapy, I'd found confronting deep psychic issues to be highly overrated, but the guy could give a quote. His words made a forceful lead.

After my piece ran, Dr. Winters received many calls and subsequent press mentions. This annoyed Aaron, who said his ex-fiancée, Lori, had recommended Dr. Winters for HIM, not me, and that in one session, I'd extracted a marriage proposal (which came on November twenty-second, right on schedule) and turned his new shrink into a media whore.

In my favorite wedding photograph, Aaron was gallantly sparking my long menthol cigarette with my father's silver lighter.

A week later Claire, my best friend in the universe, with whom I'd chain-smoked since I was thirteen years old, suddenly quit smoking after two sessions with some guru doctor in Boston. I felt as if she'd left cigarettes in order to leave me, since I had sort of left her by tying the knot with Aaron. Not being able to smoke with Claire shook up my life more than my new nuptials.

"I'm not quitting just because you did," I warned her. I wasn't ready yet.

"Who asked you to?"

"I'm not flying to Boston. I hate Boston." I felt abandoned and jealous.

"Who said you should go to Boston?" she asked. "Why don't you call Dr. Winters?"

"I'd have to be a masochist. Why would I pay somebody who's already telling me I'll have to feel like hell for a year?"

"Because this is the man who got you married," said Claire.

Chapter 2

OCTOBER 6, 2001

10 A.M.: Woke up and stuck nicotine patch on my arm, determined to once and for all quit cigarettes. Wrote list of reasons: live seven years longer, please my husband Aaron, have healthy children, be socially acceptable. Tore up list and made better one: look younger, have fewer wrinkles, spite enemies. Scratched patch, which itched like hell. Went out to buy carrots, celery, grapes, ten packs of Juicy Fruit, lollipops, and rice cakes. Finished it all by 11 A.M., desperately craving cigarette. Went back out though it was pouring rain. Bought four packages of fat-free Entenmann's brownies. Tried to work. Instead polished off brownies and took nap.

12:30 P.M.: Woke up feeling ill from brownies and cold caught walking in rainstorm. Took a Sudafed. Felt better. Felt delirious. Tried to work, but couldn't concentrate on anything but wanting to smoke. Read in newspaper that schizophrenics and manic-depressives in mental hospitals committed suicide when their cigarettes were taken away. Decided never to have children. Called brother Brian, the trauma surgeon, who'd been sending X-rays of cancerous lungs, asking him to send 65 more nicotine patches. Took another Sudafed. Was there a Sudafed group in the city?

2 P.M.: Tried to work. Developed bad cough and sore throat. Read another newspaper, scanning obits for people who died of lung cancer, happy to see one in his sixties. Took another nap. Dreamed I was stuck in the middle of a tidal wave and lit up, then felt sad I fell off the wagon. Woke up and found I wasn't smoking but wanted to be. Remembered that my friend Irene warned me about weird patch dreams. Called my cousin Miranda, who said that after she quit, her concentration didn't come back for a year. Took one hundred deep breaths. Breathing was overrated. Read touching article on recovery mission at Ground Zero, noting only that rescue worker in picture was smoking. Felt exhausted though I had just slept, read, and eaten all day. When it stopped raining, took a walk, counting that nine stores and bodegas on the block sold cigarettes. Called my friend Roger, who said, "My neighbor quit in three days on Nicorettes. Try Nicorettes," though I told him I tried them and threw up, then went out and smoked two packs to get the taste out of my mouth. Read that nicotine's harder to quit than heroin. Took another Sudafed. Thought about smoking. Brian called back to say don't even think about smoking with patch on, somebody's fingers fell off.

4 P.M.: Spent twenty minutes on exercise bike. On *Oprah:* "Mothers Who Want Their Violent Kids Taken Away" put problem into perspective. Called my sister-in-law Monica, who complained every time I took out a cigarette for twenty years but now said, "I can't talk to you when you're like this, you're too intense." Tried to work but realized it was impossible to be a freelance writer, nonsmoker, and thin in the same

year. Sudafed was losing its bite, e-mailed Aaron to pick
up Comtrex on his way home from work. Negotiated self-
destructive behaviors: decided that taking sleeping pill, smoking a joint, getting drunk, and making myself come was better
than a cigarette and Oreos, though not if done on the same
night.

5:30 P.M.: Felt depressed and edgy, sweating and coughing
up phlegm. Hand shook while reading another paper, where
tobacco company executives said nicotine wasn't addictive.
Made list of ten seventy-year-old smokers still alive. Had dinner with Irene, who kicked habit and gained twenty-four
pounds in four months, sure it was the smart choice. Considered heroin. Stopped at Duane Reade to buy pacifier, pretending it was for my two-year-old niece. Pondered how anyone
could expect morality from people who plastered penis-faced
camels all over the country. Bumped into novelist pal Kathy,
who blew smoke in my face while saying, "It's great that you're
stopping." Tried to come up with one famous writer who didn't
smoke or drink.

6:30 P.M.: Forced myself to gym. Did high-impact aerobics,
weight machines, sat in steam room, had a Swedish massage.
Walked out of health club, longing for cigarette. Glared at
smokers on street, enraged they looked so beautiful and happy.
Added up money saved from not smoking. Spent $100 on
Swedish massage, $46 on way home for seven boxes of fat-
free cookies, twenty-seven cinnamon sticks, and three Lean
Cuisines. Snapped rubber band around wrist one hundred
times. My father the oncologist e-mailed, "The patch doesn't
really work," forgetting that the last time he quit his thirty-
five-year three-pack-a-day habit he gained thirty-five pounds
and smoked a six-inch cigar every night. Decided neurosis
was genetic. On stationary bike watched *Saturday Night Live*
rerun, which quoted tobacco company execs saying that the
400,000 annual smoking-related corpses weren't really dead.

Downstairs neighbor complained bike made too much noise. Did serenity exercises. Pictured sitting on a tropical beach, where I was happily smoking.

8 P.M.: Ate more celery, fruit, salad. Polished off Oreos. Felt bloated and constipated, dying for cigarette. Aaron came home with Comtrex and roses to congratulate me on my first smoke-free day. Burst into tears. "Maybe you want to call Dr. Winters?" he asked. Screamed, "No! Fuck you!" Unable to sleep all night, wondering why I was perfectly healthy smoking two packs a day for two and a half decades but got so sick on the day I quit.

Chapter 3

OCTOBER 2001

"I smoked for twenty-seven years," I said, crossing my legs, a little nervous. It was easier to be bold and flirty last time, with Aaron to blame everything on. Now, sitting on Dr. Winters' light-blue couch, I felt self-conscious and married. "My last cigarette was three weeks ago."

"I bet you feel like hell," he said.

"No, it's not as bad this time."

Although five years had passed, he looked exactly the same. White shirt, brown pants, beige tie—did he always wear a tie to see patients? No jacket this time. He must have turned fifty, as Aaron had. It annoyed me how well they both had aged. No bald spots or wrinkles. I'd made the appointment for six P.M., but Dr. Winters hadn't called me in until six-fifteen. Was he running late? I hated people who were always late; I was always early. I was glad I'd worn my black jeans and tight black sweater. Had I chosen my high-heeled boots, which I couldn't walk well in, because they were sexy? I'd never seen a male shrink alone before. I felt like I was cheating on Aaron with one of his friends.

"I enjoyed that article you wrote, about ways New Yorkers quit cigarettes," he said. "Especially when you brought yourself into it, with the oncologist father who smoked. And the surgeon brother sending pictures of tumorous lungs. Was that true?"

Quoting what I had written was a smart way to disarm me, though I already found Dr. Winters fascinating. He was the only one who knew exactly why my husband had married me. He had me in the palm of his hand by the ring on my finger. I bet he was surprised that I'd called to request a solo session.

"How's married life?" he asked.

"Never better." I feared I looked older.

"How's Aaron?" he asked.

"Good." I was five years younger and less dour when I'd first met him. Or, I hated to realize, I was much funnier and more charming with cigarettes. I'd lost my smoke screen. "We moved too; we're two blocks from here," I said.

His new office was more modern and three times the size of his old one. There was mauve carpeting, two small rugs, built-in bookshelves, a whole bunch of framed diplomas hanging on the wall between two huge plants. I wasn't a fan of indoor plants—even the real ones looked fake. But I liked having Dr. Winters close, within walking distance—just in case of a storm or emergency.

"What's really going on?" he asked.

It had been a difficult year. I'd turned forty and felt afraid of dying for the first time. Then two planes hit the World Trade Center, two miles away, as if to underscore my fear of how little time could be left. It wasn't just me being morbid. All my downtown neighbors and friends were emotionally raw, drinking, smoking, having "trauma sex." Claire had gone

back to cigarettes again after five years clean, just as I had
quit. I seemed to be having "trauma sobriety." Broke in the
eighties, happily married during *Sex and the City*—I was always out of sync.

"Why do you have six diplomas?" I asked. "Undergrad,
master's, Ph.D. What else is there?"

"I did postdoctoral work in substance abuse," he said.

I recalled seeing that in his brochure. "Tell me about your
addiction therapy," I said. "I've tried to quit smoking a hundred times. I'm on the nicotine patch. I never heard of doing
talk therapy sessions just for addictions before. What approach do you use? The twelve-step method?"

"My own approach."

"I minored in psychology in college. Addiction treatment is
usually behavioral, right?" I asked. "Like AA, with the meetings, or SmokEnders, where you smoke brands you hate and
snap your wrist with a rubber band?"

He shook his head no.

"Well, what do you call it?" I was a writer, I needed a name
for it.

"It's psychodynamically oriented," he finally offered.

"Why so vague?"

"Why do you want to quit?"

"Smoking cigarettes is like killing yourself slowly," I said.
"I think I've decided that I want to live."

"Don't reduce it to significance." He was dismissive, bored
even.

"It's time to get healthy."

"Why now?" he asked.

"Midlife crisis?" I tried. "I recently turned forty."

"Kind of cliché."

His unflinching stare bothered me. I looked around the
dimly lit room, the shades drawn. The same artwork was dis-
played on his walls as last time. I recognized the pretty pink

and blue three-tiered collage; I found it soothing. Just as I was about to miss his antique clocks, all telling different times, I found them hiding on the bookshelves behind me. Instead of in his waiting room, he'd put them in his inner office now; he'd wanted them closer.

"Aaron hates when I smoke," I said. "Not that a spouse can demand you stop doing something self-destructive. Well, maybe heroin. Isn't nicotine harder to quit than heroin?"

He scrawled in his notebook, then looked at me. "Aaron is not the reason you came here."

"No, he's not the reason," I said. Whenever Aaron told me to quit, I told him to fuck off and worry about his own bad habits. I'd never had any use for masculine authority. I adored my husband, father, brothers. Yet I'd never felt that any male had ever really understood me or penetrated the idiosyncratic inner workings of my brain. Until that one gonzo therapy session with Dr. Winters, who got me right. Or at least he got me Aaron.

"Tell me what you want," he said.

"The things in life I want most, I can't get."

This seemed to wake him up. He jumped in quickly. "What do you want most?"

I'd walked in feeling sure that I needed to quit my fierce twenty-seven-year smoking habit once and for all. I recited my long list of reasons to myself. I wanted to get healthier, live longer, be a good role model to my students, overcome my father's smoking curse, please my husband, have a baby. Instead I shocked myself by blurting out: "I want to get my book published."

"Is it any good?" he asked.

"I think so. But I can't find an agent. I might just start sending it to editors myself. I'm known for getting everyone else's books published. Five students last term. It's a perfect paradox."

"What's stopping you?" Go deeper, he was demanding.

"It feels connected to smoking," I tossed out. "Or my not being able to quit smoking. What the hell does psychodynamically oriented mean?"

"What do you think it means?"

"Something about how past experiences still motivate you?" I asked him.

"Isn't it better to have a literary agent send out your book to editors?" he asked me.

"Yes, an agent is better," I answered. "But the agent I was hoping would represent it, this woman Lilly West, wants me to make all these changes I'm not sure about."

"Do you think she's smart?"

"I wouldn't send my work to an agent I thought was dumb. Lilly's brilliant," I said. "Still, what good is that if she's not interested?"

"She didn't say she wasn't interested."

Why did he seem more curious about my book than my bad habit? "She said make all these changes that would involve months of editing without a guarantee that she'll take me on as her client." I was warm, I shouldn't have worn a turtleneck. "Don't you know the way it works with agents?" I snapped. "They only want you when you don't need them."

He glanced at his notebook and said, "You have to listen to everything Lilly West tells you."

"I've had a successful twenty-year career without an agent." I resented his tone. "I'm a very self-sufficient person. Everyone in my family works for themselves. We don't play well with others."

"You depend on substances, not people," he said.

Aside from his black leather perch and my blue couch across from him, there were two empty chairs by his desk. Why so many? Did he do family therapy in here? I thought of my mother, the compulsively cheerful overfeeder, and my father, the chain-smoking oncologist. Dr. Winters was right. All the independent souls in my extended sect were obsessed with either food or cigarettes; that was your choice.

"For me, the substance is singular," I said. "It's just the cigarettes." I didn't depend on other people because they always disappointed you.

"Really?" He looked skeptical.

He was wrong. In my case it was singular. I'd never been a big drinker—I just had enough wine at dinner or champagne at a party to get me a tiny bit tipsy. I was too needlephobic to shoot up, too much of a control freak to drop acid. In college I used speed to cram for finals, and ate magic mushrooms at a few outdoor Bob Dylan concerts, but I'd never really been addicted to anything but nicotine. Unless he counted junk food. Or chewing ten packs of Juicy Fruit gum in ten minutes. Or drinking too much caffeine. Or having hot sex with the wrong men in grad school. Or marijuana, in which case I was in trouble. I'd been a stoner since junior high, but assumed that toking fell in the "smoking" category.

"My personality can be described by that line, 'The problem with instant gratification is that it takes too long,'" I quoted *Postcards from the Edge*.

"Exactly," he said. "You have an inability to delay gratification or stay with bad feelings. You've cut corners for twenty-seven years, never learning how to cope. You survived by smoking a pack a day."

"Two packs a day," I admitted. "Is it too late? What do I do?"

"What happened last time you quit?"

"I gained twenty-three pounds in three months, couldn't write a word, and wanted to kill myself." I said it quickly, like it was a joke. "I know everyone says you should only stop one bad habit at a time but . . ."

"Of course, you have to diet too," he said, as if it was stupid to think otherwise. "But you can't take away something you depend on without replacing it."

"What do I replace it with?" I asked.

"A program that involves group meetings or exercise classes or—"

I cut him off. "There's no way I'm going to join groups or take any classes. I can't stand groups and I teach four classes a week at NYU and the New School. I don't have time to take them." His advice pissed me off because it was so generic, as if he were counseling any moron who walked in off the street.

"Okay," he said. "Then keep using the highest dose of the nicotine patch every day. And keep seeing me."

"How about once a month?" I suggested.

"That's not enough," he said.

"How much is enough?"

"Twice a week."

"I can't afford that." I was a freelance writer and part-time teacher. Did he think I was made of money? I'd already done a dozen years of therapy with Dr. Goode, who'd had a sliding scale. She'd danced at my wedding, which seemed the equivalent of graduating with honors. Then I stopped seeing her. I didn't have the time or energy to reenroll; I just needed a brief refresher course to get me off tobacco.

"At least once a week for a year, then," he said.

The thought of fifty-two sessions was overwhelming. I couldn't afford that either. I felt as if I were on a second date with a guy who was already clamoring for a commitment. He could be a snake who wanted my money. He was too good-looking.

"And you have to do everything I say."

I laughed out loud. "You're kidding?"

He shook his head no. He was not kidding.

"You mean with the addiction stuff?"

"I mean with everything," he said.

"Is this like giving yourself over to the higher power in AA?" I asked, needing the words for it. "You're God now?"

He smiled.

I had long ago reconciled being a raging feminist with my rape-me-ravage-me fantasies. Yet feeling this vulnerable, with him having all the power, now seemed cerebrally sadomasochistic, as if I were paying him to hurt my mind slowly. I didn't want to admit it, but there was something exciting about taking a subservient role for a change.

"What happens in a year?" I asked.

"You will be an ex-smoker and your book will get published," he said.

"What if I relapse?"

"If you smoke, even once," he warned, "your book won't happen."

That was the most ridiculous lie I'd ever heard in my life. What an arrogant bastard he was! Or was connecting my book's publication to staying on the wagon an ingenious ploy? It was the one temptation he knew I couldn't resist.

"I can't afford you," I told him.

"What can you afford?"

After the couples' therapy appointment that led to Aaron's proposal, I'd recommended several friends who were still his patients. I'd also provided him with free press. I decided that Dr. Winters should charge me the same as he'd charged Aaron in the past. "One twenty-five a session," I said, calculating that I'd be paying him two dollars and fifty cents a minute. I couldn't afford that either, but somehow he'd managed to make me feel that I couldn't afford not to try.

He nodded.

"It's a deal. I'll give you a year," I said. "I'm ready now, I'm feeling less tense. It'll be easier this time. I'm happily married. We've redone our apartment, it looks good. You should see …"

As I was talking, Dr. Winters pulled out one of his business cards, wrote on the back of it, and handed it to me. It read: "Underlying every substance problem I have ever seen is a deep depression that feels unbearable."

Chapter 4

NOVEMBER 2001

"It was instant love, the first second," I told him. "I was thirteen years old."

I pulled a black-and-white photograph from my purse and handed the worn picture to Dr. Winters. It was a tourist shot, taken in Italy, the summer I was thirteen years old. I was wearing a tight blue halter, denim skirt, and high-heeled sandals, my long chestnut brown hair flowing behind my shoulders. Standing on the street with my right arm outstretched, it looked like I was holding up the Leaning Tower of Pisa. The other illusion was how slender I looked. Something about the odd side angle made my legs appear longer, my breasts bigger, and my waist tiny. When my mother first saw it, she said I looked like a model in a fashion magazine.

He had started our session twelve minutes late; he was always running late. Though he added the time to the end of the session, this was not a good pattern. I'd never brought a visual aid into therapy before. The last month I'd been feeling so old and frumpy. Did I want to prove to him that I was once young and pretty? He stared closely at the five-by-seven image.

"You certainly don't look thirteen," he said, then returned it to me.

"Interesting that it's a trick photograph," I said, slipping it back into my purse. "Don't you think?"

"Because you tricked the world into thinking you were okay?" he asked.

"I was okay," I said. Or had I tricked myself?

I described how I talked my parents into letting me go on the student program in Europe that summer my world changed. Mostly juniors and seniors had signed up, but the teachers in charge reassured my folks that I'd get academic credit and enhance my transcript. Luckily my mother, who'd grown up poor, was living vicariously through her kids, determined to give us everything she'd never had. She convinced my father this trip was the ticket to get me into a good college. Thus, at thirteen, I spent three months traipsing around Italy, France, Germany, and England, with students from all over the world.

By day I visited the Louvre, the Tate Museum, the Jeu de Paume, and studied intensive French, Renaissance history, and romantic poetry. By dark I ditched my nerdy schoolmates and hit the nightclubs with my new best girlfriends, two bubbly blond eighteen-year-old party gals from North Carolina. (I told them I was eighteen too.) I'd sneaked a few of my father's cigarettes before, but the Southern blondes taught me to blow smoke rings with their Gauloises and Gitanes, and how to seductively suck smoke from my mouth to my nose. We sipped sloe gin fizzes with skinny Italian men who said *"Ciao bella"* and tried to stick their tongues in my mouth. Preferring French inhaling to French kissing, I didn't let them, but I liked how hard they tried.

Though still a virgin, I returned to suburban Michigan twenty pounds thinner, quoting Baudelaire, and swearing in three languages. I started wearing makeup and perfume with my torn jeans and high heels. At five foot seven and 127 pounds, I got picked up more than I got carded, but soon I had a stack of fake I.D.s just in case. Since I couldn't find foreign brands in West Bloomfield drugstores, I smoked a pack a day of More Menthol Lights, which were thin, brown, and twice the length of regular cigarettes. They looked like anorexic cigars.

"You had an array of fake I.D.s when you were thirteen?" Dr. Winters was surprised.

"Everyone did," I said. I was suddenly intrigued with the idea that, at such an early age, I'd needed so much false identification.

I was nervous when Claire's family visited Michigan for her brother's bar mitzvah in the fall of 1974. Our families had been close forever; our mothers were pregnant four times in a row together. Mr. Lyons, an automobile executive, kept moving Claire's clan to different countries in Europe and South America. We'd sent each other confessional twenty-page letters, presents, and school pictures, but after two years apart I wasn't sure that Claire and I would easily reconnect. While our dads and brothers played touch football on the lawn, our mothers were the cheerleaders and lemonade and cookie servers. Claire and I sneaked to the man-made beach.

"You look great," I told her. "You're so thin."

"No, you're thin. I'm fat." Though we'd both grown to the same height, had dark hair, big shoulders and feet, I noticed her breasts were bigger.

"What are you, a C cup already? I'm just a B." I pulled my shirt up to show her my bra. She pulled hers up to show me.

"What base are you on?" she asked.

"Pinto, an Italian guy I met in Rome, stuck his tongue in my mouth and grabbed my boobs over my shirt, but I pushed him away," I admitted. "Does that count?"

"Pinto? My guy in São Paulo was named Paco," she said.

"What if he's the same guy?" I joked.

Sitting down on the broken picnic table, she pulled out a blue and white box of Rothman cigarettes from her shirt pocket, a pack of matches hanging off the plastic. I pulled my More Menthol Lights from my purse.

"You smoke cigarettes too? I'm so glad you smoke," she said as she lit mine and I lit hers.

"Yours are so fancy, what are they, European?" I asked.

"Yours are too long, like skinny black dicks." She giggled.

I cracked up, thrilled that my transformation had miraculously paralleled changes in Claire. I took it as a sign from God. All the sophisticated, fascinating people I liked best were smokers.

In high school the ritual of smoking fit me perfectly. I'd puff away while listening to Bob Dylan or Motown music and scrawling really bad poetry into my black spiral notebook. I fancied myself a beatnik, unaware I was a little late. I bought a cheap black lighter. Having the pack and black Bic in my denim shirt pocket (copying Claire) made me confident, as if I were armed and protected. I felt instantly worldly, cooler, happier. When Claire (my only true friend until now) went back to Brazil, I soon became popular without her. I secretly attributed it to the cigarettes.

Joining a Jewish youth organization called B'nai B'rith, I'd spend hours at Howard Johnson's restaurant on Northwest Highway with a gaggle of girlfriends. We sipped diet soda, chain-smoked, and flirted with Southfield boys for hours. Since I couldn't yet drive, every night Arlene, one of the cool older girls in my chapter, would honk her horn and I'd rush outside, ready to rock and roll, or at least table hop. My mother was as pleasantly shocked by my newfound popularity as I was. She didn't like that I smoked, but how could she stop me when my father smoked too? I appeased my parents by acing advanced placement classes and the SATs. I soon ordered

New York City college catalogs. My father quoted a line from my new Steely Dan album: "The things that pass for knowledge I can't understand." My brothers joked, "How are you gonna keep 'em down on the farm, after they've seen Paree?"

"Just thinking about that summer makes me want to be young and smoke again. Everything was so much better when I came home," I told Dr. Winters. "It seemed like the cigarettes were magic."

"They certainly fixed a lot of problems for you," he noted.

It was as if I'd prescribed myself appetite suppressants, relaxers, and antidepressants, to be taken between twenty and forty times a day. Whenever I felt hungry, happy, sad, hyper, or nervous, I lit up and let the smoke soothe me. No wonder I was so attached to the ritual.

"What was it like before you started smoking?" he asked.

"Not so good. I had a rough early adolescence."

"Tell me about it."

"It was horrible. No friends. I was ugly, fat, alone."

"Describe home."

"I'm stuck in my pink room in a big white house in the bleak Midwest with three brilliant science-brain brothers I can't compete with. My dad is this important handsome medicine man. My mother is a gorgeous, warm, redheaded fertility goddess. I flunked being her."

"How did you feel?"

"Miserable. From another planet. Claustrophobic, like I was doomed to a life of domestic insanity. I couldn't wait to get out of there."

"You have to go back," he said.

"I spent twelve years delving into my past with Dr. Goode. I talked about it, analyzed it, wrote about it. I'm sick of my childhood," I said. "Everyone's sick of my childhood."

"You were smoking when you underwent therapy," Dr. Winters said. "It was like you were wearing armor."

"I miss my armor." I started to cry. Why had he chosen mauve carpeting, beige blinds, and blue couches? There was too much stuff in here, it was too busy. Everything clashed; it was giving me a headache. "I hate being scared and wimpy like this," I complained. "I used to be so brave."

As a headstrong, adventurous teen, I couldn't wait to prance through Europe. I'd fled to college at sixteen, two years early, and boldly reinvented myself as a troubleshooting New York City journalist in my twenties. Now, at forty, I could barely leave my apartment. Instead I sat on the couch with the covers over me, as if I were recovering from a serious illness. All I could do was teach my classes, read, and scrawl incoherent lines into my journal in between sobbing jags.

"Where has Aaron been?" Dr. Winters handed me a box of Kleenex.

"He's never around. He's too busy working twenty hours a day on two animated TV shows at the same time. Working on one show is time-consuming enough. I can't compete with two."

"It's like he has two mistresses," Dr. Winters opined. "Let's call his jobs Angela and Shirley."

I cracked up. "How about Laverne and Shirley?" Blowing my nose, I kept the box next to me on the couch. "So he was busy with his harem until two A.M. last night. When he got home, we had a fight."

"Why?"

"Because he showed up with a bunch of those lollipops I like, even though I told him you said I'm not allowed to have them anymore."

Since nicotine gum made me nauseous, I'd replaced cigarettes by chewing regular gum and sucking on Blow Pops, the kind with bubble gum in the center. They worked wonders because the candy shell lasted for a long time and the white stick jutting out of my mouth simulated a cigarette. It seemed like an innocent rite, but in no time I was eating twenty daily. At Dr. Winters' request, I found out they were fifty calories each. That meant I was consuming a thousand extra calories a day, he said, solving the mystery of why I'd gained twenty-three pounds so quickly the last time. It wasn't metabolic changes, it was the sugar I kept shoving into my mouth.

In anticipation of my new stop-smoking attempt, Aaron had stocked up on Blow Pops. He'd hidden them all over his den, shelves, and briefcase so that, like he did before, he could hand me one whenever I was edgy and I'd be quiet. I thought I could handle a few Blow Pops a day. Dr. Winters thought otherwise. I was still on the twenty-one-milligram patch, the highest dose available, slowly weaning myself off nicotine, yet he'd insisted I quit the Blow Pops cold turkey.

"I miss my lollipops." I started sniffling and laughing at the same time. "When Aaron gives me one I feel like he's my mom, sticking a pacifier in my mouth to shut me up."

"Did she do that?"

"Picture having four little kids in six and a half years, no help, a workaholic husband. He's a smoker, she's an over-feeder. Whenever I was upset, they'd just stick something in my mouth—a bottle, pacifier, food, anything to mollify me." It occurred to me that my favorite doctors also used to give me lollipops. Except this withholding son-of-a-bitch doctor, who was taking them away. "Aaron's trying to sabotage me and make me fat."

"He is not," Dr. Winters said. "He just hates to see you hurting."

The way he said it made me love Aaron again. Poor guy, working so hard while having to put up with my recent mood swings, misplaced rage, and overwhelming sadness.

"I'm barely functioning," I said. "My editor at the *Times Book Review* e-mailed to ask if I would review a new Holocaust memoir. Usually I'd be thrilled. Today I just started bawling. I'm not sure why. What if I can't concentrate enough to get it done?"

"Is that why you were upset?"

"No. I can't bear to read any more books about the Holocaust, I want my own book to get published, and after fifteen years he's still assigning me three hundred words for a hundred dollars."

"Why don't you say no?"

Was he nuts? "Of course I'm going to say yes. I could never say no to *The New York Times*."

"This time say no," Dr. Winters said. I'd mistaken his inflection. It wasn't a question, it was an order. "Stop freelancing."

"You're not serious?" By the stern expression on his face, I could see that he was. "Why? I've been freelancing for twenty years."

"How many pieces have you written for them?" he asked.

"I've had more than a hundred bylines in the *Times*," I answered quickly; I'd counted. "Starting in 1985, I've been published in four different sections of the paper—the Book Review, the City Section, the op-ed page, and the Sunday magazine."

He didn't look the least bit impressed. "Stop chasing bylines you already have. It's too much stress," he said. "You mentioned that Aaron is working on two TV shows. Can't you live without the money you make freelancing?"

Aaron's TV work paid ten times my salary. He was so glad I was quitting cigarettes, he had offered to pay for my addiction therapy. I nodded yes to Dr. Winters, then had second thoughts. Producing a steady stream of bylines for prestigious publications was like keeping a gold star glued to my forehead. I prided myself on getting seven pieces a week in print. Was that another addiction I had to quit? No cigarettes, no lollipops, no hot new clips in the paper that everyone would read. I was used to the recognition and praise. Who would I be without it?

"I should quit teaching too," I said. After ten years of leading classes three nights a week, I looked forward to a well-earned break. My life would be so much mellower without a hundred needy students in my face, calling and e-mailing and begging me to edit their endless rewrites.

"No. Keep teaching at night and work on your book by day. That's all," he declared. "Do not write anything else."

It figured that teaching, the one exhausting activity that I couldn't wait to quit, he was forcing me to continue. "Why can't I take off a term or two?" I asked. A poorly paid, overworked adjunct professor of journalism, I pictured calling the heads of my programs to tell them I was giving myself a sabbatical.

"Teaching uses a different kind of energy," he said.

"I'm sick of it."

"You're good at it and it balances your life," he argued. "Plus you like your students."

That I did. I was relating to the kids in my classes more and more, especially the young, shy undergraduates. The weaker I felt, the more sensitive I was to their fragility.

"Aside from teaching and seeing you, I'm afraid to go outside. I get hurt too easily. I feel like I'm twelve years old again." I sniffled. "I can't go back there without armor."

"You're already back there," he said. "That's why you brought the picture to show me."

"I was so pretty and happy then," I said.

He shook his head no. "You already told me it was only a trick."

When had I told him that?

• • •

On my way out he handed me another card. In tiny letters on the back he'd written:

1. *Crying is good*
2. *Hug Aaron for an hour every night without speech*
3. *Drink water*
4. *What you're doing is very brave*

Chapter 5

DECEMBER 2001

The very first cigarette I smoked was my father's.

It was late at night. My parents and brothers were asleep upstairs. I was wearing the pink lace nightgown my mother bought me for my thirteenth birthday. I wandered through our big quad-level white house, as I often did before dawn. Tiptoeing down to my father's den, I turned on the lights. His built-in wooden shelves were filled with hardcover medical texts; I ran my fingers over their sharp edges. He loved to be alone in there, reading, hiding from the world. He'd sit on the worn leather couch, books and journals on his lap and newspapers stacked by his feet, half-hidden in a curtain of smoke. My father's den always scared me.

I used to stand behind the door, listening to him dictate complicated medical words into his small microphone: "Patient developed substernal chest pains radiating down her arms and neck ..." He had a skull paperweight on his desk.

An X-ray of a cloudy skeleton was still attached to the unlit light box. I opened the top drawer. Inside was a tangle of paper clips, stethoscope, cotton swabs. I rummaged through electric bills, health insurance forms, family photographs.

"What were you looking for?" Dr. Winters asked me.

After a dozen years of therapy, that one was easy. "His love," I said.

I touched the wrinkled pack of my father's Chesterfields. There were five cigarettes left. I took one out. Sitting where he liked to sit, in the corner of the couch, I held his cigarette to my lips. Lifting his square silver lighter, I touched the tip of the cigarette to the orange-blue flame. I sucked in quickly, the way I'd watched my father inhale for as long as I could remember. I thought it would burn my throat, like hot, spicy food. But it didn't hurt. It felt warm. I exhaled, then puffed again. I was a little dizzy, the inside of my throat tingling. I blew out slowly, feeling older, lit up, wildly dangerous. Afraid that he'd catch me, I stubbed it out in his green glass ashtray. I left it lying among his white ends and ashes, half hoping he'd smell the stolen smoke and know I'd been there.

"How far do I have to go back?" I asked.

"As far as you can," Dr. Winters said.

My grandfather Harry Shapiro, who smoked Lucky Strikes, was the least lucky guy you could ever meet. My father often spoke of his father's lousy life. His mother had deserted him in Poland, and didn't come back to get him until Harry was six years old. Although he was extremely intelligent, he was poor, uneducated, stuck running Shapiro's Windowshades on Delancey Street. He was tricked into marrying Yetta, who was a dozen years older than she'd said, hiding frail health. He resented my father, his only male child, perhaps because my father had a mother who'd adored him. Harry never forgave him for leaving the window shade business. He was the only Jewish parent in the world who didn't want his son to be a doctor.

My father's only sister, Shirley, was a smoker too. She kept Kool 100's in a black leather cigarette case with a loop on top for her black lighter. As a young woman, she was a fiery, stubborn, raven-haired beauty. "You're just like Shirley," my father used to tell me. He thought it was a compliment, but the comparison upset me because her life wound up being tragic. My father linked her sadness to Harry's, who thought girls didn't need degrees and refused to pay her college tuition. Instead Shirley married too young, found she couldn't bear children, and was widowed at twenty-six.

Shirley's second husband, Frank, was a very charming, funny guy who made her laugh. But Frank was either thin and unemployed, or fat and rich. He could never watch his weight and work in the same year. (Even the spouses of my family members seemed to depend on substances.) Frank got caught committing a white-collar crime and wound up skinny in jail. Shirley took to drinking along with smoking.

At first Harry had also refused to pay my father's NYU tuition. Family lore had it that my grandmother Yetta stuck her head out the window and threatened to jump headfirst. He finally relented. Yetta died young, of breast cancer. It was the same disease that killed Shirley. Picture the helplessness my father felt, not being able to save the first two women he loved. I had always thought it was the reason my father became a cancer doctor.

Harry lived to be eighty-five. "The monsters always live," said my brother Michael, a cardiologist whom I called "the heart doctor."

My father's first cigarette was a Lucky Strike he'd stolen from his father's pack when he was thirteen.

"How do you know?" Dr. Winters asked.

"I called to ask him yesterday," I said.

My mother once showed me a picture of my dad on the corner of East Broadway, hanging out with a group of friends. He was wearing a black leather jacket, the cigarette dangling from his lips. He was "handsome as a gangster," she'd told me. He remembered that first day too. "Her hair was bright red, same as her nails," he said. "I walked her home for hours."

They dated for the next five years. Supposedly he then proposed by saying, "I just got into medical school in Chicago. You coming or not?" She came, worked her way from secretary to buyer in a chain of drugstores, putting him through medical school. They moved to suburban Michigan, where they had four kids in six years. I was the oldest and the only girl, born during my father's residency.

Although there were obvious links between cigarette smoke and cancer by the 1960s, my father ignored them. He smoked at home, in his 1959 light blue Chevy, in the office where he had a private practice, at the hospital where he was chief of medicine (until the middle '70s, when they made him smoke outside). In one childhood picture, I'm sitting atop a stone elephant sculpture in front of the downtown Hudson's. My tall, dashing, dark-haired dad held me up there, a cigarette dangling from his lips, like the first time my mother saw him. I wondered if he was smoking a cigarette in the hospital on January 23, 1961, the very first time I'd laid eyes on him.

"How old were you when you first lit up?" I asked Dr. Winters.

"In high school," he said. "About sixteen."

"Was it hard for you to quit?"

"Yes, very difficult," he said.

I was so glad that he really wasn't one of those annoying faux smokers who could have one or two cigarettes a day or quit easily when they felt like it.

"It was really hard for my father to stop too," I said.

Picking up a notepad from his table, he put it down again. He seemed uncomfortable when I compared him to my father, who was twenty years his senior. Dr. Winters looked so young, I bet he was touchy about his age. I guessed that was why he liked antique clocks. Or was I the one in a time warp? At the beginning of our sessions, I never thought about his wife in New York, or his ex-wife and teenager in California, whom he'd mentioned on a few occasions to Aaron. Yet lately I'd been trying to picture his daughter. Dr. Winters, who was not a strict Freudian, didn't believe shrinks should keep their private lives secret. I wished he would. The long-distance daughter I'd heard about was now stuck in my head. Instead of Aaron's rival, Dr. Winters was turning into my father. As I regressed, she was my phantom rival for his attention.

My real doctor father was fifty, Winters' age, when he first tried to kick the habit. He smoked six-inch cigars every night instead. "They're phallic," my father told my mother, with a smile. "You wish," she said. Realizing he was inhaling the cigars and actually smoking more, he quit cigars too. He switched his addiction to oversized oatmeal-raisin cookies and gained twenty-five pounds. I've never met anyone who didn't gain a lot of weight when they quit smoking, and for years I used this as the reason I couldn't stop. My brother Brian, the trauma surgeon, conceded that nicotine was an appetite suppressor and it boosted your metabolism. "But here's your choice," Brian said. "Gain twelve pounds or die of lung cancer."

"He's smart," Dr. Winters said.

"If he stopped drinking, he'd lose thirty pounds," I countered.

Quitting cold turkey, my father was smoke-free for a whole decade. Then my mother said she started smelling smoke on him. She confronted him. He said no, he wasn't smoking again. Soon the neighborhood newsletter declared, "We have a Marlboro Man in our midst," reporting that someone was sneaking empty red cigarette boxes into other people's garbage late at night. My insomnia was inherited.

So was my oral fixation. My mother had tried to smoke once, when she was thirteen. "I took one puff and coughed my brains out. I thought I was going to die. Never again," she said. She grew up poor and an orphan; food on the table meant everything was okay. Everything had been more than okay for decades, but she still needed proof. A svelte size six for most of her life, my mother didn't smoke, drink, or overeat. She obsessively overfed. It was part of her identity. Every night she would serve huge bloody steaks, lamb chops, or brisket to my father and brothers, gleefully fetching them salt, steak sauce, green beans, mashed potatoes, sour cream, and butter. I gave up meat and ate alone in my pink room.

After Michael, her youngest, went to college, my mother started a party-planning business. Our basement was stuffed with Mylar balloons and baskets of Nutter Butter popcorn, sprinkled treats, and many kinds of dark and light chocolate. Neighborhood kids nicknamed her "the Candy Lady." I assumed her choice of profession was an excuse to overfeed the rest of the world.

"It's because nobody ever gave her a birthday party," my father told me. "You become what's missing."

My mother hated smoking. This was a serious problem, since the people she was closest to were always lighting up around her. With a tobacco-addicted dad, older sister, husband, and daughter, she might win the award for most exposure to secondhand smoke. My mother told me that her beloved father, Hyman Goodman, smoked a pack a day of unfiltered Lucky Strikes, the same kind as my paternal grandfather. She recalled that her father's fingers and teeth were stained yellow and that their Clinton Street tenement reeked of smoke. He died when my mother was twelve. After that she went to live in New Jersey, with her older sister, my aunt Ettie, a redheaded chimney. When her husband (a Marlboro smoker) died young, Ettie came to live with us in Michigan for two years. An overeater and a smoker, she took us weekly to Kmart to stock up on oversized Hershey's milk chocolate bars and cartons of Dorals, both of which she still enjoys at eighty.

When I pointed out that one could smoke and live happily until eighty, my brother Brian scoffed at me and said, "Aunt Ettie's had two heart attacks and needs a pacemaker."

"But she's had a happy life," my brother Eric piped in.

"It all comes down to genes," added my brother Mike.

"We were both blessed with three brothers," my mother told me all the time. Although all three of her brothers were short-term smokers, none of mine ever picked up a cigarette. If there was a smoking gene, as I strongly believe there is, I alone was the heir. Then again, I'd wanted the distinction. In a family of boys I'd felt weak and inadequate. Cigarettes made me bolder, unafraid of the world, less hungry. They gave me something to do with my hands and lips, literally creating a wall of smoke to protect me from getting too close to other people.

I've often pondered why I started smoking at the age of thirteen. My oldest brother, Brian, was already heavily in training for his bar mitzvah, the all-important day, according to ancient ritual, that a Jewish male becomes a man. Girls at our conservative temple didn't yet have bas mitzvahs. By picking up a cigarette, unlike my mother but like my father, I had decided who in the house I was going to emulate. Lighting a cigarette at thirteen, I was christening myself masculine.

"Isn't christening a Christian ritual?" Dr. Winters asked.

"Okay, it's a mixed metaphor," I conceded. "I meant to initiate or purify, as if being a female was bad or dirty."

"Worse than bad or dirty, in your perception it was powerless," he said, handing me my message of the day. It read: "You can adore your father and leave him at the same time."

Chapter 6

JANUARY 2002

"My first lover was a smoker," I said.

"Of course he was." Dr. Winters smiled.

A brown-eyed, curly-haired Canadian, David smoked Marlboro reds in a box, which he'd roll up in his T-shirt sleeve to show off his muscles. He lit my cigarettes, which seemed sexy and chivalrous when I was fifteen. I was impressed with his lighter, a black rectangular contraption with a digital clock in it. He said he bought it in Japan when he'd accompanied his father on a business trip. By sixteen, I'd switched to Virginia Slims Menthols, the brand all my girlfriends liked. I felt graceful smoking my long white filtered cigarette, cruising down Woodward in David's silver Camaro.

High-school summers David would take me to outdoor concerts at Pine Knob, where we'd light up twice. He showed me how to roll bags of strong, light-green dope into thin pin-sized joints. Long, slow drags of cigarettes were soothing, while holding in smoke from the joints made me feel emotional and intense. If nicotine was my drug of choice, marijuana came in a close second, and the combination was sheer bliss.

A premed student from a good family, David pretended he was a heathen. He said I was "an old sea hag" who had "breeder's hips" and "violent eyes." The cigarettes and dope fit with his bad-boy air. I was a good student who enrolled in the University of Michigan early, but I longed to be a bad girl. On weekends David drove to Ann Arbor to visit. We listened to Bob Dylan's *Blood on the Tracks,* smoked a joint before sex and a cigarette after. We went out, off and on, for five years, until my senior year of college. It was clear he was sleeping with my roommate when I found his hard pack of Marlboro reds and his black Japanese lighter in her purse.

My next boyfriend, Brad, a brawny Grosse Point WASP, was a nonsmoking, nondrinking, workout fanatic. He hated cigarettes and loved the cliché: "Kissing a smoker is like licking a dirty ashtray." Brad would remove the cigarette from my lips and break it in two. When we started sleeping together, I would brush my teeth before we kissed and leave his apartment after sex, in the middle of the night, to have a cigarette. It was the only afterglow I cared about.

Though Brad's constant carping about my smoking was annoying, I noticed two kinds of antinicotine zealots: those who didn't like cigarettes because "they're bad for you," which at least seemed like they cared about my health, then the more selfish ones who just didn't like the smell. Brad was both.

When I moved to Manhattan to get my master's degree at NYU in 1981, everybody in the big city seemed to smoke everything. Hippies passed around joints filled with marijuana and hashish in Washington Square Park, where you could buy ten dollars' worth of dope, twenty-four hours a day. Dime bags were also sold in fake East Village grocery stores or by drug dealers who delivered! Friends took me to Brooklyn cafés where Arab men smoked flavored tobacco in elaborate pipes that looked like bongs. Homeless people bummed cigarettes daily on Midtown streets. The Indian guys at my neighborhood bodega sold "loosies," one loose cigarette for an overpriced quarter, to those who couldn't afford a whole pack.

That December my little brother Michael visited New York for a weekend. I'd been excited to show him around, but we didn't get along too well. He hated my friends, as well as the Broadway play and downtown restaurants I took him to. At the time he was just a teenager, so I accompanied him on the cab ride to La Guardia and went inside to see him off. His plane to Michigan was delayed. I waited with him, buying him dinner at the airport and Yankees and Knicks caps and T-shirts to bring home for my other brothers. After he left I realized I'd spent all my cash and didn't have enough for a taxi home. (It was a Sunday evening, and years before the proliferation of ATM machines.) I boarded a Carey bus back to the city, which only cost four dollars. The closest it would take me was Wall Street. I'd have just enough money left for a seventy-five-cent subway token to get home.

I was the only rider on the bus. Sitting in the back, I felt lonely and tried not to cry as we headed out of the terminal and onto the highway. Suddenly the driver, a uniformed black man who looked in his thirties, asked if I was okay. Sniffling, I told him about the difficult weekend with my brother. He told me his name was Troy, and that his brother didn't like him either. He asked if I minded if he smoked. I said, "Of course not, I'm a smoker too." Troy opened his window and lit up. It smelled funny; it wasn't a cigarette. It was a thick joint.

Troy asked if I wanted some. I inched up to the first seat and he handed it to me. I took a hit and immediately felt dizzy. It was the strongest joint I had ever tasted. He told me it was laced with cocaine. Troy and I drove around toking, exchanging stories about being the black sheep of our families. After three frustrating days with my cranky kid brother, it seemed like a miracle. This was why I loved New York—you never knew what was going to happen next! In my stoned twenty-year-old brain, I decided that God was rewarding me for being so nice to my brother.

"Where do you live?" Troy asked.

"The Village," I answered.

"What street?"

Instead of dropping me off at the Wall Street bus stop, Troy drove me straight to my door. My doorman gave me an odd look when I got out of the Carey bus. I waved goodbye to Troy. In my pocket was another cocaine-laced joint that he'd slipped me on my way out. When I told my roommate Ellen the story, she said I was an idiot who could have gotten raped, had a drug overdose, or been killed in a traffic accident. She was worried that Troy knew where we lived and would come back. He never did.

I didn't tell her about his goodbye present. The next day, when Ellen was at work, I smoked the whole laced joint myself. It made me gleeful and hyper and I danced around my apartment naked for hours, listening to Motown music. Best of all, I didn't eat for two days after. Or realize that I'd basically smoked crack years before it wreaked havoc on the streets. Still, I never took the Carey bus again and always wondered about Troy when I'd read about bus accidents.

Cocaine seemed like a lot of fun, with a diet pill thrown in to boot. Yet at a hundred dollars a gram, it was too expensive. At forty dollars an ounce, I could barely eke out enough for my own bag of marijuana. I was bizarrely practical with my addictions. Cigarettes, which were then about a dollar and fifty cents a pack, remained my main fix.

My old shrink, Dr. Goode, also thought the Troy bus-ride episode could have been dangerous and questioned why I would do drugs with a male stranger driving the bus I was on. How depressed was I about my brother's rejection? Was I being blatantly self-destructive? I assured her I wasn't suicidal. Lighting a cigarette and inhaling a few times, I promised her I'd be more careful.

At the start, Dr. Goode let me smoke during our therapy sessions, assuming I would have one cigarette. After I smoked six or seven at each appointment, she asked me to stop. Even with two open windows, I assumed that she couldn't bear the smell. Yet she said the reason I had to refrain was because I lit up whenever I was upset, or coming to a subject that was difficult to talk about. I'd inhale and get quiet or change the subject. "You're sucking in too much," she explained.

In my twenties, I was a confessional poet obsessed with getting to the truth. I penned poetry and essays in revealing first-person style and founded a writing workshop based on sharing accurate, insightful criticism. I was politically outspoken and personally determined to examine my psyche deeply and honestly. All of my identities demanded candor. I wanted to face my faults. Hell, I reveled in them. Dr. Goode's comments were jarring, as if I were lying to her or myself. Could cigarettes be repressing my true feelings? It was the only reason to stop smoking that had ever made sense to me.

My favorite English professor, Joseph Brodsky, smoked unfiltered Lucky Strikes during his Modern Poetry lecture. I'd sit in the front row and light his cigarettes for him. (Nobody else was allowed to smoke during class, just him.) When he was done he'd throw his butt to the ground near me and I'd stomp it out. Once, during a particularly emotional dissection of Auden's "September 1, 1939" (which he made us memorize), he gave me a petrified look. I realized he'd run out of cigarettes, and I quickly reached in my briefcase and handed him one of mine. He glared at my long Virginia Slims Menthols with disdain.

"Beggars can't be choosers," I mumbled.

He took it, broke it in half so it was the size he was used to. I lit it for him. After that I carried an extra pack of unfiltered Lucky Strikes just in case. I hoped that wasn't why he gave me an A. With a several-pack-a-day habit, I wasn't surprised to learn he had serious heart problems. Were his continual cigarettes connected to his onetime imprisonment in Siberia? Missing his family in Russia? The sadness of exile? It was the first time I traced a link between smoking and depression.

I was heartbroken when he died, fifteen years later, in his early sixties, of a heart attack. Like my other intellectual idol, the pipe- and cigar-smoking Sigmund Freud, Brodsky's lifelong addiction to tobacco is what killed him. At least physically.

After finishing my master's degree, I landed a job as an editorial assistant in *The New Yorker* library. You weren't allowed to smoke in the magazine's large reference room. So I took many daily cigarette breaks, sitting on a shabby couch right outside, on the eighteenth-floor hallway, by the stairs. All the smokers gathered there. Confirming my belief that the most fascinating human beings lit up constantly, I met some of the world's greatest writers because of my bad habit. Yet I also knew that professional scribes tended to be more emotionally damaged and committed suicide in greater numbers than other people. I tried to make a list of all the famous writers who never drank or smoke, but I never came up with any.

Around this time I fell for Richard, a Dylan biographer with a mutt named Oscar. Though we had a Dylan obsession in common, Richard didn't like the smell of smoke (the selfish reason). I told him I didn't like the smell of dogs. After I moved into his two-bedroom railroad flat in the Village, he declared the apartment was nonsmoking. I wound up offering to walk Oscar in order to sneak cigarettes. After we split, he married a dog-loving nonsmoker. It was the second time it occurred to me that smoking could be a liability. Many personals in *New York* magazine asked for "a nonsmoker." I'd never met anyone through advertising, and the fact that a lot of men who took out ads didn't like women who smoked seemed a good reason to keep lighting up.

Still, the first time I really tried to quit smoking, when I was twenty-nine, was because of a man. George, the handsome theater professor I was dating, was very athletic. He ran and swam every day. He complained that his half-pack-a-day habit was ruining "his wind." I began working out with him and we decided to quit together. We planned a day at Jones Beach. He picked me up early that morning in his beige Honda Civic. After six hours, I was sweaty and itchy. I kept coughing, suffering through withdrawal with serious shakes. Ignoring my condition, George ogled passing bikinis. A screaming match resulted in my taking a cab back to the city, stopping to buy cigarettes on the way. That night he came over and apologized with yellow tulips from the Korean deli. "It's worse for you," he said. "Your dad smoked. I didn't know it would be so hard."

I also had no idea it would be such a battle to stop. When I smoked, I felt absolutely fine. Every time I ceased cigarettes, I got sick. My throat became sore, I coughed up phlegm, I was groggy, couldn't write, and all I wanted to do was eat, cry, or take a nap. My brain knew that these symptoms showed how dangerous cigarettes were. Yet avoiding the horrid withdrawal became another reason to continue.

As a compromise I cut down a little, trying to keep it to eighteen or nineteen cigarettes a day, telling myself that if I ran out, I couldn't buy another pack until the next morning. Sometimes it worked. Other times I'd desperately go through my garbage to find half-smoked butts, get edgy, and call the local deli to have another pack delivered at three A.M. I switched to Capri Menthol Lights, which were white but skinny, half the width of other cigarettes, with less tar and nicotine. Though medical experts wrote that low tar and nicotine barely made a difference, it made me feel better. For a smoker I could work out pretty well. Doing weights and running five miles in an hour on the treadmill daily, I was soon in the best shape of my life. So I was shocked when I learned that George was having an affair with one of his protégées.

To make matters worse, right after George left, I had a cancer scare. My trusted gynecologist, Dr. Cherry, called to say that my yearly Pap smear showed precancerous cells on my cervix. I feared it was from smoking, that I'd given myself a serious disease. My father, perhaps scared he could lose another female relative he loved to cancer, ordered me to see a doctor he knew at his Michigan hospital. I flew in for a biopsy. The next day the bad cells were lasered away, quickly and completely. There wasn't as obvious a link with smoking and cervical cancer as there was with lung cancer. Still, except for evidence that cigarettes helped schizophrenics in mental hospitals cope, nobody had ever implied that smoking was good for anything.

When I turned thirty I tried to halt my habit, this time with newfound urgency. On another Midwest visit, I had my father write me a prescription for the nicotine patch, which wasn't yet sold over the counter and cost twice the price of cigarettes. I put it on every morning. The patch itched and gave me spooky dreams. I gained weight and noticed lines under my eyes. I wasn't sure if it was worry or sadness that suddenly turned strands of my hair gray. I stared into my full-length, pink-framed childhood mirror and it hit me for the first time: I was no longer young. The last day of my trip, I went with my mother to her beauty shop and had my hair dyed back to its original color. I was raven-haired and immortal again. At least until the roots grew in. Two weeks later I started smoking again.

"Do you mind if I smoke?" I'd asked Aaron on our blind date. It was a casual question and a serious test. If a guy hounded me about smoking, I'd never go out with him again.

"The first woman I slept with was a smoker, so I associate cigarettes with sex," he said.

It was a good answer. It made me picture him in bed with a bohemian nymphette. Though he had never smoked, for the three years we dated, Aaron never bothered me about my smoking. He lit my cigarettes for me, never pointed out the smoking-will-kill-you articles in the newspaper, never relayed stories of chain-smoking relatives who'd died gruesome deaths of lung cancer, and said my tobacco dependency was my own business. So I married him. One week after our wedding in 1996, Aaron turned to me and said, "Now you have to quit smoking."

"Very funny." I wasn't laughing.

"I'm not joking." He wasn't either.

"I asked on our first date if you minded my smoking. If you said yes, I wouldn't have married you," I said. "I wouldn't have even gone out with you again."

"I know." Aaron shrugged.

It wasn't a terrible strategy. He knew that, at age thirty-five, after many horrible breakups, not to mention our three-year courtship, three engagement parties, three showers, two wedding ceremonies—one with a rabbi, one with a judge—and closing on a two-bedroom, two-bath, downtown Manhattan apartment, there was no way I was going to divorce him. Unless he was gay, having rampant affairs, or hitting me. But how could I leave him for smacking me with a mandate to improve my lungs and perhaps protect our future children? Part of the reason I wanted to get married was to be healthier, damn it.

It didn't seem fair. Aaron was ordering me to quit a personal custom he had actually implied turned him on during our courtship. The minute we'd closed the deal on our new living quarters, he'd turned into a Nicotine Nazi. I would not be forced to walk outside every time I wanted a cigarette. I thought of walking out altogether. Yet I'd just moved in, couldn't afford to move out again, and deeply loved him.

I had spent my life escaping male domination. I left my father's house at sixteen and lived alone for a decade and a half. Part of the reason I didn't wed until age thirty-five was my suspicion that marriage would be too imposing and intrusive. Now my worst fear was coming true: A man was in control of me. I rebelled against Aaron's orders by smoking more than usual. Unfortunately this only gave me a bad cough and headaches. Since I was actually getting sick of the disgusting and stupid daily ritual, I decided to quit in September.

For this attempt, I attached the nicotine patch to my back every morning when I woke up, and I bought a treadmill, which I forced myself to run on four days a week. The only thing that really helped were the Blow Pops, preferably grape flavored. (Though late at night even the despised strawberry would do.) Copying Kojak, I pretended I looked cool, surmising that the sugar tasted better than nicotine. When I got up to twenty lollipops a day I realized that, like my father and his oatmeal-raisin fetish, I'd just switched addictions. Still, weren't suckers better than cigarettes?

More disturbing, I could no longer write. I couldn't concentrate for more than a few minutes. I took naps during the day and continued to have bizarre patch-induced dreams. In a month the only work I did was update and resell the "Ways New Yorkers Quit Cigarettes" piece, where I'd quoted Winters, and pour out a new rant called "Quitters Never Win." It was a humorous take on going crazy trying not to smoke. My *New York Times Magazine* editor, who'd never smoked, said it made him want to try. "Quitters Never Win" became my most resold piece, currently in five different anthologies.

"See, you can write when you don't smoke," Dr. Winters commented.

"No, I can't," I insisted. "That was just a fluke."

After three months without a cigarette I was angry, tense, bloated, antisocial, reclusive, and idle. All the ways that I'd identified myself—as a writer, attractive woman, cheerful friend, and sexy wife—seemed to disappear. In December I stepped on the scale to find I had gained twenty-three pounds. I was hysterical. Aaron, six foot four and twice my heft, didn't understand what the big deal was.

"Oh no!" I shrieked, pointing to the scale. "I'm a hog. I look hideous!"

"You are not, you're still beautiful!" Aaron said, hugging me.

"Stop patronizing me, you idiot!" I screamed, pushing him away.

Luckily he was still occasionally seeing Dr. Winters, to whom he ran confused, complaining that I'd become verbally abusive when he called me beautiful. Aaron came home that night saying, "Okay, you look hideous." That made me feel better. Or was it the pack of Capri Menthol Lights I'd just finished?

I ate less when I was busy smoking, so I soon lost all the weight. I felt better, slept more easily, wrote for hours every day like I used to. Whenever Aaron complained about the smoke, I ignored him. I learned that you can't quit anything because somebody tells you to. Aaron didn't bring it up again. He knew that if he forced me to make a choice, I would rather be smoking than be married.

I had actually chosen cigarettes—and my right to smoke them—over him.

Chapter 7

FEBRUARY 2002

T. S. Eliot had it wrong—February was the cruelest month. At least for a sun-worshiping East Coast tobacco hound who hadn't had a cigarette for five months. I'd switched from the large to the medium-sized patch, going from twenty-one milligrams to fourteen a day. I felt like I needed something to replace the lost nicotine. (Seven milligrams lower was, after all, the equivalent of seven cigarettes less a day.) I began drinking wine at dinner and sipping hot cognac late at night while chewing on cinnamon sticks, which helped me work.

"I finished my rewrite for Lilly, the agent," I told Dr. Winters. "I dropped it off at her office."

"Good," he said, barely looking at me. He was fourteen minutes late today and seemed preoccupied, his head somewhere else.

"Did I tell you that Lilly's from Michigan, exactly my age, and she has three little kids?" I asked.

"You told me that six times," he said. I hated when he was preoccupied like this, as if everyone else in his life was more important than I was.

"I think you were wrong about doing the revision for Lilly. As a writer you have to trust your own instincts," I said.

"An addict's instincts are misguided," he said. "They lead you to continue using."

I didn't care about addicts in general, I cared about me and my book. "I can tell it isn't going to work out with Lilly," I lamented.

"Why?"

"It's like I showed her my baby and instead of saying, 'He's beautiful,' she said, 'He might look okay after serious plastic surgery.' "

"It doesn't sound like plastic surgery. More like minor re-construction. All on the surface." He jumped right into my book-is-my-baby metaphor, which almost made me like him again.

"I'm too attached to the project. It was hard to hear any criticism."

"You should have three babies too, like Lilly. If you only have one baby you'll make him too crazy. Spread the neurosis around," he said, taking it a little further than necessary. The concept wasn't even original. I thought of the theoretical baby in Edward Albee's play *Who's Afraid of Virginia Woolf?*

"I'd love more books, but I can't write without smoking," I said, killing all the babies off. "This was rewriting. An editor friend wants me to update an old essay, and I'm not even sure I can handle that."

"Say no," he said.

"I have time. What else am I going to do?"

"Wait for Lilly's response."

"It's a miracle I can rewrite." I decided to admit the way I'd really been able to finish reworking my two-hundred-and-thirty-page manuscript. "I can only work when I drink half a glass of wine at dinner or cognac later. Or toke half a joint. Or leave an unlit one in my mouth." I knew that smoking more dope now was dumb and that I had to stop. I was merely re-creating the way it felt when I used to write and chain-smoke cigarettes. I was sure he was going to order me off marijuana.

"Stop drinking alcohol," Dr. Winters ordered.

"What?" What did alcohol have to do with anything?

"Quit alcohol now!" His voice was angry, as if I had screwed up his entire day.

"I barely drink," I mumbled. "Having half a glass of cognac, wine, or champagne helps me write. Why should I stop?"

"You've mentioned cognac, wine, and champagne so far. What else have you been drinking?" he demanded to know. I felt like a teenager who'd finished off the liquor cabinet while her parents went out of town. Now they were back and I had to face the music.

"Nothing else," I swore, then remembered it wasn't true. "Well, I had one wine spritzer and then a rum and diet Coke at a book party last week. And half of Aaron's Kahlúa and cream after dinner on Saturday night. Does that count?"

"Everything counts," Dr. Winters reminded me. "You need to stop drinking."

"Okay," I said sheepishly. "If you tell me why."

"Because alcohol is addictive, has a lot of empty calories, and lowers your resistance to cigarettes, dope, and food."

"You think I'm going to quit cigarettes and become an alcoholic?" I laughed.

He didn't laugh back. "Addictions do not get smaller. They get bigger," he said. "They can overlap."

"My primary substance is cigarettes. That's definitely not the same as being a drunk," I argued.

"My treatment for heroin, cocaine, pills, nicotine, alcohol,

gambling, cigarettes, and food addiction is interchangeable,"
he said. "Just switch the word and it's the exact same story: I
want it, I need it, I can't get through the day without it."

Heroin users tapered off with methadone. AA members
chain-smoked and guzzled coffee instead of liquor. My dad
had swapped cigarettes for cigars and oatmeal-raisin cookies,
while I'd used pot and the nicotine patch. If there was no such
thing as a clean break, was the trick to keep switching to
healthier substances, trading up, until you were healed?

Wallowing in book surgery allegories, I was stunned later
that week when a real medical trauma surfaced. My mother
called to tell me that doctors had found a suspicious spot on
my father's recent X-rays. He feared it was cancer. Thankfully
the next day more tests showed it wasn't a tumor. It was a hip
fracture. After second and third opinions, he quickly scheduled an appointment to have his right hip replaced at his own
hospital.

I had always avoided the freezing Midwest in the winter,
but this time I made a reservation to fly to Michigan for ten
days. I had the day off from teaching for Martin Luther King's
birthday and rescheduled my other classes. In five months I'd
never canceled any appointments with Dr. Winters; he was
my priority. I told him in advance I needed to reschedule two
sessions in a row. I felt as if I had to sacrifice seeing my fantasy
father to run back to the real one.

I flew home the night before the operation. My brother
Eric picked me up at the airport. Brian and Mike were at my
parents' house when I got there. Nobody in our immediate
family had ever needed to be in the hospital for a week; we
were all nervous. Especially the doctors of the bunch, who
were notoriously bad patients.

"It's because we've seen what can go wrong in a hospital,"

Brian said. He explained that Dad had his own blood taken several times in case he needed a transfusion during the operation, which would cut down on the chance of a blood mix-up.

There was one nice surprise waiting for me. The twenty-four-hour lung cancer scare had scared my father straight—he was off cigarettes, for good, he swore. He was about to turn seventy, I was forty-one, and it was the first time we'd ever been nonsmokers together. It made me feel closer to him. I went for a run around our neighborhood and hurt my own hip. (Never run in walking shoes.) Obviously I was overidentifying with my dad. It seemed to run in the family. The day before, Eric had smashed his leg playing soccer, also (I thought) in sympathy.

"I hear about athletes who need their knees and hips replaced all the time," I said over an early dinner the night before Dad went in.

"Sometimes it's genetic," Brian said.

"Didn't Grandpa have bad arthritis?" Eric asked.

"Sure. Your grandma did too," my father said.

"Could be normal wear and tear," Michael offered.

"Your grandfather Harry made me carry blinds and shades up and down broken steps of decrepit old tenement buildings," my father said. "You don't know how heavy those blinds were."

"How long did that last?" I asked.

"All through school. From when I was ten to twenty-two, for twelve years. He paid me three dollars a week. We'd fight and I'd go get an after-school job working for somebody else. I was big for my age. When I was thirteen I told people I was older so I could get hired at other jobs."

I looked much older at thirteen too. I'd never made that connection before.

"That's one of the reasons he couldn't wait to leave New York. I would have stayed," my mother offered. "I always wanted to open up a little clothes boutique in Greenwich Village."

Instead of blaming my parents for all my problems, I switched to blaming their parents. I felt enraged that my father's mean dead father, Harry, who had cursed him with nicotine addiction and lack of love, was haunting him again. I already thought my parents were escaping Harry when they fled New York, where I should have been born. Now he was the cause of my father's injured bones. Or was it the fault of my great-grandmother, who'd deserted Harry as a baby and thus ruined him?

We drove to the hospital together at five in the morning. I told my dad I loved him right before he was wheeled into surgery at six A.M. For the next six hours I pretended to stay calm, but thoughts of losing my father consumed me. I felt helpless, in total turmoil, bargaining with the God I didn't even believe in. I would stay off cigarettes, alcohol, Blow Pops, and freelancing forever if only my dad could be okay.

Although he had nerve damage in his left foot, and it would be three months before he'd walk without a walker or a cane, we learned that my father was going to be absolutely fine. I visited the hospital every day with my mother. On day three Dad quit being a patient and decided he was a doctor again, making rounds in a wheelchair to see his patients in the hospital. Aaron laughed when I told him. I laughed too. But when I landed back in New York, I felt like I'd been through a war.

I was greeted by lots of good news. While I was gone Aaron was offered a job to write and produce a new animated TV show he was excited about. His new health insurance would cover almost half of my addiction therapy. Furthermore, I learned by e-mail that Lilly West loved the rewrite of my memoir and had decided to take me on as a client.

"Did I tell you that Lilly's new office is on Fifth Avenue and

Thirteenth Street?" I asked Dr. Winters during my first post-Michigan session.

"At least ten times," he said in a bored voice. "She's from Michigan, she has three kids, she's five blocks from here."

He didn't understand why it was so important. Lilly worked on the same avenue as Dr. Winters, in this very neighborhood. If psychologically I was embarking on my second childhood, the two of them had become my Greenwich Village mother and father.

"It's interesting that my dad's father caused his hip problem to begin with," I said.

"It's interesting that you think his father caused it," Dr. Winters said.

"For ten days I didn't get high, smoke a cigarette, or drink," I reported. "Though I think I'm still allowed to have a glass of wine if I feel like it."

"You are not allowed any alcohol," he admonished.

"Well, I didn't want any alcohol. But I was in sheer agony the whole time."

"That's very good." He nodded, looking surprised, as if I were a C-minus student who'd just aced the final.

"Why is being in agony good?"

"Instead of self-medicating, you let yourself feel bad."

According to Winters, the remedy wasn't to quit smoking by switching substances. He was recommending a sort of emotional detox, where I had to experience what was behind the desire to use, letting the darkness unfold, no matter how much it hurt.

"Now I get it," I said. "Feeling is the enemy of addiction." My vision of the world was starting to look reductive and cartoonlike, as if sober superheroes were constantly doing battle against their own evil urges.

"Feeling real and suffering is what substances are supposed

to numb," he said, looking at his appointment book, signaling that our time was up.

"My version was better," I said, looking at my watch. We'd gone seven minutes over, as if he sensed I'd needed more of him today.

The list on the back of this week's card said:

1. *No alcohol at all, ever*
2. *Make room for more feelings*
3. *Think first before you express those feelings*
4. *Don't trust any impulse, your impulses are always wrong*
5. *Bring me a copy of your book to read*

Chapter 8

MARCH 2002

After Blake Falls finished his inspiring hour talk about breaking into the publishing scene, my students applauded and crowded around him. They were enthralled that the editor of a hip downtown magazine was so accessible and willing to hire new freelancers and interns. About fifty, in jeans and a flannel shirt, he resembled an aging rock star—but a clean-cut one from the Midwest. At least he usually did. He looked off-kilter tonight.

"Thanks. Your speech was terrific. Even more inspiring than usual," I said, staring at Blake, trying to decipher what was different. His hair was longer than it was last time I saw him, messy too. He looked sexier but more frazzled. "New hair?" I asked him while handing back last week's papers to my students and collecting this week's assignment. "Are you having a midlife crisis?"

"Yeah, I am. How did you know?" he asked. "I'm smoking again too." He caught my eye.

My mouth opened. "Smoking again? Oh no. But you quit for . . ."

"Eight years," he said.

"I haven't smoked in six months. I was so excited to tell you." I shook my head. "This screws up my whole world."

"Sorry," he mumbled. "We always switch."

If I divided everybody I knew into two categories, the smokers and nonsmokers, most of the people I really liked in my life still lit up. Smokers were more intense and complex, I continued to believe, and they had darker senses of humor. Amid our kind was the small subgroup of successful quitters. In that tiny pool, Blake had been my role model. Eight years ago he'd simply quit cold turkey. He began working out daily, turning the five pounds he'd gained into muscle. For the last eight years he'd been hounding me to quit, saying how foolish cigarettes were and how much better off I'd be without them.

"Can I buy you a drink?" I asked.

I had an urge for a glass of white wine even though I'd have to order diet soda since I was reluctantly following wicked Dr. Winters' all-out ban on alcohol. I put on my coat. Blake put on his too, still shaking hands and waving to the female fans gathered around him, as he answered questions I was no longer hearing. I'd always been drawn to Blake, loved the few times a year he would come by to speak to my class. I always asked if I could take him out afterward. He always said no. I'd assumed he had to get home to his wife.

Tonight he said, "Sure."

Something was obviously up. As we walked out of the building and parted ways with the throng of fawning students, he pulled a pack of cigarettes from his backpack and lit one. Marlboro reds, like my sexy ex-boyfriend David. I felt threatened, as if I would suddenly want to smoke again too. Oddly, I didn't. Watching Blake light up so fast and desperately now appeared dumb and ugly to me. I wondered what was so bad that he'd gone back to smoking after eight years.

"Thanks for hiring my student Naomi as an intern," I said. "Isn't she a kick?"

"She's sharp as hell. And a hard worker," he said. "Not like that little slacker jerk you sent me, Pete. The short kid from New Jersey."

"Pete was your fault," I said. "You made him a star when you put that piece about his Joey Ramone obsession on your cover."

"I know. After that he was too cool to file or get anyone coffee," he laughed. "How's Aaron doing?"

"Good. Working late. On a new show. How's your wife?" I asked, leading him across Twelfth Street. I'd met his wife once, at a party. I'd liked her, though I couldn't remember her name. She seemed nice, smart, my age.

"I left her," he said, sucking in smoke.

"When?" I bet not remembering his wife's name was an omen. I tried to recall how long they'd been together. "What happened?"

"Few months ago. I moved out."

I was right, the cigarettes were a sign denoting internal war or devastation. "Blake, I'm so sorry. Are you okay?"

"Fine." He nodded, puffing a few more times. I watched him stub out the butt on the sidewalk. I knew he wasn't fine.

Walking past the fancy Gotham Bar & Grill, I noticed it was half empty, unusual for nine-thirty on a weekday night. I led the way inside, wanting to be somewhere softer and prettier than the neighborhood dives I usually frequented. I asked for a table in the bar area, where he was allowed to smoke. I remembered how essential that used to be. I used to scan every social venue for a way out, a place with an ashtray where I could light up over and over without being bothered by nonsmokers, those pesky prudes who rolled their eyes and complained that they were allergic to smoke, had asthma, or that it was a nonsmoking section.

As soon as we sat down, Blake lit another one. It looked manic.

"You have to quit. It's not good for you," I told him, as if I had a vote in the matter. We really had switched roles. After six months without a cigarette, I knew that I was a nonsmoker now, every bit as intrusive as he used to be. Damn, I had become one of those annoying, horrible, boring, preaching, self-righteous former smokers! At that moment I saw that I'd crossed over to the other side.

Blake ordered a Scotch on the rocks, I ordered a diet soda. I asked the waiter for menus. I had a strong impulse to feed him, take care of him. I sensed that he needed to be taken care of. Quitting smoking and drinking had made me feel thin-skinned, raw, and fragile, as if I might fall apart at any second. Weak as that sounded, there was an upside to experiencing such extreme emotions. All the deprivation and suffering had made me more empathetic than I'd ever been. It was as if all the pathways to people I cared about had been cleared; there was less separation. My radar screen was picking up intimate fluctuations in my friends' movements, facial expressions, and voices. Yesterday I'd called my colleague Faye. When her voice sounded a little different over the phone, I asked if she was pregnant. She'd said, "I just took a pregnancy test. I haven't even told my parents yet. How did you know?" I was seeing, hearing, and intuiting more than I meant to.

"What happened with your wife?" I asked Blake. "You want to talk about it?"

He was usually a man of few words. But if he needed to confess, I was more than willing to play priest. I'd been revealing too many of my darkest secrets to Dr. Winters; the role reversal actually felt like a nice relief.

"After September eleventh, I just couldn't do it anymore," he said. "Lisa's a great, sweet, smart woman, but after ten years together . . ." He paused, then said, "It just felt like a lie. I walked out."

"Wow." I'd fallen deeper in love with Aaron after the disaster. Since I'd quit smoking we'd been getting closer. I needed him more—for pep talks and long hugs that made me feel safe. Having him hold me for an hour without talking every night had turned out to be my favorite of all Dr. Winters' wacky prescriptions.

"There's someone else in the picture," Blake offered before I could ask. "She's way too young. Completely inappropriate." He hit the cigarette one more time, deeply, as if he were sucking in a joint. I couldn't help staring, strangely fascinated, surprised that I still had no interest in smoking myself.

As a monogamous middle-aged married woman, I expected to feel sisterly outrage about his affair, but I didn't. He was a good friend. Aaron, Dr. Winters, Blake—I was gravitating toward smart, supportive men a decade older than I was. Blake was once my mentor, printing my first-person rants at a time when I'd desperately needed the money and byline. He had also hired many of my NYU and New School students and published their first essays, book and music reviews. Whatever Blake had done, I was ready to forgive and rationalize. Yet in my mind, worse than leaving his nice, nurturing wife was returning to tobacco. How could he? *That* felt like a personal betrayal.

I ordered seafood, pleased that he ordered pasta. I wasn't pleased that he wanted another Scotch and a glass of red wine. When I'd read that ninety percent of addictions were caused by depression, I didn't believe it. I was beginning to. Though I missed the fun feeling of being tipsy, I was glad that Dr. Winters had convinced me to stop drinking. Blake smoked his third cigarette in fifteen minutes. The alcohol and chain of smoke were difficult to observe. He was in pain, trying anything to make it go away.

"Are you in therapy?" I asked.

"I hate therapy," he said. "Think it's bullshit."

It was rare to find someone in Manhattan who had the same close-minded view of therapy as my family in Michigan. I thought the people most in need of psychoanalysis were the ones who trashed it. "Why do you think it's bullshit?"

"A lot of my friends waste tons of money on therapy. The shrinks always seem to need their patients more than the patients need them," he said. "Ever notice how they never let you end therapy?"

"You grew up Catholic, right?" I switched tactics. "You're obviously beating yourself up over this."

He nodded. "I was, but now I'm okay with it."

"Okay with being Catholic or beating yourself up?"

"Both." He chuckled. "How did you finally kick cigarettes? The nicotine patch?"

"The patch, and I have a secret weapon." I guessed that Blake would think it was wimpy since he'd gone cold turkey. "I've been seeing this incredible addiction specialist. His name is Dr. Winters."

"Getting Prof. Sue off cigarettes—that was no mean feat." He put out his cigarette and sparked another one. I felt an urge to take the stupid cancer stick out of Blake's hand and snap it in two, the way my annoying college boyfriend used to break my Virginia Slims Menthols whenever I'd light up in front of him. My brothers used to sneak into my purse and throw my packs of cigarettes in the garbage. But I had no right—Blake and I were not relatives or lovers.

"I know." I nodded. "I started when I was thirteen. I smoked two packs a day for twenty-seven years."

"What's his method?" he asked. "Black magic?"

"Suffering," I said.

"Really?" He laughed, but I wasn't joking.

"Well, comprehensive suffering. You're supposed to let yourself feel what's underneath the urge to smoke. He also believes the more ways you go at it, the better. So I'm trying an all-out assault. I'm using nicotine replacement, I'm on a diet, and I'm seeing Dr. Winters once a week."

"You just sit there and talk to him about how much you want to smoke?" he asked, making it seem stupid.

I felt defensive, wanting Dr. Winters' strategy to sound smarter and more technical. "Well, he uses talk therapy and a cognitive behavioral regimen," I explained. "It's not just stream of consciousness. He tells me specific techniques I should try in order to better tolerate the cravings."

"All the writers I know smoke and want to quit," Blake said. "You should do an article about this for me. Not the psychobabble part, just the getting off the stuff."

Maybe Blake wasn't making fun of me. I hoped he was interested because he wanted to quit again himself. "I can't. Winters won't let me do any freelance work. He says I'm chasing after bylines I already have and it's too much stress."

"This guy sounds way too controlling."

It was funny, the men in my life had more trouble with Dr. Winters than the women. Were they competitive?

"I know. I've become a Dr. Winters Moonie," I admitted. "When he asked to read my memoir, I rushed out to xerox a copy and just handed it to him at our next session."

"What did he say?"

"He said: 'This is fantastic. It'll definitely sell.' " I'd written Dr. Winters' words down in my notebook and read them to myself several times a day, as if he could control my book's destiny as well as my own. I finished my diet soda, chewed on the ice.

"That's a vote of confidence."

"It's been so mind-blowing." When the food came, I asked the waiter for a refill.

"How is it mind-blowing?" Blake asked, putting out his cigarette and digging right in. A hearty appetite was a good sign, I thought. Unless it meant that he hadn't been eating.

"At the first session Winters slipped me a note that said, 'Underlying every substance problem I have ever seen is a deep depression that feels unbearable.' "

Blake looked up, put his fork down. "I don't have to pay somebody to tell me that I'm lying to myself. I already know that," he said. Then he picked up his fork again, spinning the linguini around it. "Want to taste?"

I shook my head no. "I hate mushrooms. At least you're getting laid. What's her name?"

"Lola," he said.

"That's her real name?" I tried to suppress my smile. "How inappropriate is she?"

"She's a twenty-three-year-old Spanish lesbian," he said.

"You mean bisexual, don't you?" Having resided in the Village for twenty years, little about relationships shocked me anymore. I knew lots of people who experimented with their sexuality. A bunch of my young NYU undergraduates called themselves "LUG," which stood for "Lesbian Until Graduation," or "BUG," which meant "Bi Until Graduation."

"I'm her first man," Blake said. "She says she can only truly love a woman. I'm falling in love with her, though I know she's going to wind up dumping me."

"It's the ultimate unrequited love. Do you have a cold, unreachable mother or something?" I asked. I was so preoccupied with my therapy I noticed I was now psychoanalyzing everybody I came in contact with.

"My mother's dead. That's pretty unreachable," he said, laughing and reaching for his drink. "I was close to my mom.

But I have an older sister in Fresno who's kind of closed off. I could never get her approval."

"Is your sister gay?" I asked.

"I don't know." He shrugged. "She's in her fifties and single. Never been married. I haven't met any guys she's been involved with in a long time, but she doesn't really talk to me much."

How could one not know if one's sibling was straight or gay? "What if trying to get Lola is like trying to convince your sister to love you?" I asked. "How did you meet her?"

"Lola works in my office."

It was worse than I had suspected. He was screwing up his life. "Let me guess. You were this healthy married guy with a stable job who was too normal. So you're trying to break everything, like one of those post office workers who shoots up the whole office."

"That bad?" he asked.

"Well, I know your publisher. He's a married guy with three kids. I bet he's faithful."

"Straight as an arrow," Blake confirmed.

"Of course you're making it in the office, where you could get caught with your pants down," I said. "Come on. You're obviously trying to get yourself fired."

"Not consciously." He lit another cigarette, which he puffed in between bites. I vaguely recalled how I used to smoke and eat at the same time.

"A writer into crazy sex, smoking, and booze. How original. Here, try this." I forked some fancy seafood onto his plate.

"It's good," he said.

When I'd first met Blake, before I was married, I'd fantasized about having an affair with him. I was so glad I'd chosen Aaron, who was boring and not addicted to anything. Except me.

"Last week I took Lola to Las Vegas, what a ride. We hit

some strip clubs. She was more into the naked women than I was. I got incredibly jealous. I was thinking that I should write about it."

"It'll be your memoir," I jumped in.

"I'll call it *My Year of Lesbian Sex.*"

"Call it *Her First Man,*" I told him. I could already see the book jacket. "For the climax you should remeet your sister and figure out what you're really doing."

"What an idea," he said, putting his cigarette in the ashtray and then lighting another one.

"Stop chain-smoking!" I snapped. "George Harrison dying didn't do it for you? Fifty-eight years old, worth three hundred million, with a beautiful wife and kid he adored."

"I know. He quit, then started again," Blake said. "Got throat cancer that spread to his brain."

"Made me feel less stupid," I said.

"Knowing that rich, famous, talented people have trouble quitting too?" he asked.

"Exactly."

When we finished dinner, I insisted on treating. I hugged him goodbye on the corner of University and Twelfth Street, feeling clean and clairvoyant, as if twenty-seven years' worth of smoke had been cleared from my eyes. Before he left, I gave Blake one of Dr. Winters' business cards. At my last appointment I'd sneaked a bunch of them into my black briefcase. I made sure it wasn't one of the cards with a special note scrawled on the back.

"Therapy's not for me. But don't worry, honey," he said, slipping the card in his pocket anyway, then lighting another cigarette. "Everything'll be fine."

Aaron was on a business trip to L.A. The apartment was quiet. I pulled out the stack of personal essays I had to grade. The paper I'd assigned this week was to write a first-person New York story, something that could only happen in Manhattan.

"Shrinking" was on top. It was by Naomi, my twenty-four-year-old Jewish neurotic student who was interning for Blake's magazine. Naomi was funny; she reminded me of a young me.

Her piece was about falling in love with Dr. Latsky, an Upper East Side psychiatrist who'd been treating her for the last two years. She used to complain to him that there were no cups in his bathroom. Then she agonized for months over whether or not to buy him a Hanukkah present. She wound up getting him a black leather photo album with pictures of Freud inside. All he'd said was "thank you." Last week she found a Dixie cup dispenser on his bathroom wall and took it as a sign that Dr. Latsky had developed deep feelings for her too.

I thought it was hysterically funny, though Naomi wasn't going for laughs. She had no sense of irony at all. I scrawled "This is fantastic, but double space and look up 'transference' " in the margin and put an A on the top of her paper. Then I wondered what I should get Dr. Winters for a present and how he would respond.

Chapter 9

APRIL 2002

"I want you to see another doctor."

That was how Dr. Winters began our Monday session. It was 2:42; he was twelve minutes late. I hated seeing him in the afternoon, I preferred nights. It was the same fifty minutes but I felt slighted, as if he'd switched our important eight o'clock dinner date to a quick two-thirty cup of coffee.

"No fucking way!" I yelled.

What a shocking betrayal. I was devastated. He was sick of me, I was too boring and depressed. I should never have lent him to my friend Irene; I was sure she was using up all his good hours. Irene had admitted to me that she was hooked on painkillers, and stupidly refused to tell her husband about it. I'd insisted she call Dr. Winters and tell him it was an emergency. He got her clean in one week, confirming my belief that he really was the James Bond of drug treatment. But then Irene kept on seeing him, which got on my nerves.

"If I'm not seeing you, I'm not seeing anybody," I told him.

It was bad enough that the editor who'd been loving my book for seven weeks had just turned it down and Lilly hadn't returned my last phone call. Now I was being rejected by my own shrink. He looked different today, everything was amiss.

"Not to replace me," he said calmly. "I would like you to see a psychopharmacologist. Just once. To see if there's a medication that can help you through this. You're suffering too much."

First he wanted me to suffer, now I was suffering the wrong amount. He should make up his mind. Dr. Winters had a Ph.D. in clinical psychology and a bunch of postdoctorate diplomas. Yet he had no medical degree, so he couldn't prescribe medicine. With his huge ego, I imagined he wouldn't ask for help if we didn't really need it.

I tried to chill out. After six months smoke-free, I'd thought I was on the mend. Instead of staring longingly at skinny, beautiful models puffing down scenic West Village streets, I'd begun to catch obese old coughing smokers huddled outside, looking idiotic as they desperately sucked in poison. Following all of Dr. Winters' ridiculous rules (dieting and avoiding all alcohol, freelancing, and Blow Pops), I'd gradually weaned myself from the seven-milligram patches, the smallest dosage, until I was completely patch-free. It seemed like cause for celebration.

Yet instead of feeling better, this final nicotine withdrawal step totally upset my system. I had an emotional relapse, and while eating the same way, I gained seven pounds. As a big-boned, big-footed, five-foot-seven-inch forty-one-year-old woman, I'd come to terms with weighing a fairly average 137 pounds. But at 144, I felt bloated and disgusting. I was afraid I was revisiting the eating craziness I'd conquered years ago, before I was aware that I was using cigarettes as my own private pharmacy.

Dr. Winters had told me, in our last session, that I should get used to feeling vulnerable and overly sensitive. I had shed the armor that used to protect me from the world. I was like a burn victim, he'd said. I had no skin. Going outside was difficult. Even the air hurt.

"I don't want to go."

"Why?" he asked.

"I don't need antidepressants. I've tried them. They depress me," I said. "Only dope seems to make me feel better."

Long before the pill-popping problem, my fellow Winters groupie Irene had quit cigarettes by becoming a pothead. One very high year later, she quit marijuana. Her attitude was: Nix one indulgence at a time. Interestingly, Dr. Winters did not seem to think my smoking three joints a week, at night with friends, was an urgent problem. But he didn't know that since I'd given up the patch, I'd been cheating by toking alone, in the afternoon.

"Would you make one appointment, for me? Please?" he asked in a patronizingly soft tone, as if I were five years old.

"Why?" I yelled. "Because you don't like seeing me this enraged?"

"I don't like seeing you in this much pain," he said.

I noticed that he'd gotten his hair cut. It was way too short; I didn't like it. That was what Irene meant when she'd e-mailed that she'd had "a breakthrough session with Dr. Buzzcut last night"—an evening appointment she'd obviously usurped from me. I couldn't stand it when she gave him nicknames. It reduced my metaphysical quest for enlightenment to junior-high-school gossip. I swore I wasn't sharing Dr. Winters with anybody else anymore ever again—unless they were dying.

"I don't need any more doctors. I hate doctors. I come from a family of doctors. I've always hated doctors," I said. "I don't have any more money to waste on this recovery shit."

"We figured, at two packs a day, you spent three thousand dollars a year on cigarettes," he said.

"I'm spending six thousand this year on therapy," I retorted. "What the hell is the difference?"

"You tell me."

"I'll live longer," I mumbled. "And supposedly sell my book, which nobody in the fucking world is buying."

"What did we say?"

"I can't call you a liar and kill you until October." I stuck out my tongue.

"I can recommend two really good doctors," he said, ignoring my protests. "There's Bob Heinke, this Upper East Side German guy nicknamed 'the Chemist.' If he's too overbooked or out of town, I can give you the number of Leonard Steiner, on Thirteenth Street."

"If I go—I'll go to Steiner," I said. I already didn't like the overbooked German chemist. I wanted the downtown Jew.

"Well, Heinke has done some serious work with nicotine addiction—"

"I don't care. I'm only seeing Steiner." The more Winters argued, the more determined I was that Steiner was my man, which, I later worried, was Winters' strategy.

"You'll have to sign a release," he added.

"Sign a release for what?" It sounded ominous, as if I were a schizophrenic checking myself out of a mental institution.

"Saying that you give me permission to confer with Dr. Steiner." Dr. Winters pulled out an official-looking form that said I was waiving my rights to patient confidentiality. "Because we don't work for the same organization."

"Fine," I said, signing it at the bottom. "Confer away."

When I came home, I left a message on Dr. Steiner's machine. He called right back. Perhaps he heard desperation in my voice, because he said, "Want to come by five-thirty today?"

His West Village office was in a huge old building I didn't like. I didn't like his antiseptic waiting room either. I cursed Dr. Winters for pawning me off. This was a mistake. I needed to get off things, not get on more of them.

Dr. Steiner opened his door and came out. He was a tall, friendly-looking guy with shoulder-length blond hair and thin silver-framed glasses. He was wearing black jeans, a black sweater, and black sneakers, like I was. He said, "You're Susan?"

"Dr. Steiner." I stood up and we shook hands. "Hi."

"Call me Lenny," he said. "Come on in."

His inner office was antiseptic too, no carpeting, no blinds covering the windows, no pillows on the beige leather couch. Dr. Winters' warm, overstuffed space could double as his living room, while Dr. Steiner appeared to be sharing an office rental a few afternoons a week. I stared at the one painting on the wall, which looked familiar. Though not effeminate, something about Dr. Steiner seemed gay and comfortable with it. Good, I liked gay men better than straight men these days, when I wasn't hating everyone.

"How do you know Dr. Winters?" I asked.

"I went to Williams with Danny," he said.

Williams with Danny? How bizarro! Hearing new personal data on Dr. Winters wigged me out. I couldn't bear to think of him existing outside our sessions. Learning he'd been seeing my friend Irene steadily was rough enough. I didn't want to know he'd been young once, and had studied in western Massachusetts. That made me imagine an undergraduate Granola Guy hiking in the woods with a backpack. I had pictured Dr. Winters as an urban rebel, bashing out controversial theories with angry chain-smoking socialists in a dank basement in downtown Paris.

"He said he used to smoke in college," I threw out.

"He did?" Dr. Steiner asked. "I don't remember that."

Aha! Had Dr. Winters lied or exaggerated his bad habits? I knew it!

"I just spoke to him on the phone," he said.

Just? I feared that after my session with Dr. Winters had ended, he'd picked up the phone to his colleague and said, "Hey, Lenny. Ya gotta get a load of this one."

"What did he tell you?" I asked.

"He said, 'I'm sending you the worst case of nicotine withdrawal on the planet.' " He smiled, as if this were funny.

"He said that?" That was why Dr. Winters had made me sign that dumb form—so he could legally trash me to his friend? I was offended and wanted to sob. On second thought, I was flattered. At least I stood out. I was special, I'd warranted a superlative, as if being Dr. Winters' sickest patient would make me his favorite. I'd always known I was an extremist. Though didn't men in the hinterlands inhale four packs of Marlboros a day for fifty years? With the long and slender Virginia Slims Menthols, More Lights, and Capri Menthols I'd smoked, I assumed that my habit was comparatively dainty. Dr. Winters hyping it up to Dr. Steiner made it official. No wonder I was miserable. I didn't have an average affliction—it was epic!

"Tell me about it," he said.

There was something sweet and jovial about this Lenny. If he'd gone to college with Winters he had to be fifty too, but he looked a decade younger. What was in that Williams water? I spilled the entire megillah (how after twenty-seven years I'd quit cigarettes and was recovering okay—until I quit the patch), then shared the Cliffs Notes version of my overanalyzed past (the trick photograph of the Leaning Tower, the either-smoke-or-be-obese family freak show) and my most recent symptoms: how tired, idle, mindless, boring, and hostile I'd become.

"How are you sleeping?" he asked.

"Like a baby."

"Nervous or shaky?"

"I have no major physical symptoms," I admitted, afraid my abnormal withdrawal wasn't so hideous after all, just my usual inability to deal with any kind of discomfort. "Except that I gained seven pounds. I weigh 144, which is average and not worth an eating disorder, but I hate its guts."

"You have to be comfortable," he said. A gay guy in good shape, he totally understood.

At his request, I listed all the antidepressants that had previously failed me. Wellbutrin, an old drug renamed Zyban and relaunched as "a smoking-cessation medication," gave me such bad headaches I thought I was having seizures. When I read Zyban's warnings on the back of the bottle, it said "seizures." Prozac and Paxil made me fat, sexless, and workless, so I'd nixed them within weeks. While I had a captive audience, I lamented how I'd never publish my memoir or be able to write again. My *New York Times* obit would depict me an accomplished teacher but not an accomplished writer.

"At least you know you'll be getting a *New York Times* obit," he noted.

"We each have ways of deceiving ourselves. The important thing is to believe in one's own importance," I said.

"André Gide," he nodded. I nodded back; we were now sympatico on everything.

Instead of asking me about the classes I taught at NYU and the New School, he surprised me by asking what I'd been like as a student.

"A in English, drama, and psychology," I said. "I think I got a D-minus in everything else."

"You flunked classes?" he asked.

"Yeah, 'cause I skipped everything else."

He pulled down the thick *Physicians' Desk Reference* on his makeshift shelf and paged through it. Stopping in the middle, he read me a passage about a drug called Adderall. Similar to Ritalin, it was used to treat attention deficit disorder, colloquially known as A.D.D., something I never in a million years thought I had.

"I don't have A.D.D. I did my master's degree in poetry when I was twenty. I've written long pieces for *The New York Times Magazine, Washington Post,* and *Village Voice* on twenty-four-hour deadlines." I'd been throwing my credentials around a lot lately. I'd also been wearing my diamond engagement ring everywhere, which was unusual. Feeling lousy and worthless, I thought any identity was better than the one I was missing.

"It sounds like you couldn't concentrate on most subjects," Dr. Steiner said.

"I'm like the Edie Brickell song," I told him. "Not aware of too many things. But I know what I know, if you know what I mean."

He wrote in his notebook. I liked that he took notes, like Dr. Winters. They were probably just doodling, but it was a good technique, made you feel your words were significant. Though I'd been quoting others too much lately. Being smokeless had made me voiceless, a nightmare side effect for a writer.

"Let's just try a low dose of Adderall for a week," Dr. Steiner decreed.

By coincidence, Esther, my editor friend at *Jane* magazine, had penned a cover story on Adderall, the hip new drug of choice on college campuses, where coeds were sniffing it to stay up all night to cram for exams. A notorious late-nighter, it sounded cool to me.

Since amphetamines could be highly addictive, Dr. Steiner wanted to monitor me. Your average hyper six-year-old could handle ten to twenty milligrams of Adderall a day, but he wrote me a prescription for just seven tablets of five milligrams each. I wrote him a check for $200, filled the prescription on the way home, and began my new medication on Tuesday, taking one tiny blue pill in the morning. The dose was so low, I didn't even think I'd feel it. But feel it I did. Within half an hour I wasn't the least bit hungry, felt joyous, and wrote for twelve hours straight; I could barely drag myself away from my laptop.

After six days, I lost the seven pounds I'd gained and felt thrilled to be lighter. I was also randier and jumped Aaron three nights in a row. (Pleasantly surprised I was human again, he seemed eager to oblige.) This Adderall was obviously an aphrodisiac. It was especially wonderful after two hits of a joint. I was literally dancing and singing in the streets. On Monday I couldn't wait to thank Dr. Winters for hooking me up with my new best friend Lenny.

"You're on it now?" Winters asked as I sat down on his couch.

I nodded, smiling. "I love Dr. Steiner. I had a great week. I lost seven pounds and pulled out my old novel and started a new one. I've been writing really well again, feeling hotter. Aaron and I had sex three times in a row. This is incredible—"

"Get off," Dr. Winters said.

"What?"

"You're too hyper." He was insistent. "Get off."

Now I felt like he was the overbooked chemist and I was his failed lab experiment.

"I don't want to get off," I said, crushed by his disapproval. "I like being on."

"That's why you have to get off," he said. "Don't do it anymore."

"Come on. I'm using the dose they give five-year-olds. How about if I only take one pill every other day?" I begged. I was petrified that, Adderall-less, I'd get fat, bloated, slow, and miserable again. I'd had a brief reprieve from my seven-month funk. Having retasted joy, I just couldn't let it go so easily.

"What are you using it for—a diet pill?" he asked. "That's really stupid."

"What if I have A.D.D.?"

"You don't have A.D.D." He rolled his eyes.

"How do you know?"

"People with A.D.D. respond to that drug with serenity," he said. "It slows them down."

"Really?" I wondered if he'd made that up. "So it's an anti-depressant."

"You said that antidepressants depressed you and took away your sex drive. You don't seem depressed." He scrawled quickly into his notebook. I imagined he was writing: "Call that idiot Lenny."

"I want to see Dr. Steiner again," I said. Currently I liked him a lot better than creepy Dr. Winters, who seemed invested in keeping me miserable.

"Fine," Dr. Winters said in a way that made it seem not fine at all. "Let Lenny decide." Just then the cell phone on his table rang. He picked it up. I was mortified that he was going to take the call to spite me, but he looked at the number and put it back down. "In case of emergencies," he explained.

"Hey, remember that editor Mary who rejected my memoir?" I asked. "It turned out she didn't reject it. She loved it and wanted to make an offer, but then she got laid off. Can you believe it?"

"That's good news." He sat up taller, and seemed impressed, as if I'd almost redeemed myself from the Adderall debacle.

"How is it good?" I asked. "It sucks the big one. Lilly finally finds an editor who loves it and she gets canned the next day. My obit is going to say, 'After twenty-one years of writing, she almost published her book.' "

He laughed. "If one editor loved it, that means it's lovable."

I didn't believe him. "You and Lenny went to Williams together undergrad?" I asked. "Were you close friends? Is he gay?"

Dr. Winters nodded yes to all three.

"How old were you when you stopped smoking?" I demanded to know.

"I was thirty-six," he said without hesitation. Didn't seem like a lie.

I noticed the pink and blue three-tiered painting on his wall that I'd always admired. It was the same style as the one in Dr. Steiner's office. "Who's the artist?" I asked, pointing.

"Right. That's Lenny's work," Dr. Winters said. "He's a doctor part-time, and a painter part-time."

No wonder Dr. Steiner had found a way to give me my art back.

"Did you study together?" I was dying to know the inside scoop on both of them.

"Actually, neither of us studied psychology in college. He was an art major and I have a degree in philosophy," he said. "We both went back to school."

Knowing this I didn't like, as if Dr. Winters got stuck with psychology and me by default; we weren't his first love.

When I left Dr. Winters' office, I called Dr. Steiner from a pay phone on the street. He said to come by at five o'clock that afternoon. I sat down on his couch and immediately came clean. "Dr. Winters doesn't like me on it."

"You're on it now?" Lenny asked.

"Yes."

"Why doesn't Danny like it?"

"He thinks I'm too hyper."

"You don't seem that hyper to me," he said. "How do you feel?"

"Sexier. Faster. Happier. I love it," I said. "I already lost the seven pounds and I've been writing like a demon. Can I try a lower dose?"

"Five milligrams is pretty low," he said. "The average is ten or twenty a day."

"I've been too sensitive to everything, physically and psychically. Dr. Winters says I'm like a burn victim who doesn't have any skin. When I go outside, even the air hurts."

"Trenchant metaphor," he conceded.

"What if I just take it four days a week?" I asked.

He looked at me, then glanced at his notebook again.

"Just two days a week?" I pleaded.

"I think it's okay at this small a dose two days a week." He wrote me a second prescription for another eight pills. Then he added, "With due respect to Danny."

Was it a pissing contest between Dr. Winters and Dr. Steiner? Perhaps their rivalry had started in college thirty years before. I totally dug being in the middle of it. Okay, one guy was gay, the other was married, and I was paying them both astronomical sums I couldn't afford to hang out with me. While Aaron the workaholic was too busy and oblivious, in my warped little addiction-addled mind, two really cute guys were fighting over me.

I took one blue pill on Friday. I had so much fun that, instead of waiting and spreading them out over the week, I took another pill on Saturday. At dinner at a local Chinese restaurant, I drank three diet Cokes, forgetting that I shouldn't overcaffeinate while I was on other uppers. Aaron, too inside his own head to notice I was acting any different, went to sleep alone at midnight. Reading the Sunday papers early, I was wide awake, jumpy. My heart was racing, my feet and hands were fidgety. After an hour fast-dancing, playing and replaying my Macy Gray CD with lit candles all around my apartment, I realized what was going on: I'd become a speed freak.

I sat down on the couch, thinking of Claire's famous line: "Let yourself know what you know." I knew that taking amphetamines was ignorant and could lead to heart attacks. I was already too wound up, without the added ten caffeine-laden diet sodas a day. That plus the Adderall turned me into a hypermaniac. With my easily diagnosed addictive personality, I'd been tempting fate. If my doctor father and brothers had a lifelong mandate, it was to never take any unnecessary medication—not even aspirin. Dr. Winters, the man I currently trusted most in the universe, had told me to stop in no uncertain terms. As if that wasn't enough to convince me, when I stood up, I fainted. A few minutes later I came to, crawled to the couch slowly, and yelled for Aaron, who came running out of the bedroom.

"What's wrong?" he asked.

"Nothing," I said. "Just hold me."

"I decided not to take Adderall anymore," I told Dr. Winters at our Monday meeting. I didn't mention winding up on the floor unconscious. I was no longer seeking his guidance on the issue. Despite having little willpower, fear of instant death had provided sufficient motivation.

"Good," he said. "You don't need it."

At home from my session, I noticed that I'd mistakenly worn two different black boots that didn't go together. One heel was higher than the other. The right one zipped on the side, the left one zipped in back. I took a stab at the subtext. I was feeling mixed up, not normal, unable to take the next step? If I had to be misdirected, I was glad I had Dr. Winters to turn me back around; I felt safe in his hands. Not that Dr. Steiner had steered me wrong. He'd listened carefully, found a way to relieve what was hurting and get me working again. If I'd taken my tiny dose twice a week like a prudent patient, and cut down on caffeine, it might have been my magic. But I was a hungry hedonist with no sense of moderation, the reason I was the perfect lab rat for all this addiction therapy to begin with.

I wound up recommending Lenny to two pals, hopefully stemming the rivalry I had been creating by sharing Dr. Winters with too many of my girlfriends. My passion for writing returned just as the weather became warmer. I never gained back the seven pounds or touched the six leftover peppy pills in my medicine chest, though for some reason I liked knowing they were still there.

Chapter 10

JUNE 2002

After Lilly phoned to say she had just sold my book, I called, faxed, and e-mailed the astonishing news to everyone I knew in the world. Aaron called back first to say: "That's incredible, I love you," then added: "Guess this means I have to read the damn thing." Very hip and impressed by my provocative first-person confessional style while we were courting, he now became mortified whenever I wrote about my dubious past or our marriage. Still, he promised to take me to dinner at Nobu to celebrate, and not to file for divorce at least until the hardcover, titled *Five Men Who Broke My Heart,* hit the bookstores.

My mother, who had been warned that it was "a sex, drugs, and marriage memoir," phoned back next. "Oh God, you're going to humiliate me in public again," she said, only half-joking. "Do I have to leave town?" asked my father on the other extension. "Should we move to Alaska?" The benefit of waiting until age forty-one to publish sexy nonfiction was that

I no longer needed my parents' approval. They weren't my audience. Not that it had ever been hard to freak out West Bloomfield.

Dr. Winters e-mailed: "Susan—this success is real and will mean more because you worked so hard for it and deserve it." That sounded impersonal and shrinky, but I printed it out and carried the folded-up page in my purse. I pulled it out and read it on subways, buses, and before I went to sleep, as if it contained an important hidden message. Other successes I'd had weren't real? Keep working hard? Keep quitting?

I decided to invite all my friends, colleagues, and students to an impromptu book party for myself that Saturday night, before the book was out and therefore before any negative reviews or bad press could ruin my elation. It would be the first nonsmoking party I'd ever given. I knew, beyond a doubt, that I'd never smoke another cigarette. Not because I didn't want to, but because I couldn't live through getting off them again.

Everything that Dr. Winters predicted had come true in nine months, an apt length of time for a childless woman my age, though I was now focused on having books and not babies. "You've given birth to a nonsmoking writer," said Claire, who had quit again herself. "You didn't need that Winters guy, you were just ready," said my brother Brian, who I thought was jealous that he wasn't the doctor genius I'd been exalting. "You helped hundreds of other people get published," said my sweet cousin Miranda. "It was your turn; the good karma came back to you."

I didn't believe it was luck or fate. I wanted the publication of my book to be directly connected to not smoking, because then I could stop doing something else stupid in order to publish the next one. I pondered what the exact equation was. Getting what I'd wanted instantaneously (forty cigarettes a day) had been keeping me from getting more in the long run (a two-hundred-and-thirty page hardcover). Or clearing away the smoke was like personal feng shui; the tar and nicotine had been clogging me up inside, blocking the flow from my brain to my heart to the tips of my fingers.

At my Monday session, I gleefully blurted out all the details of my book deal to Dr. Winters.

"You're much too happy," he said, shaking his head despairingly. "Stop aiming to feel good."

"You can't be serious," I said. "Why wouldn't I aim to feel good?" He was being a total downer. I had to force myself to remember that he was the main reason why I was currently such an upper. "What am I supposed to aim for?"

"Aim for being closer to yourself," he said.

"Haven't you heard the joke 'If I were any closer to my feelings, I'd be molesting them'?" I asked.

He was not amused. "As an addict who was using, you were trying to lessen your suffering. You have to embrace suffering," he said earnestly. "Make it your friend."

"I have enough friends." I folded my arms in front of me, trying to figure out what was wrong with my newfound joy and why he expected me to look the proverbial gift horse in the mouth. "Is this the same thing as Freud's theory that analysis transforms hysterical misery into everyday unhappiness?"

"Similar," he said.

"Well, I've accomplished something that Freud couldn't. He never stopped smoking and died of lung cancer. Whereas I quit tobacco. I've transformed hysterical misery into everyday happiness!" I proclaimed.

"There is only one way for an addict to feel happiness, and that's by using," Dr. Winters proclaimed.

"I'm talking about a different kind of happiness. Career satisfaction," I said. "I used to argue with this former professor of mine about whether achievement was redemption."

"Achievement is not redemption," he said.

I sort of knew it really wasn't, thinking of all the rich, successful people who'd committed suicide or otherwise self-destructed. But why did this feel like redemption? "When you told me my book would sell, were you manipulating me to quit smoking?"

"No," he said. "I just saw that."

"Like a psychic sees things?" I asked.

"No. I wasn't operating in a vacuum." His tone was sickeningly rational. "You had enough success behind you so it was a reasonable prediction."

I wanted to think he'd been psychic. Or better yet, that when he'd read my memoir in manuscript form, he thought it was so fabulous he knew it would sell. But he'd told me it would sell before he'd even read it. "What if you'd hated it? Would you lie and say you liked it?"

"No. I'll never lie to you. If I didn't like your book I would have said, 'This isn't my taste but I'm no predictor of what publishers want.' " He was so dull and matter-of-fact, I believed him.

"You did like it?" I wanted his reassurance and praise.

He nodded.

"You said it was fantastic." I wanted him to say it again.

"Did I?" He smiled. He wasn't going to flatter me anymore; he was too busy punishing me for feeling too good.

"I can't believe how well the therapy worked," I marveled.

"Don't use past tense," Dr. Winters scolded. "You're not finished yet."

"I know. I'm chewing too much gum and I have to quit dope." I was so hyper I could barely sit still, as if I were back on the Adderall, which I wasn't. "I know toking is connected to the cigarettes."

"First you have to quit gum," he said.

"You already made me give up my Blow Pops," I whimpered.

"How much gum are you chewing?"

"A lot."

"How much?"

It was gross and tactless, how he always wanted to know the nitty-gritty. It was disgusting to say out loud, because that made it real. "Around twenty packs of gum a day," I mumbled.

"You're chewing one hundred sticks of gum a day?" he said loudly, looking shocked. "Why didn't you tell me that before?"

"You didn't ask." It had never occurred to me before that it was important. "Not sugarless gum either," I threw out. "I hate sugarless gum. The sorbitol gives me stomachaches."

"A hundred sticks of sugared gum adds an extra five hundred calories to your diet daily," he calculated.

"Some of the packs have seventeen sticks in them." Might as well confess to everything. My oral fixation was endless.

"You have to stop gum now!"

"Why?"

"Because you're killing your teeth," he told me. "What does your dentist say?"

"That I'm killing my teeth," I said.

"It's too many calories," he added. "Sugar affects your mood."

"Can I switch to sugarless?" I begged.

"No," he answered. "It gives you stomachaches."

That was the problem with honesty; it always came back to bite you in the ass. "I don't think sugarless gum would hurt anything," I argued inanely.

"Well, you're wrong. Your excessive gum use is the same neurotic instinct as smoking. You haven't really quit, you've merely switched addictions," he said. "You're still medicating yourself hourly, trying to take the emptiness away. You want to fill an endless need that can never be filled. You'll never get enough."

Nothing like plunging back down to earth with a thud.

"You said it would take me a year to get over the cigarettes and publish my book. It only took nine months." I tried to resign myself to my chewless fate. My mouth already felt lonely. "How long will it take me to get over gum?"

"Three months," he said.

I could tell his answer was completely arbitrary. He was winging it, making up the numbers as we went along. I was probably the only serious chewing-gum junkie on the planet; there was no scientific data available. Still, Dr. Winters was three for three: marriage, cigarettes, memoir. I was keeping all my money on him.

Walking home I passed a newsstand, a Korean market, and Ricky's, where I usually bought pink Spice Girl gum and bags of yellow candy-coated Gold Rush. I leered longingly at the gumball machine at the cheap jewelry store, where I used to buy twenty-five-cent colored gumballs. They sold gum more places than they sold cigarettes. This was too hard; I couldn't do it.

Smoking at least was vilified socially, among doctors, and in the press. Chewing gum was as innocent as apple pie. I thought of the Doublemint twins on TV commercials and cute kids blowing gum bubbles that burst in their faces. I wasn't going to be able to convince myself that gum was evil. The only argument that seemed to work was Dr. Winters' comment that, like cigarettes, my desire for gum was endless. One pack wouldn't ever be enough; I'd always want more. It was an eternal hole I could never fill.

I had a long history as a gum whore. As a child, I started with a normal brand—yellow Juicy Fruit was my favorite. Then I added Beeman's and Teaberry. I liked gum so much that at first I swallowed it. By the time I was six years old I'd learned to spit it out—but way too quickly. I'd throw it in my mouth, chomp hard a few times, suck out all the flavor, discard the remnants, and move on to the next piece.

It was an action that reflected my personality, Aaron suggested.

Okay, my greediness for gum had always been compulsive. Anytime I could earn, borrow, or steal a dollar, I would buy stacks of penny Bazookas with comics, a pack of baseball gum (I'd give my brothers the cards), flavor-coated Chiclets (I'd eat the red and purple ones first), and tiny-sized Chiclets in yellow pouches, which I'd pour into my mouth in one upward swoop. Though I couldn't stand Nicorettes, my regular gum usage increased tenfold when I wasn't smoking. Most recently I'd taken to thick juicy grape Bubble Yum and pink bubble gum tape, which came in a pink plastic container shaped like a tape measure. As an adult I still had a little kid's taste in gum.

My chewing was legendary among my students, who would watch in awe as I'd consume multiple packs of gum while the guest editors lectured. I kept the garbage can close, to keep tossing out the wrappers and gnawed carcasses. Perhaps, like filled ashtrays, I needed to leave a trail. When my foreign pupils traveled home for the holidays, they would bring me back local gum. Marta presented me with Kataboom, from Ecuador, which resembled orange Chiclets. They were filled with a sugary liquid, like Chewels, which made them seem more like candy. Joris returned from England with Airwaves, which were sugar free, honey and lemon flavored. It said "vapour release" on the yellow package. Unfortunately, that meant that on the second bite, they took on the flavor of cough drops. Jamaican gum tasted like hot pepper, Elma gum from Greece appeared to be a clone of Dentyne Ice, and Bon Bon Bum lollipops from Colombia were the smaller, Spanish twin of my beloved Blow Pops. America definitely was the gum capital.

No wonder I had horrible teeth, too many cavities, crowns, and a weight problem. Deep down I'd always been a sugar freak. I'd been in denial.

For a while I entertained the notion that I could savor a few sticks of gum, like those moderate alcoholics who could handle a beer every once in a while. Then I realized that Dr. Winters was right. I'd have to give up chewing entirely and forever. My first few weeks gum-free, I missed it desperately, as much as I'd missed cigarettes. It felt like I'd broken up a fun long-term affair with someone who lived right in my neighborhood. I had to zigzag, avoiding everything: bodegas that sold cigarettes and an array of gum, along with Duane Reade, which had all my brands of smokes and Chiclets. Not to mention bars, restaurants with smoking sections, and all liquor and candy stores.

Meanwhile, as Aaron always said, "Things coexist." In the midst of mourning gum, I was also positively cheerful about the publication of my memoir. I called my wonderful, extremely patient agent, Lilly, every day and set up a meeting with my new editor, Dina. I was thrilled to learn that Dina lived downtown, just four blocks and an avenue away. Dr. Winters' office was on Ninth Street and Fifth Avenue, Lilly's office was on Thirteenth Street. Dina was in the neighborhood too. It was fate, a New Yorker's wet dream: no need for buses, subways, or taxis. All the essential people were miraculously within a ten-block radius of my apartment!

Dina knew from my book that I was a night owl, so she suggested skipping the usual writer/editor Midtown lunch and having our first meeting over dinner in the Village. When we sat down at our table in the nearby seafood restaurant she'd chosen, I said, "What a cool blind date. I'm already in love with you, you know everything about me, AND you're already supporting me." Although she soon proved herself to be brilliant, perceptive, and hysterically funny, externally Dina was my opposite: a conservative, calm, tactful team player. We were the perfect duet. She was my female rock and voice of reason. I was her evil twin.

Shocking myself with my ability to readjust, I was over the worst of my gum withdrawal in ten weeks. I no longer felt desperate for my beloved sugar sticks; reality appeared to be satisfying enough. When I found a lingering pink Spice Girl in my old purse, I quickly threw it down the garbage chute in the hallway. I e-mailed Lilly and Dina several times daily, as well as Aaron and Dr. Winters, as if I were transferring my compulsion from constant substances to constant people. At least I was hitting on the right ones.

At the start of my next session, I told Dr. Winters that I had an important question I needed to discuss.

"There's something I want to bring up too," he said, seeming worried and very businesslike.

"Can I see you twice a week?" I blurted out first. He was very expensive, in a lot of ways. But I had more substances to stop and books to sell. I was nervous that without him, I would ruin all my newfound sobriety and success.

"Well, listen." His face was so serious I got nervous. Was he moving away from Manhattan? Dying? Breaking up with me?

"It's about our payment. I need to raise your fee to one hundred fifty dollars a session. In fact, when new patients come to me I now ask for two hundred a session—"

"Done," I cut him off.

"It's not a problem for you?" He looked a bit taken aback, as if he'd had his argument all plotted out.

"No problem."

I didn't tell him that, now that I could afford it, I would have gone up much higher just to keep him around. I couldn't imagine being without him. Not that I was ever without him. I was perpetually arguing with him in my head and in my notebook. Dr. Winters had been creeping into all of my conversations. He was even intruding into my sleep. In an amusing reversal, my unconscious kept casting me as *his* hero, the female James Bond. In one dream, after the World Trade Center attacks, he was hurt, lying bandaged, lost, and bloody in a cave, like the Ralph Fiennes character in *The English Patient*. That was when I found him, identified him, brought him home, and nursed him back to health. In my next eerie evening reverie, he was imprisoned at Payne Whitney's mental ward, where I crawled into his hospital bed before helping him escape.

With Dr. Winters holding my hand, I managed to banish cigarettes, alcohol, Adderall, freelancing, chewing gum, and rejection from my existence. I felt fearless, absolutely certain that I could live without anything.

Chapter 11

JULY 2002

That summer my husband stopped screwing me.

To be more accurate, Aaron stopped initiating sex. I'd decided to stop being the aggressor to see how long it would take him to grab me or say, "Want to fool around?" After six lonely weeks with no action, I was getting worried. While I was acing sobriety, I feared I was flunking marriage.

"Let me get this straight," Claire said. "You've got this sweet rich brilliant hunk who'll jump your bones whenever you snap your fingers. But you don't want to snap your fingers? I really feel sorry for you."

She had just split up with the fellow architect she'd been dating, and her thirty-year-old kid brother was marrying a gorgeous girl Claire had introduced him to. Plus she'd requit cigarettes for two months, gained twelve pounds, then started again. Now, she said, she was single, smoking, and fat. She definitely was not the right person to commiserate with over my husband's lost passion for me.

Instead I called my wonderful new friend Jasmine, an English professor who seemed blissfully married to Glen, a district attorney even taller than Aaron. He was a hunk too, and a great father to their three daughters. To my surprise, Jasmine admitted that Glen wasn't sexually aggressive either. "His work takes so much out of him. His boss is a stressed-out maniac. We're always broke. His parents are crazy and draining. When he gets home, I don't think he wants to risk rejection," she explained.

"You don't feel let down having to initiate it all the time?" I asked.

"Well, I give him a break. I let different things count as aggressive. If he says, 'You look beautiful in that dress,' or holds my hand, then I take it from there," Jasmine said. "Always with compassion."

Jasmine was so compassionate that for a second I felt sorry for modern men; surely the mixed messages from multiple waves of the women's movement had paralyzed them. Aaron was exhausted, working crazy hours at three jobs. He had also been assisting me with my addiction therapy, going along with Dr. Winters' semi-kooky mandates—holding me for an hour while we watched TV without talking every night, throwing out all candy or junk food in the house, taking long walks with me when I got antsy.

Dr. Winters' latest written edict ordered: "Sex for Medicinal Purposes." I waited for the appropriate time to show it to Aaron over the weekend, as if it were a "Get Out of Jail Free" card.

On Friday night, we had a fight when Aaron did the laundry but just happened to forget to do *my* laundry. Then, afraid his clothes would shrink in the dryer, he hung them up all over the bathroom and living room, until our sleek Manhattan high-rise looked like *Fiddler on the Roof*'s Anatevka. Since Aaron had dropped twenty pounds lately, why would he care if his jeans or shirts shrunk a little bit? He'd been coming home from work every night at midnight. He wasn't sleeping or eating well. When I found a toothbrush and clean pair of polka-dot boxer shorts in his briefcase, I worried that he was having an affair. Then I worried that he never even thought of having an affair.

Too preoccupied with stemming my own self-destructive impulses, I realized that Aaron wasn't just acting like a male jerk. He was being insaner than I was. I suggested he call Dr. Winters to make an appointment for himself. To my surprise, he didn't argue. Winters, always the nonconformist, thought it was a good idea that we saw him separately. I suspected that Aaron was becoming jealous of my fascinating weekly discussions with the good doctor. At least I hoped he was.

"I'm seeing him at eight forty-five Thursday morning," he told me when he came home at midnight on Monday.

"That's so funny, because my appointment is for eight forty-five Thursday night. We'll be Dr. Winters' bookends. There's a screenplay in it, like *Rashomon*."

"Let's fuck with his head," Aaron said. "Make up bizarre conflicting stories to see if he's really listening."

I was not thrilled to share my shrink, though I had originally stolen him from Aaron, who had stolen him from his ex-fiancée. I feared that oedipal triangles and dormant sibling rivalry would resurface all over the place. Yet how could I not trust the guy who made Aaron make an honest woman out of me? Not to mention morphing me into a smoke-alcohol-and-freelance-headache-free soon-to-be published memoirist who weighed 137 pounds, a miracle all by itself.

Instead of leaving well enough alone, I'd made the mistake of admitting that the best way for me to stay off nicotine would be to nix ten pounds. That way I would relinquish the reason I'd always gone back. Thus Dr. Winters' latest torture involved giving up bread products—since that was the quickest, healthiest way I lost weight. (Aaron had lost weight this way too.) I could eat unlimited protein, fat, fruits, and vegetables, while I said goodbye to my cherished pasta, potatoes, pizza, pita, pancakes, sandwiches, pastries, cake, and Entenmann's fat-free brownies. Worse, I'd sadly bid adieu to the fried rice, shrimp dumplings, cold sesame noodles, scallion pancakes, egg rolls, and almond cookies that I had been ordering in weekly from Sammy's Noodle Shop. I was still in the throes of serious Sammy's withdrawal.

Adding sex to the taboo list was killing me. It was deprivation overload. Making myself come wasn't really satisfying. Sort of like eating hard-boiled eggs when I was dying for French toast made from challah. I was feeling desperate. I figured if Dr. Winters had gotten me married, clean, and published, chances were he could get me laid.

At my 8:45 Thursday night session, before I could even say "hello," he looked at me and said, "Stop criticizing Aaron."

"Why?" I asked. "Aaron criticizes me constantly. He says incredibly mean things. If I take out his garbage, I'm an 'anal neat-freak.' When I didn't let him order garlic naan at Café Spice, he said, 'You're such a controlling cunt.' Did you know that when Lilly sold my memoir, Aaron had the nerve to tell my close friend Susie, 'Thank God my father isn't alive to read it.' How passive-aggressive is that? He didn't tell it to one of his best friends, which would have been bad enough. But he told it to one of mine!"

"What did you say to him?"

"I said, 'Go chew on yourself,' which my brothers used to say to me. Sometimes I ignore him. I don't care. Growing up with three rambunctious kid brothers, I'm used to fighting."

"Stop fighting with Aaron," Dr. Winters insisted.

"Why do I have to be more sensitive than he is?"

"Because criticism doesn't bother you but it bothers him," he said.

"That's ridiculous." I crossed my arms. "What a double standard!"

"You can eat anything you want in front of Aaron because it doesn't affect him. But if you watch him eat one french fry, you'll start sobbing and shove twenty-two pieces of bread in your mouth. That's why he's no longer allowed to eat any bread products in front of you. Remember?"

"He knew I was a castrating ballbuster when he married me," I argued. "That's what he wanted. A woman who could do hard jokes. He'd dated enough actresses and suburban dolts who just wanted to cook and have babies. He didn't want a Kewpie doll."

"Both of you have changed in five years," Dr. Winters said.

"I can't smoke, drink, chew gum, freelance, or order in one goddamn egg roll from Sammy's and now I have to play the barefoot wifey who makes him feel big?" I screamed. "Why don't you just give me a lobotomy?"

"Who does it benefit if Aaron feels big?" Dr. Winters asked.

"Some men love brilliant, argumentative women who voice their opinions when they feel like it!" I felt like punching him.

"Who?" he yelled back. "I never met one."

"Come on. I've had relationships with strong men who can handle a real woman. My old boyfriend Brad loved to fight with me. We'd argue and wrestle and have hot makeup sex afterward...."

"Brad?" he asked. "Isn't he the guy who just married the quiet twenty-five-year-old graduate student?"

I knew I'd regret letting my shrink read my memoir in manuscript form. I also knew Dr. Winters was right. Not because he was a sexist pig trying to keep me sweet, quiet, and nonthreatening—which he clearly was. But because making my husband feel big would get me more love, which was what I needed to replace the bread.

"No men like tough, argumentative women?" I inquired in a softer voice.

He sternly shook his head no. "Not to live with."

I walked dejectedly back to my apartment, exhausted from my war of words with horrible, haughty Dr. Winters. Aaron opened the door for me. It was 9:45; he was home earlier than usual. As I stepped inside and hung up my coat, he wrapped his huge warm arms around me and said, "Hi, beautiful."

"Thanks. You feel so good," I whispered as he rubbed my tired shoulders.

"Want to fool around?" he asked.

Before I could say yes, now, and/or hallelujah, he grabbed my breasts and kissed me hard on the lips like he used to. I pushed him down to the floor, tumbling on top of him while stripping off both our clothes.

Later, lying naked in the middle of the living room, I asked, "How did your shrink session go today?"

"He wrote down an adage on the back of his business card," Aaron said.

I was heartbroken. I had imagined that Winters' mini-messages, in his black felt pen, were just for me.

"It's much easier to live with an addict who's using than an addict who's in recovery," he recited.

I wondered what Dr. Winters meant by that dumb little ditty. That it was more fun to be around someone self-anesthetizing and in complete denial than somebody who was bravely confronting all their demons?

I looked up to see that our blinds were wide open. The people in the building across the street could probably see us, but I was too blissed-out to care.

"Sorry I've been such a bitch lately," I told my husband.

"Sorry I've been elsewhere." He kissed my forehead. "How was your shrink session? What did you talk about?"

"Nothing important, sweetie," I said, noting that it was the first time I hadn't craved a cigarette after sex. Now I wanted a bagel.

Part Two

Chapter 12

OCTOBER 2002

"Do you really need to wear that blazer for your book photo?" asked Claire. She was scrutinizing me with her head tilted and arms folded, biting her lower lip.

"What's wrong with it?" I felt insulted. "I always wear blazers."

"When?" She brushed my bangs out of my eyes, then stepped back to inspect me again.

"When I teach and go to meetings. Why? You don't think it looks good?"

"Do you want to look serious?" she asked.

"I don't know. Don't I?" I went to the bathroom and looked in the mirror.

"You're publishing a sexy book. How about a tight T-shirt that shows some cleavage?" she suggested.

Claire had come over to help style me for the author's photo that would appear on the back of my book. It was being taken by Darren, a freelance portrait photographer who charged $500 for the whole job—from the shoot to the proofs. My publishing house would have picked up the bill. But then the photographer would have handed the negatives and contact sheets directly to them and they would get to decide which pic we would go with. I wanted to control my own image, so I decided to have them done, and pay for them, myself.

Darren was the son of a writer friend. His claim to fame was taking the author photos of famous old male poets for the back of their Knopf and Farrar, Straus and Giroux poetry collections. Ten years before, I had wanted to look like a serious poet on the back of a Knopf or Farrar, Straus and Giroux poetry collection. At forty-one, having sold a lust-filled memoir I hoped would be a commercial hit, I'd prefer to look mysterious and seductive, like Mary Gaitskill on the back jacket of her terrific, dark, and twisted short-story collection *Bad Behavior*. Claire was right. I took off the blazer.

"What time is the photographer coming?" she asked.

"Soon, around four o'clock," I said, pulling down the V-neck of my black sweater. "How do I look?"

"Nervous," she said.

"I need to get high." I went to the wooden box from Jamaica on my shelf, where I kept the joints of strong light-green weed that I'd rolled the day before.

"This Winters guy still lets you smoke joints?" She looked surprised.

"Yeah. He said we don't have to worry about dope yet. Didn't I tell you?"

I opened all three living-room windows and lit up the thick doobie, sucking the sweet smoke in deeply. One hit and I already felt mellower. I handed it to Claire, then opened the windows wider. The only problem with getting high after I'd quit cigarettes was that there was nothing to camouflage the strong smell of pot. Aaron came home one night and told me it reeked from the minute he walked out of the elevator. Although it was Greenwich Village and many people in the building got stoned, I needed to get incense or air spray to mask the scent.

"How long have you been off cigarettes now?" Claire asked, sitting down on the couch.

"It's been a whole year. The longest I've ever gone, since I was thirteen." I put on Joni Mitchell's *Blue,* the album we used to get high to in the seventies.

"Blast from the past." She smiled.

"How have you been doing with the cigarettes?" I sat on the couch next to her. She looked sad.

"Off and on," she admitted. "Tell me that line Winters told you again."

I had already told it to her in a fax, two e-mails, and several phone calls. "Underlying every substance problem I have ever seen is a deep depression that feels unbearable," I recited, then sucked in more smoke.

"That's so heavy," she said.

"I know. He's such a genius." I could hear the reverence in my voice, as if he were a cult leader and I was his moonstruck minion.

"Are you sort of in love with him?" She took the joint back.

"Sort of." I nodded. "But I was sort of in love with Dr. Goode when I was seeing her too."

"I know what you mean. I think I'm in love with Denise," she said of the shrink my old shrink had recommended for her several years ago. When I had first suggested Claire share my shrink, Dr. Goode nixed the idea. She thought treating me and my best friend could create sibling rivalry—especially since Claire and I had three brothers each and already suffered from sinister bouts of actual sibling rivalry.

"I think you're allowed to fall in love with a few of your shrinks and writing professors. But only the ones who change your life," I threw out.

"Didn't you sleep with one of your writing professors?"

"Yeah, but I wasn't really in love with that one," I said.

When we finished the joint, I put the leftover little roach back in the box, opened the windows even wider, and sprayed perfume around the apartment. Back in my closet, I pulled out more clothes. Claire followed me in there.

"How about this?" She held up a light purple T-shirt.

"Really?"

"With a push-up bra," she said.

"If you say so." I tried the bra and purple shirt on and looked at fake cleavage in the full-length mirror.

"That's nice." She nodded in approval. "When do you think Winters will make you quit dope?"

"I don't know. I'm not even over quitting gum or bread yet," I said, trying on a black T-shirt with the push-up bra, which looked much better. She shook her head no, so I put the purple one back on.

"I can't believe you quit gum. Remember those bags of yellow Gold Rush we used to buy at the candy store?" she asked. "Didn't you used to swallow it?"

I nodded yes.

"Do you miss it?"

"A little," I said, putting the blazer on over the T-shirt. She was right, a little lilac with cleavage was prettier. "Winters said the gum was killing my teeth. I was gaining weight from all the sugar."

"You do look thin," she said.

"So do you." I cracked up.

"What's so funny?" she asked.

"We've been the same height and weight since we were ten."

"No wonder you look so good," she said.

The room filled with her long light laughter, which I'd loved since we were kids.

The doorman buzzed to say that my photographer, Darren, and his assistant were here. They came in, shlepping a lot of equipment for a short photo shoot—three black leather bags, flashes, a camera stand, and three cameras hanging over their shoulders. Darren had long hair and torn jeans. He was a good-looking thirty-year-old hippie who looked twenty. He introduced his assistant, Chris, who was twenty but looked fifteen. I introduced Claire as my stylist while they unpacked their gear and scoped out my apartment.

"I was thinking I should stand in front of the bookshelves," I offered.

"Are you wearing that blazer?" Darren asked.

"Why? You don't like it?" I hoped the dope would chill me out, but I was as uptight as ever, maybe worse.

"You look kind of professorly," Darren said. Was that a word? He looked like one of my students, the type who would miss four classes in a row to go bungee jumping in Belize, then wonder why I gave him a B.

"She is a professor," Claire said.

"I'm just a lowly adjunct," I clarified.

"A sexy professor," she added.

I was embarrassed, then realized she was flirting with them.

"Okay. Stand over there," Darren instructed me as Chris set up a black umbrella-shaped stand in front of me.

"You're using color film, like we said on the phone, right?" I asked.

"Most author photos are black and white," Darren said.

"I don't look good in black and white," I said. "And I look better from a few feet distance," I added, feeling spacey and ancient. "I don't look good up close anymore."

• • •

A week later Darren came by to show me the proofs and get paid. He handed me an invoice for seven hundred dollars.

"You quoted me five hundred dollars on the phone," I said.

"I had to shoot four extra rolls," he said, taking the contact sheets out of the envelope. "Some of them came out pretty good. I like this row." He pointed.

"Why did you shoot four extra rolls?" I asked, looking at the strips of my faces.

"Well, you didn't like the test shots I tried, so I just kept going until I got something I thought you'd like."

How was I supposed to know how many rolls he'd taken? I hadn't been keeping track. I was too stoned and preoccupied.

"They're not bad," I said, but I was disappointed. The first two rolls of colored film were okay. Claire was right, the purple T-shirt with cleavage looked nice. The next two sheets were filled with black-and-whites. "I told you to just use color film and not to do any close-ups."

"Most author shots are black-and-white close-ups," Darren repeated. "You don't like them?"

"No, I don't." How arrogant was this cute young hippie? I was a cute young hippie before he was even born! "I knew I wouldn't like them. That's why I told you to take color shots from a few feet away." I had a strong urge for a cigarette. I went to my purse and wrote him a check for seven hundred dollars. He was my good friend's son; I didn't want to fight and—for once—I could afford not to worry about an extra two hundred bucks.

Before he left, Darren turned to me and asked, "Did you get stoned before the shoot?"

I was taken aback. "Why do you ask?"

"You look high in the pictures. That's the problem with them," he said. "Check out the close-ups I took. You're squinting your eyes. You seem kind of elsewhere."

I handed him the check and said, "You should have listened and shot them farther away, like I asked you to."

When he left I stared at the film for a long time. The color shots were decent, but for some reason I looked really different in the rows of black-and-whites. I hated to admit that Darren had a point about the pot. My eyes were elsewhere, half closed. I'd never seen exactly what I looked like high before. It never dawned on me that being stoned could alter the way my face appeared in a photograph. It scared me.

I put Joni Mitchell's *Blue* back on, sat on the couch, and smoked another joint while staring at my faces on the black-and-white film. I looked hollow, lost, and haunted. Then I tore up the contact sheets, marched to the hall, and threw them down the chute so nobody would ever see that I was a drug addict. Not even me.

Chapter 13

NOVEMBER 2002

"Since I've quit cigarettes and alcohol, I've become ludicrously sensitive," I told Roger, a young book-editor friend I was having dinner with at Café Spice, a downtown Indian restaurant. "I find myself overreacting to the smallest insult or slight."

"I know how that feels," Roger said. "You know, I'm a recovering alcoholic and drug addict."

"You are? I didn't know." I was oddly pleased to learn this, as if he'd just told me that we were from the same home state. No wonder he'd always ordered soda or tea at restaurants, and had made excuses to opt out of the late-night parties I'd invited him to.

He nodded. "I've been clean for four years. I was afraid to go outside for the first six months."

"You were really vulnerable too?" I asked, ogling the piece of warm bread, smothered in garlic and butter, that came with Roger's vegetarian platter. If the warm, puffy pita was by my plate, I'd down it in a second and want more. Lately it felt safer to stay home, where there were fewer temptations. Then again, Dr. Winters pointed out, I lived in the center of Manhattan, where I could get any substance I wanted delivered within twenty minutes. That was why, he insisted, I had to learn self-control.

"Of course I was vulnerable," Roger said. "How could I not be? I'd been using cigarettes, booze, and drugs to get love or be cool or fit in. It was a huge crutch. Without them I felt scared and naked. I had no self-esteem."

Roger was only twenty-six. When had he found time to indulge in that much partying, clean up his act, and do the therapy to undo—and understand the root of—all those addictions? Was Drew Barrymore his role model? He'd accelerated the process; he was way ahead of me.

"How old were you when you started?" I asked.

"Twelve," he said. "Junior high."

He'd started even younger than I did. "How did you get off everything?"

"I went to AA meetings every day," he said. "It saved my life. It amazed me to be around so many people who felt as fragile and scared of relapsing as I did."

I'd considered going to Nicotine Anonymous, Smok-Enders, or smoking-cessation meetings sponsored by the American Cancer Society. But coming from a clan with four kids too close in age, I'd always felt diminished and uncomfortable in group settings. The typical dynamic seemed to involve being constantly interrupted and overriden by the loudest (usually male) bully in the bunch. Group interactions always called up the suffocating sibling rituals I had moved to Manhattan to escape. I responded better to individual attention, as if I needed a few more years of one-on-one parental guidance.

I never minded leading groups. When I taught, I tried to be

patient and fair. I would ask questions, then go around the room to make sure everyone had a turn to speak. I encouraged shy students with such comments as "No question is ever stupid," and "What a brilliant observation! I'm so glad you brought that up," making sure that nobody in my classes ever felt intimidated or invisible.

"Do you think everyone quitting stuff feels overly sensitive?" I asked Roger.

"Sure. Don't you know the AA joke?" he asked. "If a normal person gets a flat tire, they call a tow truck. If a recovering addict gets a flat tire, they call the Suicide Hotline."

I'd thought my addiction therapy was idiosyncratic and profound. I didn't know I was just a recovery cliché.

"I had no idea you used to drink and do drugs," I said.

"Booze, blow, and cigarettes were my poison, with a few pills thrown in whenever they were free." He picked up the bread and took a bite. "I think I even did heroin a few times. At parties, by mistake."

"Did you smoke dope?"

He nodded. "Pot too. I used to keep a bong on my nightstand. I was an insomniac for years. The coke and nicotine would pick me up, the dope would get me to sleep. I call it the substance shuffle."

" 'Cause you'd just switch off?"

"Yeah. Some weeks I'd say, 'I'm never doing coke again.' I would be real proud of myself, forgetting that I was drinking more. Or I'd stop drinking but then start chain-smoking two packs a day. It took me a while to see there was no real difference between what I was using. The forms varied but it was the same escape. Now I'm a sober, nonsmoking vegan and I just quit caffeine," he continued. "I still go to AA meetings three or four times a week. I've never felt better in my life."

I felt competitive with Roger's extranicotine addictions. His former coke, booze, pot, pills, and accidental heroin use clearly trumped my pot, gum, and bread. He had quit meat and dairy too; he was off more things than me. He looked thinner than I was *and* he was still allowed to shove naan into his mouth. Life wasn't fair.

Later that night, while smoking a leftover joint, Roger's words echoed. "The forms varied, but it was the same escape." He was four years clean; I wasn't. I'd gone from getting high a few times a week with friends to toking every day alone. In an open, honest two-hour talk with Roger about addictions, I'd neglected to mention that little factoid. I'd been lying to him and myself. It was time to face the truth: Doing my own substance shuffle, I had become a middle-aged pothead.

I had started getting stoned at thirteen, around the time I had taken up tobacco. I loved to smoke, so it seemed like an ingenious invention—a cigarette that packed a punch. At my liberal private school, I'd gravitated to an older, artsy crowd. I became friendly with Mitch, a suave seventeen-year-old with a mustache and glasses who drove a red Trans Am and smoked cigars. Mitch was a member of a weekly Transactional Analysis group that met on Sunday nights at the home of our psychology teacher. Though I already hated groups, I developed what Claire deemed "a serious crunch" on Mitch. I joined in order to ask Mitch for a ride. When he picked me up, two of his friends, Larry and Alex, were in the backseat.

My father thought TA sounded like '60s mumbo jumbo (though it was the '70s). My mother was pleasantly shocked to learn that Mitch, Larry, and Alex were nice Jewish boys on their way to law and medical school. My " 'rents," as Mitch called them, allowed me to convince them that our Sunday night pseudopsychology party was an educational activity.

On the way home after the first TA session, the guys lit a joint and passed it around. I wasn't sure if I caught a buzz that initial time or if I was just overwhelmingly excited to be the mascot of three cute senior boys. For a second I feared they could all take advantage of me sexually. I was disappointed to find the trio was much more enthralled with $1.95 special roast beef dinners, complete with coleslaw and hash browns, at a local Arby's restaurant. My interest quickly shifted from TA to TLC to THC. By the time Mitch and my romantic escapades ended, I had replaced him with regular reefer madness.

At sixteen, I started college, two years early. Freshman year I couldn't wait to attend Ann Arbor's Hash Bash, the infamous annual smoke-out where most of the campus went cannabiscrazy, lighting up in the diagonal square in front of the graduate library. The night before, I sat on the floor of my dorm room, twisting twenty tiny pin joints with Bambú rolling papers out of my new boyfriend Peter's thick forty-dollar bag. I smoked one first, listening to an album by Bob Dylan, who—as legend had it—was the one who'd originally turned on the Beatles.

Rolling the bag involved taking out the seeds and twigs and crunching it into powder. I'd first used a rolling machine but was soon able to roll a small one quickly in my fingers, a talent I was proud of. Peter taught me how to shotgun, putting the whole joint inside his mouth, fired-up side first. While he blew out, I opened my lips and inhaled. It was like a kiss of smoke and I loved it.

Dope provided me with instant relief from anxiety and insecurity—my mental state from junior high on. Two bong hits and everyone seemed cooler, funnier, and more colorful. Even puffing the strongest stuff, I never hallucinated, though I faked it a few times, to keep up with the stories of classmates. One managed to tie himself naked to a tree during an acid trip and wound up in a documentary; another claimed that cocaine was the cause of a botched gas-station robbery.

The only time I lost control was in bed, where getting high had the same pleasing effects as popping a few drinks, loosening me up without the calories or nausea the next morning. Puffing just a quarter of a joint made me less inhibited. For an uptight, overly cerebral neurotic, this was no small feat. A tiny dose of this dazzling drug transformed me. In mere minutes I morphed from Diane Keaton in *Annie Hall* to Cher in Las Vegas.

Like Roger, I was a lifelong insomniac. I noticed that toking before I went to bed helped me crash and get a good night's sleep; it must have been a mild sedative. My friends found that grass gave them the munchies, but I actually ate less in my stoned states because I was too busy dancing, having sex, or smoking cigarettes. Fellow tokers agreed that it was an instant cure for constipation. I read how the nifty narcotic had provided poetic inspiration for the nineteenth-century *Club des Hachichins* (the Hashish-Eaters' Club), whose members included Gautier, Balzac, and Baudelaire. I used this to justify my addiction, as if my pot-smoking implied a higher artistic calling (though I found it better for blurting out ten-page first drafts than for fixing grammar and punctuation). No wonder I'd been under the spell for three decades.

I recalled a graduate-school party centered around pot brownies, which took longer to get you stoned but the high lasted for six hours. I'd smoke bowls while giggling with Claire for hours about nothing, no doubt the reason some referred to pot as "Laughing Grass" and "Good Giggles." I'd passed around joints while dancing to Aretha Franklin's "Respect" in the middle of my wild thirtieth-birthday soiree. It was held at an artist friend's Soho loft, where even nonindulgers got a contact buzz. A cartoonist I dated drew me a comic strip starring Marijuana Girl, who was way mellower than Superwoman and lived high on planet Greenwich Village.

Rethinking the image of the merry Marijuana Girl, I forced

myself to acknowledge the downside of dope. I'd once wound up in a dangerous neighborhood on the Lower East Side late at night to meet a dealer who never showed up. Upset and stunned, I'd called Claire from a pay phone.

"Duh. Drug dealers are known for being space cadets," she said. "That's 'cause they're usually on drugs."

Later that night, a street dealer in Washington Square Park sold me a ten-dollar dime bag that turned out to be dirt. I was stuck, broke, and straight. What was I going to do? Report him to the police? Call the Better Business Bureau? I quit for a year and a half after that. I was a broke freelancer who wasn't sleeping with anyone at that point anyway. Dope's aphrodisiac elements weren't worth the hassle.

I didn't start again until I met Stu, a long-haired, fairly reliable struggling musician who delivered ridiculously expensive $100 quarter ounces of the strong green stuff door-to-door. At this stage I bought extra and made sure I always had enough. The only problem with my new system was that Stu wanted to hang out and chat, and often needed to use my phone. He then had to wait around for his next customer to call back.

Pot made me horribly paranoid once, when I was on my way to a dentist appointment. Dr. Panzer was a nice and gentle man, but I'd always hated going to the dentist. (Given my gum obsession and mouthful of cavities and crowns, it wasn't an irrational dislike.) I was afraid he would need to give me novocaine shots and drill my teeth, which was my definition of loud death. I thought getting high before I left would chill me out, as it usually did. This time it didn't, it made my dread worse. I had an anxiety attack and almost didn't make it to Dr. Panzer's office. Finally I forced myself to hop a taxi. When the driver started driving fast, I was positive I was going to die in a car crash. I didn't, and luckily Dr. Panzer didn't drill or give me shots that day. Some said marijuana merely enhanced whatever you were feeling. I never got high before going to the dentist again.

Marijuana wasn't supposed to be habit-forming. Since I'd been able to quit for that year and a half after graduate school without missing it much, I assumed I wasn't dependent. That began to change. One evening I ran out of stash and desperately called every toker I knew, trying not to jones out. I finally rummaged around my apartment, blending little leftover roaches with tobacco to eke out one pathetic last high. I started buying it in larger amounts so I would never again be stuck dry. Surely there were better uses for the $1,500 to $2,500 I calculated I'd spent on pot annually.

I realized that getting stoned had been making me exhausted and spacey, giving me a dry mouth and a sore throat. I recalled the voice of a prudish NYU poetry professor who had warned that dope damaged your brain cells. He used to list writers whose careers went to seed from too much wacky weed. I worried that dope did indeed thwart motivation. For a decade and a half I had been a busy freelancer, penning seven pieces a week for newspapers and national magazines. I was convinced this productivity proved that dope didn't deplete my energy or slow me down. But now I heard Dr. Winters' voice saying, "Addicts can be very stupid," and saw that years of excuses were only a rationalization.

In truth, smoking had always helped me concentrate, but only for brief periods. For two decades I had mostly worked on very short pieces, between three hundred and three thousand words. In order to make my mark as a writer in the world, I needed to work on two- and three-hundred-*page* canvases. ("A page a day is a book a year," a successful—and clean-living—writer friend with ten books out often reminded me.) At the age of forty, I'd finally been able to successfully sustain a longer narrative with my memoir. Anti-drug crusaders had always insisted that marijuana induced short-term memory decline and impaired judgment. I feared that was why I hadn't been able to publish a hardcover book sooner. Professor Prude had been correct: My fine dope fetish had fried my brain.

Addictions transported you, took you someplace else. All I had to do was inhale three hits of good ganja to be lying on a Jamaican beach, rocking out at an outdoor concert, a teenager again. But taking a few tokes with stoner friends at midnight dance parties downtown wasn't the same thing as toking every single night by myself. I tried to make a rule that I had to do all my work without pot. When I was done, I would allow myself to indulge. Instead of nine o'clock, I began craving highness by six. It was the only reason I considered seeing Dr. Winters in the early afternoon. That way, I could work, see him, then get off after our session.

I kept my stash in a box right over my desk that I'd begun staring at in between paragraphs. Sometimes I'd let myself hold the unlit joint between my lips while I was at the computer. Soon I was lighting up before I finished working. Then one night, right before I left for my Thursday meeting with Dr. Winters, the temptation was too great and I took a few hits before walking out the door. I had never done that prior to a therapy appointment. Uh-oh. By going to see him high, I was crossing a line. I brushed my teeth twice and sprayed perfume so he couldn't smell it on me. I put more makeup on my eyes so they wouldn't look red. I was sure that Dr. Winters couldn't tell the difference.

"I got high before I came here," I blurted out the second I walked in, as if his office were a confessional booth and he were my priest.

"Why the hell would you do that? Don't waste my time," he admonished me. Some absolution. "You're never allowed to come here high again. If you do, I won't see you. I'll send you home."

I felt ashamed. An old boyfriend once asked what I was thinking of during sex. When I told him I was picturing two beautiful strangers fucking, he accused me of not being able to have an orgasm without fantasizing. Thus I was removing myself from reality. My ex was right. I wasn't really present. Getting stoned before getting shrunk felt the same way, as if I were wearing a mask, hiding, pretending to be there when part of me had checked out. It never occurred to me that one could have fear of intimacy with one's own shrink. I questioned whether that meant I was afraid to know him, or myself.

"Okay, I won't," I said. I didn't feel very stoned, just a bit more tired than usual. I opened my notebook and read a line I'd scrawled. "You told Aaron that it's easier to live with an addict who's using than an addict in recovery. Why is it easier?" I finally remembered to ask. It had been bugging me for months.

"Someone in recovery is feeling feelings they've spent their life avoiding and don't know how to process or manage," he said. "Who wants to live with that?"

"Isn't it better to confront your demons?" I asked.

"Of course it's better ultimately, but it's not easier," he said. "You do know what all your addictions are about, right?"

"Wanting more?"

"Wanting more what?"

We'd been through my early years a hundred times. I felt as if he were springing a Psych 101 pop quiz on me. "Wanting more love," I answered.

"Why?" He reminded me of my grating fourth-grade math teacher, who wanted us to "show our work" while solving problems. This was a problem for me, since I did long division by guessing numbers and multiplying. I was eternally finding ways to cut corners, even back then.

"My mother had four kids in less than seven years," I

repeated by rote. "If I was upset or needy she didn't have time to hold me." Such mild neglect seemed embarrassingly inadequate, especially when so many writers grew up poor, abused, battered by alcoholics, and/or having sex with their stepparents.

"Nothing will ever fill that loss," he said. "Stop getting high and learn to let yourself feel bad."

"Can't I learn self-soothing?" I asked.

"Not if you keep getting stoned to block it out," he said.

It was hard to stop, and I needed his help. I wanted to see Dr. Winters regularly at this time every Thursday night. Unfortunately he was too overbooked to give me anything steady. Week by week he kept switching our meetings to different times. You would think he would start on the hour, or the half hour. But he wanted to see me Thursday at 2:10 P.M., next Friday at 3:15, on Monday at 5:45. Then he was between seven and sixteen minutes late for each appointment. The sessions would go later so it was still fifty minutes, but there was no consistency. It confused me, my work, and my dope-smoking schedule, since I was determined to see him sober.

As I started toking less, Dr. Winters seemed busier and more disorganized. He resembled a mad professor, reminding me of my father and husband. It was hard enough trying to stay straight. His more frenzied manner made me nervous. Before each scattershot slot he stuck me in, I called to confirm.

"You don't have to keep checking before you come." He sounded annoyed. I supposed he didn't want me using up valuable message-machine tape when it wasn't an emergency. I guessed that my checkup calls were conveying my feeling that he was unreliable.

After the third time he complained, implying my need to confirm our session each week was neurotic, I stopped calling. Big mistake. As I slipped into his waiting room on Wednesday night at six-thirty, there was a woman I'd never seen before sitting there. She looked older and more frumpy than me. Dr. Winters called me into his office, apologized, and said he had made a terrible mistake by double-booking the hour. He asked me to reschedule. Why didn't he ask the other woman to reschedule? If I was going to be jealous, shouldn't he at least blow me off for somebody cuter and younger?

I took a few breaths, then agreed, assuming that, because I was so strong and stable, he knew I could handle it. Whereas the frump might freak out. In order to justify the extreme level of anguish I felt about this menacing mix-up, I told him my friend Roger's great line about recovering addicts with flat tires calling the Suicide Hotline.

"I don't get it," Winters said.

"It's about how we overreact to day-to-day problems," I attempted to explain.

"Will you be okay?" he asked.

"I'm not going to smoke a pack of cigarettes or shoot heroin," I spit out. "If that's what you mean."

"What about getting high?"

"What about it?" If he was going to cancel our session, he didn't have a right to take away anything else.

"Listen, starting in January I think I'll be able to see you late every Thursday night," he offered.

That seemed a long time away when I wanted to see him that night. "I'll need to keep confirming our sessions this month," I warned. I felt like a wife who'd been cheated on who didn't want to catch her husband with his mistress again. I was telephoning ahead to send the signal: "I'm on my way over. So you better get rid of her now, you idiot!"

"You don't have to call. Really." He took out his appointment book. "I'm sorry about this. I can see you Tuesday at three-fifteen."

"You don't have any nights free this week?"

He shook his head no. "Sorry. I'm overbooked because of Thanksgiving."

"Okay," I relented, surmising that guilt had its uses. At least I'd soon nail his coveted late Thursday night slot, though he'd only thrown it in as a consolation prize.

At home, I smoked half a joint, analyzing the trade-off. I was devastated by his rejection one minute, then completely placated when he offered me a steady date. It was pathetic. I debated switching to Roger's method, relying on groups rather than depending on one person. While focusing on alcohol, too many AA members chain-smoked, I'd complained. Roger pointed out that there were special nonsmoking AA assemblages. Groups would be cheaper and safer. If a leader didn't show up, there would be others to get it going. Plus there were lots of different meetings at all times one could attend. If you were vulnerable and needy, you would never be left out in the cold. It was too bad that my past had left me no patience for clusters of people I wasn't controlling and that Winters had already hijacked my brain.

His inconsistent behavior reminded me of the sadistic game I used to play with my baby brother Michael, when I was eight years old and he was two. I would pretend he was a stranger and that I didn't know his name. As he started crying and looking scared, I would say, "Of course I know you, you're Michael," and hold him close. I had probably traumatized my brother forever, though, in my defense, I was a miserable eight-year-old with an intense case of sibling and penis envy. On the other hand, Winters was a fifty-year-old acclaimed psychoanalyst who should know better. His forgetfulness could push a weak patient over the edge. But I wasn't weak. After selling my book and ditching cigarettes, I was semisolid. By comparison, one missed appointment seemed tolerable. He was lucky that, for being crazy, I was so sane.

I never got high before a therapy session again. Next, in order to be dope-free for full twenty-four-hour cycles, Dr. Winters insisted I stop toking *after* appointments too. I was about to get the hang of it when I arrived at his office on Tuesday afternoon. He called me inside his inner sanctum. He had a confused expression on his face.

"I'm so sorry, Susan." He glanced at his list of appointments, then looked at me. "There's been another scheduling snafu."

"Don't tell me you've double-booked me again." I threw up my arms in disbelief.

"I did." He closed his black leather book.

I was stone cold sober and absolutely stunned. He was standing me up twice. This time it was for a younger woman: a distraught-looking teenage girl who, he claimed, had come to see him from out of town. To make the rejection more frustrating, Dr. Winters' second screwup was occurring right before he was going out of town. That meant that I would not be able to meet with him again—and tell him off—for ten days. A mature, intelligent, happily married woman, I realized with horror that I was now paying him to be the Bad Boyfriend. Like all the best Bad Boyfriends, he knew the worst torture for somebody like me was making me wait.

How dare he! Who did he think I was—his doormat? I didn't have to put up with this! I rushed home and got really stoned to spite him. Unfortunately this time the dope didn't make that much difference. I was just as bereft as I was straight. As my life was getting better, getting buzzed was getting boring. I no longer wanted to be high. I wanted to be with him.

Chapter 14

DECEMBER 2002

"What the fuck is your problem, blowing me off twice?" I asked Dr. Winters at our next fifty-minute tête-à-tête, which he thankfully hadn't double booked to avoid me. One benefit of not clogging my system with unhealthy intoxicants was that my mind was crystal clear. Even ten days after his second scheduling mishap, I was still distressed.

"Susan, I'm very sorry," he said. "You have every right to be upset."

"What really gets me is that two of my nights wouldn't have been ruined if I'd called to confirm, like I wanted to." I crossed my arms, then crossed my legs but couldn't get comfortable. "We were just talking about how my parents didn't have enough time for me and then you stand me up twice. It's like that joke where the patient says, 'Nobody pays any attention to me,' and the therapist says, 'Next.' "

"I know. You're right," he said, in the way that a rejecting suitor, feeling guilty about being a two-timing cad, would say, "It's not you, it's me."

"You're the one who's angry. I can tell. Why are you so angry?" I demanded. "Because I'm too needy?"

He shook his head no.

"I bet that I remind you of some strong Jewish woman from your past." I threw transference back in his face.

"I'm not conscious of it," he said. "But maybe."

That wasn't good enough. I wanted to understand what was happening inside that hyper head of his. Something was twitching him out. I couldn't bear to lose his esteem or full attention. "Because I came here high?" I tried.

"No," he said. "It was just that once?"

"Just that once." I nodded.

"You won't come here high again?"

"I already promised I won't."

"That wasn't it," he said.

"Since I don't have any skin, I've been psychic lately," I reminded him.

I wasn't usually the type to give credence to any kind of clairvoyance, mental telepathy, or extrasensory phenomenon before. I'd never gone to séances, believed in tarot cards, or had my palm read.

"I know. You have been extremely perceptive," he conceded.

"I can tell you've been elsewhere and really angry. Why? You don't like that I won't agree to see you in the morning?"

"That might be it," he said. "I think you're too rigid."

"I'm too rigid because I won't bend to your schedule? I'm supposed to change my work around to fit into your early-morning time slots so that your life can run smoother?"

"I didn't say that."

"I was blocked for months when I was getting off cigarettes, but lately I can write again. I start work the minute I wake up and keep going until at least six o'clock every day. If I take a shower, get dressed, and go out to see you at two o'clock, then I never wind up being able to get back to work. I lose half the day," I told him. "You're acting like your work is more important than mine." I figured that I might as well let out ten days' worth of rage. He was the one who'd sworn that if I could just let my pain play itself out, I wouldn't need to self-medicate it away.

"That's a good point." He nodded distractedly. It wasn't much fun to argue with him when he wasn't really fighting back.

"If you double book again, I think you should get rid of her, not me," I said, thinking he was so elsewhere today, he'd double booked his own mind.

"Okay," he laughed.

I liked making him laugh. "I'm calling you first to check from now on. Otherwise I won't trust you."

"I bet you'll never trust me again," he said.

His flagrant flakiness presented me with a dilemma. If I was single and dating a guy who blew me off twice in a row, I would simply stop seeing him. The problem was, Dr. Winters was not my lover, he was my savior. Worse, he wasn't finished saving me yet.

As a tough-talking, cynical urbanite who didn't take crap from anyone, I really wanted to dump him. But avoiding cigarettes, alcohol, and gum while cutting down on weed was hard enough. Being deprived of the therapy I'd used to replace the addictions would be too daunting. Deep down I knew that Dr. Winters was a kind, gentle man who understood me better than anyone. (Except for Claire, who simultaneously offered unconditional love while encouraging drug-taking and debauchery.) I needed to find a way to accept that he was a good, but flawed, human being.

I was constantly forgiving my husband, who also broke all

my rules. He'd recently booked a solo business trip to L.A. the weekend of my birthday, showed up forty-five minutes late for dinner last week, then apologized by bringing me the same Bob Dylan bootleg CD he'd already given me. After six years of marriage I was learning to let minor stuff go because, in his own messy, distracted male way, I knew Aaron was a good guy.

When I turned forty, I also noticed that I was fighting less with my parents and brothers. I had made peace with so many of my faults and weaknesses this past year. It seemed only fair to pardon the imperfections of others I loved.

"Are you giving me Thursday nights out of guilt?" I asked Dr. Winters.

"No. The night of my Columbia class was changed," he explained. "I really am sorry for switching our appointments around."

"You have to get our time right from now on," I warned him, adding, "I've always detested flakes."

"I am not a flake." He glared at me. I'd struck a nerve. He did not like to think of himself as flaky. He looked as angry as I thought he felt.

"Well, you acted flaky." I taunted him with the epithet, gratified I could get a rise out of him.

He shook his head and said, "Listen, do you want to know why I've been having scheduling conflicts lately?"

"Of course I do," I said. But did I really?

I wasn't sure I wanted to see any more cracks in his armor. He was, after all, my knight, guiding light, and most trusted confidant. Still, I was itching to know what was really going on with him.

"You know I live in Battery Park City?" he asked.

"Yes." I vaguely recalled that he owned a town house there. Confirming this address bummed me out. It was hard to idolize a Manhattanite who had such bad taste in real estate.

Aside from the fact that city-within-a-city complexes rarely worked in New York, the first World Trade Center attack, in 1993, should have been enough to convince him to sell it and move farther uptown. What kind of sign was he waiting for, Armageddon?

"Early in the morning on September eleventh, my wife and I went to work," he said. "We left our four-year-old daughter, Kyra, with her babysitter."

"A four-year-old daughter?" I was flabbergasted by the addition of this new Winters. Since when did he have a four-year-old daughter? "I thought you had a teenage daughter in L.A."

"I have a teenage daughter with my ex-wife, in California," he clarified.

"I didn't know that you had another daughter," I said quietly.

My brother Eric's pretty little girl, Andrea, whom I adored, was four years old. It was a great age; she was a miniature person with a big vocabulary and distinct personality. Thinking of Andrea helped me picture Kyra.

"We live across the street from the World Trade Center. Kyra and her babysitter were home when the first plane struck the tower. Ash and smoke blasted through the windows and under the door," Dr. Winters said. "It was pandemonium. People fled for their lives. Kyra and the sitter left with no shoes, no wallet. They thought we were being bombed. They were terrified. They ran to the Hudson River, where they got on a police boat and wound up in New Jersey. . . . I couldn't reach the babysitter by cell phone until late that night." His voice was quivering. "My wife went to pick Kyra up. She was physically unharmed, but I couldn't see her until Wednesday night."

I pictured that warm, eerie Tuesday afternoon, recalling that no cars or buses were allowed downtown. Police and fire trucks blocked the traffic. Everything below Fourteenth Street was closed. They wouldn't even allow newspaper deliveries. It had happened fifteen months before, but Dr. Winters was talking as if it were yesterday.

"By the time I got there, Kyra was traumatized. She couldn't talk. Her expression, all her gestures..." He paused. "She was like a different little girl. I swear I could barely even recognize her...."

The night of September 11, I'd met with a group of my NYU students who'd been evacuated from their Water Street dormitory. I felt so helpless, I was glad to give a few of them money and clothes and loan them my phone and computer to let their relatives and friends know they were okay. They were terrified and flipping out. A few foreign students wound up dropping out of school and moving home.

"We took Kyra to several doctors," he said. "They diagnosed post-traumatic stress disorder. Nothing they suggested helped. We don't even believe in therapy for kids her age...."

It surprised me that he didn't believe in therapy for little kids. Aaron told me that Dr. Winters' wife was a shrink too, one who took care of cancer patients. As an escape from such grueling work, they used to go to see all the new gory action movies on weekends, which he'd discussed with Aaron. I hated scary movies.

"Then this psychiatrist suggested we get her a pet," Dr. Winters said.

"I hate pets." I couldn't help but throw out my bias, though my friend Lisa had a cute poodle I almost liked.

"I hate pets too," he said.

"Really?" It was good to know that he wasn't an animal person either. Aaron (who loved dogs) had always maintained that Dr. Winters was not the warm and fuzzy type.

"But we wanted to help Kyra, so we tried giving her a puppy named Sammy."

"What kind of dog?" I asked.

"A Yorkshire terrier," he said. "Kyra started attributing her fears to the dog, saying things like 'Sammy's scared. But it's okay, the buildings are not going to fall down again.' It's called projective identification. Anyway, the dog was really helping her."

"When did you move back home?" I asked.

"We haven't. Our apartment was too damaged. It needed a total renovation. We've been subletting a string of places. We're about to move back, but our building doesn't allow pets. The condo board won't make any exceptions. Even in this case, when it's documented that Sammy is what they call an emotional-support animal."

"Like a Seeing Eye dog?" I asked.

"Exactly," he said. "That'll come up in the lawsuit, which involves the federal department of Housing and Urban Development and the New York State Human Rights Commission."

I thought Dr. Winters should just sell his place in Battery Park City and buy an apartment that allowed dogs. Given the downward dip in downtown real estate, I guessed he couldn't afford it.

When he was finished, he looked at me, as if now I'd understand everything. At first, my heart went out to him. I couldn't bear to envision him sad. Imagine being a brilliant swashbuckling shrink who could mend everybody in Manhattan but not his own little daughter. Then I pictured all the sublets, contractors, kid shrinks, lawyers, urban commissions, neurotic patients, and psychology students he was juggling. His life seemed chaotic, crazy, loud, ungainly. Weirdly, this cheered me up. I was more stable than my shrink! It made me appreciate my pretty peaceful existence: no kids, no dogs, no babysitters, no construction, no sublets, no lawsuits.

Despite Dr. Winters' deadly double bookings and my battles with the demon dope, for the last few months I had been

relatively joyous—still dancing around my apartment to my
Macy Gray CD every day and singing to myself walking down
Village streets.

I kept waiting for him to further connect the dots, to tell
me that the frump was his lawyer or a HUD representative, or
that both days he'd canceled on me were court dates. But he
didn't.

"You're saying that this is the reason you blew me off for
two appointments?" I asked.

"Yes. I've been very upset," he said. "Preoccupied. Calling
the lawyers. Fighting with the president of the board."

"I'm sorry to hear about your daughter," I said.

I'd started seeing him three weeks after the World Trade
Center attacks. I had no idea that his apartment had been
damaged and that he hadn't been able to live at home all this
time. To his credit he'd never given away the extent of his anguish.

"Does it make you feel better knowing?" he asked.

"No. It feels horrible." I was tired just hearing about all his
turmoil. "I thought you had one kid in California. It's hard
knowing you have an ex-wife, a new wife, a traumatized little
girl, a babysitter, a dog, a lawsuit. You're too overburdened. It
creeps me out."

He looked stunned, as if taking me into his confidence was
supposed to soothe me, or make me feel special, when it had
the opposite effect.

"Aren't shrinks supposed to keep their personal lives secret?" I asked. "Didn't Freud have strict rules about it?"

"Freud used to invite his patients to his home for tea, and
tell them all about his life and his family. The post-Freudians
were the ones who pushed the concept of therapist as blank
screen," he said. "Addiction therapy is more behavioral. I always answer any personal questions a patient asks."

"I hate knowing this much about you," I admitted.

"Why do you hate it?" he asked.

For more than a year, I'd been infantilized, spiraling back to my childhood, where Dr. Winters was my ever-attentive phantom father. This new information snapped me out of it. I could no longer be the vulnerable female child *he* was saving. I couldn't even go back to my semierotic dreams of rescuing him. Now all I could think about was his daughter Kyra, whose terrors weren't neurotic or imaginary. I wasn't a young damsel in distress. I was a grown-up woman who wanted to save the scared, real little girl in the story.

"I was miserable in a big family. It's the least sexy scenario possible," I said. Even I could hear how selfish I sounded. But this was not a friendship where we were on equal footing. He was not my colleague; he was my doctor. I was paying him to finish fixing me, or was it unfixing me? Either way, I had to be honest. "I don't want to picture your life like Ozzie Nelson's. I don't even want to see you as Ozzy Osbourne."

"How do you want to picture me?" he asked.

"You're James Bond, this well-dressed loner who kills the bad guys with tae kwon do while sipping champagne on a yacht in the Caribbean," I said, not looking him in the eye. I was worried that I'd trashed his family-man persona and hurt his feelings.

"You know you have to give up dope completely, don't you?" he asked.

"I'm not ready yet," I told him.

"Get ready," he told me.

"Within the next few months?" I pleaded for more time, feeling terrified by the thought of losing something else. "You'll show me how?"

"When it comes to drug treatment, I'm still James Bond," he declared.

He reached for his appointment book. I reached in my briefcase for his holiday present. Getting me off cigarettes alone was worth my gratitude, even if I'd recently been paying him to reject me. I had considered giving him a fancy pen, a leather-bound first edition of Freud's *Dream Analysis,* or another antique clock. When a friend with season Knicks tickets was going out of town, she'd sold me two of her courtside tickets for a January game. I didn't care much for sports events and Aaron already had plans to go to that Friday's evening game with a work buddy. While I was deciding who I owed a serious favor, Dr. Winters happened to mention that he was a big basketball fan. That eliminated much meandering over what kind of gift would be most meaningful and/or appropriate. As I handed him the envelope, I figured out why something as frivolous as basketball tickets seemed ideal: I longed to give him even a few hours of the joy he'd given back to me.

That night, I called one of my favorite former NYU students, Stephen, who was now an up-and-coming *New York Times* reporter. I pitched him Dr. Winters' little-girl-needing-her-dog story, hoping that the power of the press would help persuade his dumb Battery Park City condo board to have a heart and let her doggy stay. Stephen wound up interviewing Dr. Winters and writing a full-page, extremely emotional story for the City Section, which they headlined "A Frightened Child Versus a Rule." In case it was unclear where their sympathies lay, the editors ran a huge picture of Sammy, Kyra's adorable puppy, in the middle of the page.

This turn of events presented a psychodynamic circus. I'd called in Stephen, my fantasy son, to rescue the little daughter of my fantasy father. But who cared about all the hidden levels if I could help someone who'd helped me? It turned out that Kyra got to keep her puppy. I got to feel powerful, as if I were the James Bond of New York journalism.

Chapter 15

FEBRUARY 2003

My father e-mailed to say that he had scheduled an operation to have his left hip replaced the second week of February. The news flipped me out. I immediately called to book a flight to Michigan. Of course I had to fly home and stay with my mother while he was in the hospital, right? As soon as I made the reservation, I started to lose it. Over the next twenty-four hours I developed a fear of flying, a fear of snowstorms, and a fear of being back in my childhood house. Mostly I was scared of being without marijuana.

Although Dr. Winters had been hounding me to stop getting high, I was still taking a few hits of a joint after I finished work, on the five nights a week I wasn't seeing him. I knew I would desperately want to toke while I was visiting West Bloomfield. Yet during this phase of heightened security at the airport, there was no way I was going to risk getting arrested by carrying an illegal narcotic on board in my purse, pockets, suitcase, socks, underwear, or bra. I might have been a neurotic full-fledged addict, but I was no fool.

After twenty years in Manhattan, I no longer had any connections to herb in my old hunting grounds. The only occasion I was able to score stuff there, it was so low-grade I could barely feel it. I'd grown too accustomed to Big Apple gourmet grass. My one hometown girlfriend who was usually happy to hook me up informed me that she'd quit. From my struggles with sobriety I knew that it was rude, selfish, and downright immoral to beg somebody in recovery to get you the substance they were recovering from. I wasn't sure what to do. Finally I figured out the only solution: I'd mail myself the needed dope in advance so I could secretly toke it up during my trip.

I had a built-in excuse for sending things home in advance. Checking big bags or having too much carry-on luggage wasn't a good idea post–September 11. Before my last trip, I'd gone to Mail Boxes Etc. and sent my clothes to my parents' house for sixty-five dollars. I'd also put presents for my family in the mail so I wouldn't have to shlep them through metal detectors or random searches at La Guardia or Detroit Metro airports.

Pleased with my plan, I rolled my allotment of five joints for ten days, making them thicker than usual, in case of added stress. I wrapped them in tinfoil, put the foil in a small plastic bag, then slipped it inside the back of a perfume kit. I carefully placed the kit in a yellow padded envelope, along with stickers, Slinkys, a Barbie outfit, and a little SpongeBob SquarePants stuffed animal for my nieces and nephews. Absentmindedly, I started putting the extra Barbie, Batman, and dinosaur stickers on the outside of the yellow envelope, the way I'd taken to decorating the kids' Hanukkah and birthday presents. I suspected the pretty, bright-colored decals were a replacement for cigarettes and gum, since I now bought sheets of them on every visit to Duane Reade. Adhering them to letters and packages kept my hands busy for hours.

"I thought you regressed to thirteen years old. Now you're three?" Aaron asked that night, when he came home and caught me playing with my new sticker collection.

"Would you rather I be addicted to nicotine, drugs, and alcohol, or stickers?" I asked him.

The next night he brought me home Cubix and Pokemon stickers from the animated children's TV network he'd been freelancing for.

I debated whether making my marijuana package so colorful was stupid. I didn't want to call attention to it. If a little kid wound up with my contraband, would I be liable? On second thought, it seemed ingenious. The post office and police would assume it was a baby present. Then I flashed to a recent episode of *Law & Order,* where the criminals used babies and baby carriages as drug mules, and I felt like an idiot again. I debated whether or not to write my name and address on the envelope, fearing a package with no return address would raise too many red flags; they'd guess it was a bomb or anthrax.

I wound up printing my address, but omitting my name and apartment number. Here was my logic: There were a thousand people who lived at my Greenwich Village residence. If the yellow package did get returned, how would they trace it to me? Perhaps I should have worn gloves to avoid leaving fingerprints. I rationalized that the FBI wouldn't have time or money for a major manhunt to find the person who mailed five joints to her parents' house in Michigan. For a final irony, I sprayed the package with Opium perfume to ward off drug-sniffing dogs. Then I added six dollars' worth of stamps—which I figured had to be enough—and dropped it in the big mailbox right outside my building. Mission accomplished.

Obsessing about my upcoming visit, I'd forgotten I was going to see my clan the next weekend anyway. That was because Claire's youngest brother, Keith, was getting married in New York, at the Palace Hotel. Our families had been close since before all eight offspring were born. There appeared to be an unwritten Shapiro–Lyons law that as many members as possible would travel to one another's weddings. My father wasn't feeling mobile enough to fly, but my mother and three brothers were booked on different Detroit-to-Manhattan flights. Brian and Monica were due to get to town first, on Thursday afternoon. "Do you have any anxiety about your family visiting New York?" Dr. Winters had asked. "No problem at all," I'd answered. Then I slammed the window on my finger.

The accident happened ostensibly because Aaron insisted on keeping the window on his side of the room wide open while he slept—even if it was ten degrees outside. I woke up this particular Thursday morning nervous about seeing my family, and ice cold, teeth chattering. Still half asleep, I marched over to the window to slam it shut. My finger somehow wound up getting caught underneath. Within seconds it was gushing blood and the nail of my pinkie was hanging off to the side. When I screamed, Aaron woke up, looking dazed. He rushed to get me bandages and extra-strength Tylenol, which soon took away some of the excruciating pain.

"No anxiety at all about seeing my family this weekend," I said, as Aaron held me, petting my head.

Since I wasn't going to die from a pinkie hemorrhage, and my doctor-brothers were due in town in a few hours, I didn't go to an emergency room. Instead, I waited to get free medical advice over the phone when Brian checked in to the

Parker Meridien Hotel at noon. Brian said to keep the finger bandaged up and keep taking Tylenol. (Could one get addicted to Tylenol?) He promised that he and Mike, who was getting in to New York at five, would come over to check on me later. I assumed that "later" meant six or seven o'clock.

During a subsequent phone call to Monica, I learned that they had made reservations to take a group of friends to a chic uptown French bistro at eight o'clock. Michael was included in this plan; Aaron and I weren't. They knew that I hated the way they spent ridiculous amounts of money on overpriced liquor and fattening French food, and that I had nicknamed Brian and Monica in Manhattan "a waiter's dream." So I wasn't annoyed that we weren't invited. But I felt neglected that Brian wasn't showing any concern or hurry to check on my traumatized fingertip.

"Don't worry. Mike and I will come downtown to your place after dinner, around eleven o'clock," Brian said.

Eleven came and went. Then midnight. Aaron wanted to go to sleep, but I told him to stay up to at least say hi to my brothers. I tried calling their hotel rooms; nobody answered. I found Brian's cell-phone number and reached him at ten to one. They were just leaving the restaurant.

"Sorry, the meal took longer than I expected," Brian said.

"Are you coming downtown now?" I asked, confused.

"It's pretty late," he said.

"It's not too late." I was a night owl and Brian was known to stay up late when he was on vacation.

"No. I'm too tired now," he said. "Mike already went back to his hotel. We'll see you tomorrow."

"I've been waiting up for you guys. Why couldn't you at least call to say you weren't going to make it?" I asked.

"I forgot," my brother said.

Aaron said not to make a big deal out of it, as if that were an option. With no skin (metaphorically) and no pinkie nail (literally), this recent rudeness from brothers assumed mythical proportions. Throughout my childhood I'd felt that I was never as important as the boys. Since there were three of them, and they often had the same preferences and voted in a bloc, it wasn't my imagination. I'd spent my early years outnumbered and overpowered. This time, without my usual self-medications, there was nothing blocking my emotions. A flurry of rage, resentment, and sorrow came seeping back.

On Friday night at the rehearsal dinner, Brian apologized and attended to my bandaged finger. He said it would heal itself, and brought antibiotics to ward off infection. Placated by his attention, I sat next to Eric, the last brother to fly into town. A technology expert who lived in Ann Arbor, Eric mentioned that he was interested in teaching a computer science class. Since I'd been an adjunct professor for the last decade, I was flattered that he was asking my advice.

"The problem is that the University of Michigan's engineering school already has a professor teaching the one course I'm interested in," Eric said.

"Try to be a little more flexible," I said. "I wanted to teach in NYU's MFA program, but there were no openings. I had more luck with NYU's journalism department and their school of continuing education."

"I don't want to be more flexible!" Eric yelled. "I know exactly which school and which course I want to teach!" He got up and left the table, leaving me stunned in his wake.

"What happened?" asked Aaron.

"I don't know." I tried not to cry, replaying my words to see how I'd inadvertently offended Eric. I'd helped hundreds of my students get jobs and internships in many different fields over the years. I'd given my brother the same advice that business columnists and career books recommended, especially in a lousy economy. I didn't understand how trying to be helpful could have rubbed him so wrong.

"The computer bubble burst, so he's in a bad mood," Aaron guessed. "Don't take it personally."

All my brothers hated my guts. How should I take it—globally?

My mother asked what was wrong with Eric. I told her what had just happened.

"You know your brothers don't like it when you give them advice," she said, as if it were my fault.

Why was she defending him? Regressing back to infancy, I felt like it was all my mother's fault. She'd had too many kids too quickly when she should have just loved me.

Although I loved Keith Lyons' adorable new bride, I was not looking forward to further fights with my family at the wedding dinner on Saturday night. When Aaron and I walked into the Palace Hotel, everyone greeted us enthusiastically. My mother and her sons seemed in fine spirits, as if nothing negative had transpired. I made excuses to myself: We were all worried about my father, freaked out that he couldn't make this trip. I was just going through a rough emotional stretch. Monica came right over to say hi. She'd brought her three-month-old son, Abe, to New York since she was still breast-feeding. She'd left the baby with a sitter at their hotel, a few avenues over.

"When you go back to the Parker Meridien tonight, maybe I can come to your room with you to meet Abe," I offered. I felt I should at least lay eyes on my new nephew, since he was two blocks away.

"He might be asleep," she warned.

"That's okay. I just want to see him for a minute," I said. "I can't believe you're already so thin again."

She smiled, and for the first time that weekend, I was bonding with somebody I was related to, if only by marriage. Mazel tov!

After the ceremony and hors d'oeuvre hour, we took our

seats at a big table in the front of the room. It was too close to
the twelve-piece band, which was already loudly playing Frank
Sinatra songs. Monica said something to Brian. Then she left.

"Is she going to the bathroom? I have to go too," I said in
his ear.

"She went back to our hotel," said Brian.

I looked at my watch. It was eight-thirty.

"To check on the baby?" I asked. "She's coming back?"

"She's not coming back," he said.

"I was going to see the baby with her later," I tried to explain. "Should I go over there with her for a few minutes—"

"Don't go anywhere," Brian said. "We had a fight. When
she breast-feeds, the hormones make her crazy. Just leave her
alone."

I was the only one who took Monica's abrupt departure,
without so much as a goodbye wave, as a slight. I stared at her
empty seat at the table all night, disappointed that I wouldn't
get to meet my new nephew.

I remembered how horrible I'd felt after I'd fixed up Brian
and Monica and then had to watch them walk down the aisle
when I was still single. I went over to commiserate with Claire.
She looked gorgeous in her mauve gown. Since she hadn't
been dating anybody special, she was attending all the wedding events alone. I knew it was hard for her.

"How's it going?" I asked her.

"Okay," she said. "Gotta go dance."

She brushed by me to join the four other tall mauve-
gowned girls from the wedding party on the dance floor. The
band played a Motown medley; I joined them. Claire did not
even look at me. Each time I shimmied near her, she sashayed
away.

"What's that about? Why would Claire ignore me?" I asked
Aaron back at our table, totally miffed and morose. "She
doesn't like me anymore."

"She's hanging out with the single girls tonight," Aaron said. "You're the enemy. You're married."

I felt ignored and/or demeaned by every member of my *mishpocheh,* along with my closest comrade. At home at one in the morning, I smoked my allotted half a joint and opted out of the Sunday brunch in order not to alienate anybody else. I was a bundle of nerve endings. On the other hand, at least I'd avoided alcohol, cigarettes, and overeating.

Obviously everything was more complicated because I no longer had my old shields to protect me. With the wedding festivities over, I was apprehensive about seeing my family again the next week. If I could feel this drained during a lovely, upbeat occasion in my city, I couldn't imagine what would happen during a serious medical procedure for five times the number of days, on their turf.

"It was like watching a home movie of how I used to feel diminished," I told Dr. Winters on Monday. "My brothers stood me up, insulted me, and yelled at me. When my mother didn't take my side, I was shattered. I read that the emotional development of an addict remains stalled at the age when they started using. Do you think that's true?"

"Often it's younger," he said.

"I'm back to thirteen again?" I asked, and he nodded. "I don't want to go to Michigan next week. I want to cancel my trip and stay here, but I feel too guilty."

"Why?"

"I'm afraid my father will die if I'm not there for the operation," I admitted.

"A hip replacement isn't a life-or-death situation," Dr. Winters noted. "It's not emergency surgery."

"It's my dad, who I love, so it feels like life and death to me.

But I can't stand the thought of getting on the plane. I don't think I can handle it. Even with the joints I sent home."

"You sent joints home?" he asked.

"Well, you don't want me to bring dope aboard the plane and get arrested, do you?"

"I don't want you to get high at all," he repeated for the tenth time.

"I know. I'm going to quit toking. I just can't pick a date to stop yet. First I have to figure out if I'm flying home this weekend or not. I'm usually such a black-and-white person. I've always made decisions easily. I've never been this stuck."

"How do you feel around Aaron?"

"He's the only one who makes me feel safe," I said. "Except you. When you're not screwing up my appointments."

"What does your mother say about your trip?" he inquired.

"She says it's a routine operation, my brothers are home, and she doesn't need me there."

"You don't believe her?"

"I said I was coming and charged a plane ticket. I feel like I should keep my word. Isn't it neurotic to make reservations to go home and then cancel last-minute?"

"No," he said. "Running home for every medical procedure is neurotic. Don't go."

If I didn't already love him, I would have fallen in love at that moment. I was so grateful that he was giving me permission not to go. At my apartment, I called Northwest Airlines. For a hundred-dollar fee, I rescheduled my flight for August. I was afraid to go over the summer too, but at least I had six months to unravel that one.

I'd never canceled a trip before and my indecisiveness seemed wimpy. But I was happy to stay home, surrounded by my books and my husband, who was wonderful, except when he kept the window open during snowstorms. It had taken me twenty years to find the right man, apartment, agent, editor, and shrink, and to become so comfortable in my little New York neighborhood. No wonder I'd grown afraid to leave.

After I hung up with Northwest Airlines, I pictured the yellow package, containing my hidden high-grade dope, which I'd already sent home to my parents. Oh my God. My mother would open the perfume kit and find my secret stash. When she'd once asked, I had confessed that I'd tried dope in high school. She had no idea in the world I'd been doing it all these years. She was already petrified that my father was going into the hospital. It was surely not the time for her to find out that her only daughter was a druggie.

The only one who could help was Monica. Since I'd introduced her to my brother, she owed me a favor. I came up with a plan. Monica usually brought all her kids to my parents' house twice a week. I needed her to head off my pot package. I could tell my mother that it contained presents for all my nieces and nephews and that Monica should open it because she was the only one who'd know which kid each present was for. What if Monica was busy with the baby or too preoccupied?

I questioned whether this odd turn of events implied that, on some level, I really wanted to get caught. Or was it just another downside of being an addict? Keeping a steady stream of your substance handy could get expensive, complicated, crazy. It was one of the reasons why I knew I had to quit altogether.

My mother called that Friday to say that Dad's operation had gone even better than his first hip replacement. Happily, my father was going to be fine. When we spoke on the phone, he complained that his surgeon had insisted on regulating his post-op medication this time. Dad then insisted on checking out of the hospital after only three days. Everyone else thought this was excellent news. Since I knew that we shared the same addictive personality, I prayed that he wasn't hurrying home so that he could increase the amount of painkillers he was taking. I mentioned it to Dr. Winters, who understood my concern but told me to keep my mouth shut and focus on my own drug issues.

Every day I phoned to find out how my father was progressing. Then I would slip in a quick question at the end about my package. Every day my mother said that it hadn't come in the mail yet. It had been eleven, then twelve, then thirteen days since I'd mailed it. I wondered if it could have been lost, stolen, or confiscated by the police.

I hadn't put my name on the envelope and I'd sprayed it with perfume so it wouldn't smell of marijuana, but I had visions of the FBI finding it. Or the CIA. They'd go to my parents' home and easily trace the narcotics to me: the black-sheep writer in Manhattan. I would be arrested, written up in the *New York Post,* on the cover of *People* magazine. I'd lose my teaching jobs. None of my relatives would ever speak to me again (which, Aaron insisted, belonged on the plus side).

The next Wednesday, when I came back to my building after my NYU class, my doorman Tony handed me the fat yellow padded envelope I'd decorated with little-kid stickers.

"What happened?" I asked, staring at the package in disbelief, cradling it close, a tiny trace of the Opium perfume lingering. The staples were still in place; it hadn't been opened. None of the stamps was canceled. I was totally at sea.

"The postman just brought it back today. Anything over one pound needs to be mailed at the post office," said Tony, a handsome dark-haired Latino that Aaron and I had nicknamed "The Latin Lover."

"Since when?" I asked. "I've mailed a lot of heavy packages in that outside mailbox."

"Since September eleventh they've been cracking down," he explained. "They've recently started returning them."

"My name isn't on the return address," I said. "How did you know it was mine?"

"You always put the cute little stickers on the outside," Tony said.

My sticker fetish saved me, unlocking the mail mystery. I felt thrilled to have my package back, the federal drug bust and family freak-out averted. In my apartment, I sat down on my couch and undid the package, opened the windows (carefully), and smoked one of the thick joints in one sitting. I'd sent myself the perfect present, just what I'd wanted. Feeling stoned and serene, I was sure the package coming back to me was a sign from God. I just wasn't sure what it was a sign for.

Chapter 16

MARCH 2003

"What's shaking, babe?" was the subject heading of my colleague Blake's e-mail.

"All kinds of things," I wrote back. "When can we hang out and catch up?"

To my delight, he answered, "How about dinner tonight?"

"Fabulous!" I said, without divulging the significance of the day.

I'd been tapering off pot slowly. Now, Dr. Winters said, it was time to up the ante. I was out of weed and wasn't supposed to replace my supply. It would be my first evening without any marijuana in my apartment. My old drugstore cowboy Stu, who used to come by any time of the day or night, had disappeared. One of his other customers said he'd moved to Seattle to become a snowboarder.

My latest dope dealer had a more peculiar schedule. If you wanted to buy pot, you had to call a special phone number and leave a message on Monday. He'd call back between eleven A.M. and noon the next day to make an appointment to deliver, but only on Tuesdays and Friday afternoons. That meant I couldn't get any stuff on Thursday, even if I wanted to. Dr. Winters said that it was good to put as many obstacles between you and your addiction as possible.

I was not ready to totally abstain from toking. I'd promised myself that I'd only smoke other people's weed, once in a while at parties. I'd simply stop buying it and having it at home. If I took away anything self-destructive, Dr. Winters had warned, I should look for a healthy substitute. Getting together with Blake seemed a smart replacement. I was sure that seeing a friend I cared about would get me over whatever tiny withdrawal I might feel. Since Blake was a good-looking guy I admired, this provided the illusion that I was going out on a date. In essence, our closeness was more like brother and sister. He'd forgive me if I was still acting eccentric. He was having a rough time himself. Plus I knew he wouldn't have any pot on him. Cigarettes and whiskey were his preference. Even if he had a joint at his place, he lived in Brooklyn and I certainly wasn't going to shlep to another borough just to catch a buzz.

After he'd spoken at my journalism class last year, things had gone downhill for him. He'd been laid off from his editor job and his young Spanish lesbian girlfriend, Lola, had broken up with him. I knew this from my former student Naomi, who—thanks to Blake—had been interning at, and writing regularly for, his magazine. I'd learned more about it from the tabloid press, who had reported the firing in the newspaper before Blake's angry boss had informed him.

On the bright side, Blake said that he'd been having luck with his writing projects. He'd sent me twenty pages of the Lola memoir we'd discussed, which were hot, filled with sex-drugs-and-rock-and-roll. He'd followed my advice about calling it *Her First Man*. He had just signed the contract for a lucrative ghostwriting job, penning the autobiography of a famous actor. If he could write ten more pages of *Her First Man* that were as compelling as the material he'd shown me, I bet he could get a big advance for that book too.

He suggested we meet at an upscale neighborhood bar to have a drink before dinner. On my way there, I picked up a bottle of fancy champagne to congratulate him on his new project. When I showed up ten minutes early, Blake was already nursing a drink at the bar. I hugged him hello, sat down next to him, and ordered a diet Coke. I didn't frequent bars anymore, and if I did find myself in one, I always sat at a table. I didn't say anything, though. Since Dr. Winters had called me "rigid," I'd made a point of being more flexible with everyone else, to prove him wrong.

It was interesting to sit on a bar stool without being able to smoke a cigarette or drink alcohol. I thought it would be uncomfortable, but it wasn't as terrible as I'd expected. That was partly because of Mayor Bloomberg's brand-new smoking laws, which made it impossible for anybody to legally smoke at most indoor establishments in the city. Watching people drink had never made me want to drink. That was because I had never been a serious drinker and I could sip a drink myself, even if it was only diet soda. Watching people suck in cigarettes was harder.

"I can't believe nobody can smoke in bars anymore," I said.

I didn't admit it to my nicotine-addicted friends, but I was secretly pleased with the sweeping no-smoking restrictions. I'd had such a horrible time quitting, and it was much easier not to smoke, or ever think of smoking, when I wasn't surrounded by smokers. I was as selfish and self-righteous as the new mayor, another former smoker. Ever since I saw how much my two-pack-a-day habit had been holding me back, I thought everyone should quit cigarettes. I was hoping Blake would tell me he had stopped smoking again.

"I know. You'll have to excuse me later when I need to duck outside to light up." He pointed to a pack of Camels in his top pocket.

"You haven't quit yet, I see."

"Guess not," he said.

"Didn't you used to smoke Marlboro reds?" I often remembered people's brands.

"Good memory," he said.

"Camels aren't too strong?" I recalled trying one once. It burned my throat.

"I started with Camels when I was with Lola," he said. "All the Spanish dykes were smoking them."

"This is to congratulate you on your book deal." I switched to a more upbeat subject, handing him the bottle of champagne. Hearing about his horrible breakup on a bar stool seemed too pathetic.

"Thanks. That was so sweet of you," he said. "You look terrific."

Several people had complimented me on how I looked lately. I hadn't lost weight or changed anything. Claire guessed that my skin was more clear since I'd quit cigarettes and cut down on dope.

"Am I allowed to ask what kind of an advance you got?"

"You can ask me anything," he said.

After he whispered the number, I said, "That's great! It's the same amount I received for my book." I didn't tell him I was glad that I was getting paid for my own story and not ghosting somebody else's. "What about *Her First Man*?" I asked. "Those twenty pages you showed me were explosive. Very intense, honest, and emotional. Not to mention hot as hell. I couldn't put it down. If you can expand it to thirty pages, I'll even show it to my agent. How's that going?"

"It's not going. I can't write about what happened with Lola now," he said, not wanting to talk about it further.

When the bartender brought my diet soda, Blake pointed to his glass and said, "Hit me again, Todd. This is my friend Sue." I nodded. Blake was obviously a regular. Being on a first-name basis with the bartender was not a good omen.

"What is that?" I pointed to his drink, which looked strong and straight.

"Maker's Mark," he said. "American bourbon-style whiskey."

"How much of this stuff are you drinking?" I was an intrusive asshole for asking, but he'd know it was out of concern. For eight years Blake used to ask me, "How much are you smoking these days?" as if that were a barometer of my psyche. I would sometimes lie and say, "Pack a day, but I'm cutting down."

"I'm having three or four whiskeys a night," he admitted. I hoped it wasn't more than that.

"Well, you're looking great too," I said, and it was true. For a chain-smoking fifty-year-old drunk he certainly looked sexy. "Are you still working out?" I noticed the chiseled muscles in his arms, which his tight T-shirt showed off.

"Yup. Every day."

"You can run with all that smoking?" I asked.

"Well, I'm lifting weights more than running these days," he said.

After I had three diet sodas and Blake had four whiskeys and went out to puff a cigarette twice, he came back and asked Todd for the bill. I glanced at it, noticing the total was thirty dollars. It only listed one diet soda and two whiskeys. Blake insisted on treating. Since my soda only came to four dollars, I let him.

"Nice guy. He only charges me half," Blake said in my ear.

This worried me more. It meant that he had become such a good customer, the bartender was giving him special discounts. I regretted bringing him champagne as a congratulations present. I should have picked a book or a CD set or a coupon for a massage, which I sensed he could use.

We went to NoHo Star, a casual restaurant close by, where we were seated by the window. We chatted about the details of our book projects. After we ordered dinner, I really wanted to ask about his smoking and drinking problem, but I tried to restrain myself. It was none of my business. I was acting like a nosy narc.

My cousin Miranda, who had been through two months at a rehab center, recently called somebody a lush. Aaron later commented that she'd been spouting too much "AA crap," and if you had one beer in front of a recovering alcoholic they would call you a drunk. I could tell that was what I was doing, seeing the world through this narrow prism, judging everybody too harshly who wasn't as sober as I was. I was a smoker for almost three decades, I reminded myself. I had never listened to anybody who'd tried to lecture me. On the contrary, I would snuff them out in seconds.

"I tried an acupuncturist to quit cigarettes," Blake volunteered.

"Really?" I asked, pleased that he'd brought up the subject. "You're back to a pack a day now?"

"At least two packs a day," he said.

Interesting that it was exactly the amount of cigarettes I'd gotten up to in my heyday. "An acupuncturist in Chinatown?" I asked.

"No. An old white hippie guy in Midtown. Right near Grand Central."

"I'm afraid of needles," I said.

"So am I."

Our first course came. "Here, taste." He gave me a big

spoonful of his corn soup. It was nice, how Blake and I both wanted to feed each other.

"It's really good," I said, offering him a bite of my Caesar salad, but he shook his head. "How could somebody afraid of needles go to an acupuncturist?" I was glad he'd ordered iced tea with dinner, and not more whiskey.

"What a ridiculous idea it was," he said. "The first few thin needles he put in my earlobe and chest, I barely noticed. Then he put a few in the arch of my foot and in between my thumb and finger, and it killed me. I had a violent reaction."

"What happened?" I picked out the croutons in my salad and put them on the side of my plate. His story was making me squeamish. I was so needlephobic I had once fainted after a pinkie blood test.

"It hurt and felt itchy, then my hands and feet swelled up. He said, 'Can you last for five more minutes?' I said no. I was sweating. He had some kind of monitor that showed I had a 104-degree temperature."

"That's really high. Just from the needles?"

"Yeah. He said I was *that* filled with toxins."

I could have told him that he was overstuffed with toxins. How could he not be? Forty of those strong Camels each day and four straight whiskeys a night, it was amazing he could function.

"When he took out the needles, your temperature went down?" I asked. He nodded. "I hope he didn't make you pay for it."

"He did. I had to write him a check for a hundred dollars. He said I should come back for three more sessions. I knew I was out of there forever, had two cigarettes from his office to Grand Central."

I wanted to know if Blake had the pack in his pocket or bought them on his way home. "Why would you try acupuncture to quit smoking?"

"I have asthma, I have to stop," he said. "I go to Duane Reade and I buy cigarettes from one checkout girl and an asthma inhaler from another counter 'cause I'm too embarrassed to buy them both from the same person."

Dr. Winters had told me a story about a big fat bearded guy, an overeater, alcoholic, and two-pack-a-day smoker, who'd said to him, "I know I need to quit smoking, drinking, and overeating. I've tried everything, but nothing works." Dr. Winters asked if he'd tried suffering.

"You wanted a magic pill," I told Blake. "There's no such thing."

"Has your addiction guy made you give up drinking water and breathing the air yet?" he teased. "How much does he charge, anyway?"

"We're up to a hundred fifty a session," I admitted.

"Have you ever calculated how much you've spent on him?"

"As a matter of fact, I have. You really want to know?"

"Yes," he said. "Let's talk turkey."

I'd read an article that said New Yorkers were more comfortable spilling secrets about sex than money. If I was loudly lauding Winters' work, I wanted Blake to know the down and dirty. I explained that the first year of weekly $125 sessions had cost me about $6,000. This year, twice-a-week sessions were costing me almost $14,000. From the amount of the reimbursement checks, I'd calculated that our medical insurance covered forty-three percent of the total. So I figured the two years getting clean would run me $12,000 altogether.

"That's a hell of a lot of money." He shook his head.

"I added up how much I'm saving on cigarettes, dope, and gum, and it's worth it," I said. "Plus I wouldn't have sold my book without him."

"Who can afford ten grand to get clean?" he asked.

"A lot of people. The Betty Ford and Hazelden rehab centers cost twenty thousand dollars for a month stay. I looked it up. Passages in Malibu is forty thousand a month," I said defensively.

"It's all too rich for my blood," he said, I thought condescendingly.

Although Aaron and I had had a banner year financially and were now out of debt, we'd both been freelancers with inconsistent incomes for decades. I still saw myself as a broke left-wing suffering artist, something else I'd have to soon give up. At least I hoped so.

"You're spending it anyway, on killing yourself," I argued. "Two packs a day at this point is—what?" I took a pen out of my purse and multiplied what two five-dollar packs cost daily. "That's $3,650 a year for your smokes. Double that for the booze. Not to mention the added health-care costs you're going to have."

"I'll save money by dying five years sooner," he joked. "Look, I'm not saying I shouldn't stop. But cold turkey is cheaper. I quit that way twice."

"I know you stopped once for eight years. I remember. You were forty-two," I said. "When was the first time you quit?"

"I started smoking when I was twelve," he said.

"Wow, that young." According to Dr. Winters, that would mean Blake was really still twelve years old at heart.

"First time I stopped I was twenty-four. I was a rock-and-roller in Chicago and it was wrecking my voice," he said.

The waitress brought my cheddar cheese omelet and Blake's deluxe hamburger. I dug in, starving, thinking it was interesting that he could quit smoking when he believed that his habit impinged on his art. It was the same—and the only—reason I had ever been able to kick the habit. Dr. Winters had convinced me that I couldn't publish my memoir unless I stopped cigarettes.

"Don't you think that the smoking and drinking are affecting your work in a negative way?"

"Nope. All famous writers smoke and drink. And I just got a big book deal." He poured ketchup on his burger and took a big bite.

"I know, and that's great for now," I said. "But you're too talented to keep writing for another person who gets his name on the book and pretends he's the real author."

"It's the most money I've ever been paid for a book," he said.

"What if I told you that if you didn't quit smoking, you'd never finish your own book?" I was imitating Dr. Winters, but it didn't seem to be manipulative. I believed what I was saying. "Think of the definition of a ghost, Blake. The soul of a dead person, a disembodied spirit, a mere shadow or trace."

"Fuck you, Sue, I know." He put his hamburger down and looked at me. "I can't write *Her First Man*. It hurts too much to go back there. I'm still licking my wounds. I had the worst winter I've ever had. My boss dumped me unceremoniously in the tabloids, after ten years on the job. Do you know how humiliating that was? Then Lola split with me and moved to L.A. She just said, 'I can't do this anymore,' and took off."

"Well ..." I put my fork down too, deciding how honest I should be. I didn't want to offend him. I wanted to help.

"Well, what?" he asked. "Say what you were thinking."

"Look, one of the tricks of my memoir was that I had this mythology for each old relationship. One lover slept around, another screwed me over. It seemed like everyone did these terrible things to me. But when I remet them as an adult who'd been in therapy, I was able to pinpoint the moment where I'd fucked up each connection myself."

"All of them?"

I nodded. "Listening to you talk about Lola, I was thinking that you were playing victim, and that's not really the only level of what happened. You have to dig deeper and see what your part was."

"How am I playing victim?" He asked the waitress for another iced tea and resumed eating.

"After ten years of marriage, you dumped your wife, Lisa." Funny, now that I no longer wanted to sleep with him I could remember his wife's name. Or was it because they were split up? "Actually, before you were separated, you started up with a twenty-three-year-old lesbian who'd never had any interest in men. She wasn't even bisexual. She told you right off the bat that she'd always love women."

"She's twenty-four now," he said.

"She has a sign on her forehead that says 'I will never love you.' She's too young *and* she works for you, which is kind of unethical. I'm sure your coworkers knew about it. And your boss, a married guy with kids. I'm sure he hates you because he can't go around sleeping with hot twenty-three-year-olds in the office. Which is part of the reason why he got so angry and fired you in such a mean, public way."

"I know. I know," he said. "I've been dating four or five girls now, but I just can't get over Lola."

"Dating or sleeping with?" I asked, sensing that his current self-destruction wasn't going to be limited to substance abuse.

"Sleeping with," he said quietly. "You know I've been hanging out with Naomi."

Naomi had mentioned that they'd had a drink after Blake was fired. I'd thought she just wanted to be supportive. I didn't realize . . .

"MY Naomi is one of the four or five women you're sleeping with?" I raised my voice, feeling protective of her. Since I didn't have kids, my students were my pretend offspring. Or could I be jealous? Maybe I was just miffed that she hadn't told me herself. "Blake, please tell me you've been using protection."

"Some of the time, but—"

"Some of the time? What the hell's your goal—to give

Naomi a venereal disease, get her pregnant, or both?" I was relieved that I was an old faithful married woman, nowhere near the singles scene anymore. "You didn't use rubbers with her? What's wrong with you? You're becoming a sex addict too?" Didn't any users stick to one addiction, or was it always multiple? Why hadn't Naomi told me when I'd spoken to her the day before?

"Listen, I've been completely honest with all the women I've been seeing. They know I'm dating a lot and I'm not ready to settle down again. Second, I am not a sex addict. None of it's about the sex anyway," he said.

"Then what's it about?"

"If I spend more than two nights in a row by myself at home, I'm ready to kill myself."

"I'm sorry you feel like that," I said, thinking that Blake was reflecting every single fact that Dr. Winters had ever told me about addictive personalities.

"If I caused all my own problems, then why do I feel so fucked over?" he asked.

"I'm a Freudian. You really want my take?"

He nodded.

"Okay," I said. "You have an older sister, right?"

"Older sister. Older parents. They were Catholic. I always thought they would have been happy to just have my sister. I guessed that I was an accident."

"You grew up feeling unwanted," I said, questioning if Blake's situation was a textbook case or if I was projecting my issues onto everyone I knew. "That's probably where the addiction comes from."

"How could it?" he asked. "They were good people. They loved me. They never hit me. No abuse, no incest, no affairs, no divorce . . ."

"I know." I nodded. "My parents loved me and stayed together too. But if you grow up feeling unloved, for whatever reason, there's this void. People like us try to fill it with smoking, drinking, drugs, sex, food...."

"Isn't that reductive?" he asked.

"Yes, but we're all taught to downplay negative emotions and to buck up and pretend everything is fine," I said. "There's this beautiful W. H. Auden poem, 'The Sea and the Mirror,' a commentary on Shakespeare's *The Tempest*. The father, who is king, has to say goodbye to the son he might never see again. His parting advice is: 'But should you fail to keep your kingdom/And, like your father before you, come/Where thought accuses and feeling mocks, Believe your pain.' "

"If you don't believe your pain, you become an addict?" He sounded skeptical and sarcastic.

"No. I'm oversimplifying. I'm pretty sure that genetics is at play too," I said. "Nature and nurture. In my case my mother was an overfeeder, my father was a chain-smoking cancer specialist."

"My father drank and smoked and died of lung cancer," Blake said. "My two aunts and my grandfather smoked and drank too...."

"Are you sure you won't call Dr. Winters?" I could hear myself echoing Dr. Winters' words and theories so much, I'd become him. Lucky for Blake, my advice was a lot cheaper and I was treating for dinner.

"What part of 'I hate shrinks' don't you understand?" he asked.

"I'm worried about you."

"Even if I didn't hate them, I can't afford them. They haven't even issued the first check from my book deal yet. I owe my ex-wife money. I can barely pay my bills and I'm still in debt."

"If you got a million-dollar advance for thirty pages of *Her First Man* in the mail tomorrow, would you—"

"No," he said.

"If you ever decide—"

"I know. I will. You're a good friend."

After the waitress left the check on the table, he said, "She's really cute."

I checked her out. She did look really cute—and about sixteen years old.

"You've got enough problems," I said, throwing three twenties on the table.

He walked me home. I gave him a quick half hug in front of my building. The minute I was inside, I called Naomi. It was eleven o'clock. She wasn't home, so I left a message. Then another. Then I e-mailed her twice. Finally she phoned me back at 11:45. I told her what Blake had told me, yelled at her, and made her swear she'd never have sex with anybody without using condoms for the rest of her life.

Self-righteous about Blake's substance abuse, I'd forgotten to be vigilant about my own bad habits. Between the bar and dinner, I had stupidly drunk caffeine-laden diet sodas until ten P.M. I went to my dope box but then remembered I'd intentionally not bought more. I had nothing to chill me out and help me sleep.

Aaron came home late from a meeting, said he was on deadline, and went right to his computer. Antsy, I called a fellow stoner friend who lived six blocks away, and asked if he had an extra joint. Though it was midnight, he said yes. He also said he had an extra thirty dollars' worth of good stuff he could sell me, to tide me over.

"I have to run out to get a piece I'm editing for a friend," I told Aaron. "I'll be right back."

He nodded, too busy to question my fake excuse. It seemed the criteria for addictions was that they had to involve lying.

I went to the ATM machine across the street and withdrew money. Like cigarettes, alcohol, and gum, I saw that I could not be moderate with marijuana. I'd have to quit all the way.

I'd do it next month, I promised myself. In April, which was supposed to be the cruelest month. Rushing to get my fix, it occurred to me that I was drawn to Blake and angry at him because we were so similar. He was my doppelgänger, my dark side. We were both stuck in this complex, underground labyrinth of loss, using substances as blinders to obscure the light. By trying to convince him that it was essential to get clean, I'd been persuading myself. What finally pushed me over the edge were seven simple words Dr. Winters scrawled on the back of his latest business card: "Lead the least secretive life you can."

Chapter 17

APRIL 1, 2003

10 A.M.: Woke up and wrote on calendar "D-Day," then changed it to "No D-Day," swearing that I was ready to stop my daily dope habit. Rifled through desk and threw out Zig-Zag and Bambú rolling papers, leftover roaches, two pipes, a minibong, and plastic Baggies. Proclaimed it would be easy since pot wasn't physically addictive. Lit lilac-scented candle and watched flame flicker, feeling serene. Decided it was never about smoking, it was about being a pyromaniac. Found names and phone numbers of drug dealers in address book and whited them out with Liquid Paper. Turned page, noticing I could still read dealers' numbers backward. Whited that page out too. Drank six diet sodas in a row. Cleaned apartment, paid bills, returned phone calls. Felt productive, wonderful, so happy to be drug-free.

11 A.M.: Ordered fruit salad, newspapers, and more diet soda from local deli. Ate fruit salad and drank two liters of diet soda from bottle. Opened wooden box from Jamaica

to find half a joint left. Guessed it was stale. Sniffed longingly and considered eating it before tossing in garbage. Con-
templated rummaging through garbage to find and smoke it.
Took out trash filled with pot paraphernalia, tossing it down
incinerator. Wondered if any of my dealers were listed.

12:30 P.M.: Read in the paper that, when asked if he'd inhaled pot, Mayor Bloomberg said, "You bet I did, and I enjoyed it." Felt certain that Clinton did inhale while Bloomberg
didn't. Listed negative side effects of dope: depression, disori-
entation, dry mouth, munchies, anxiety, paranoia. Got paranoid I'd never be able to find dealers' phone numbers again.
Turned on Dylan CD. Turned off "Everybody Must Get
Stoned." Felt hungry. Lit another scented candle.

2 P.M.: Craved a joint though I'd never once toked so early
in the day. Tried to work. Went to freezer and ate forty-calorie
Smart Ones diet fudge bar. Ate another forty-calorie diet
fudge bar, proud that my pig-out consisted of only eighty
calories. Polished off box of ten Smart Ones diet fudge bars,
adding up to four hundred calories, feeling stupid. Noted that
everyone got munchies when they got high, I got munchies
when I quit. Threw away hemostat brother gave me for roach
clip. Drank more diet Coke. Wrote list of cool nicknames for
dope: Hemp, Love Weed, Love Boat, Buddha Sticks, Blunts,
Green Goddess, Wacky Tobaccy, Mary Jane, Black Gold,
Magic Smoke, Ganja, Alice B. Toklas. Started to laugh hysterically. Started to cry.

5 P.M.: Went to take nap but couldn't sleep from too much
diet chocolate and diet soda. Looked up diseases medicinal
marijuana eased: cancer, AIDS, arthritis, MS, epilepsy, and
Alzheimer's. Reminded myself I was lucky not to have cancer,
AIDS, arthritis, MS, epilepsy, or Alzheimer's as reason to keep
toking. Promised myself if I ever got Alzheimer's, I'd become se-
nile pothead. Worried I wouldn't remember promise. Recalled
Dylan admitted to lifelong toking. Looked at recent picture of

Dylan. Heard phone message from Claire. Realized she might have an extra joint, though I'd have to go to her place, at 102nd Street and Riverside. Decided it was worth shlepping ninety-four blocks uptown. Wondered if she'd give me the name and number of her dealer. Didn't pick up phone or call her back. Got headache. Took extra-strength Tylenol.

6 P.M.: Tried to work. Remembered that Jack Kerouac and Allen Ginsberg swore by dope. Admitted I never loved writing of Jack Kerouac or Allen Ginsberg. Rationalized that, since Dr. Winters said I had to quit marijuana, I could still smoke hashish. Realized I couldn't switch to hashish without being a drug-addicted liar. Pondered whether hash brownies were okay. Decided hash brownies weren't okay and would destroy both sobriety and diet. E-mailed my pal Pam that I was quitting dope. Surprised that she asked if I'd send one last $200 bag of strong New York stuff to her in L.A. Said sure. Then figured out I couldn't buy some for her without buying some for me. Saw I'd already whited out phone numbers of dealers anyway. Called her back to say no. Went to work, recalling Rastafarians' claim that cannabis was a sacrament that heightened spirituality. Admitted I'd never been religious or spiritual. Wished I could be as high and cool as Bob Marley. Recalled Bob Marley died at thirty-six.

8:30 P.M.: Turned on Macy Gray CD. Realized for the first time that songs were all about drug trips, including lyric "I just want to go get high." Wondered if street dealers still sold dime bags in Washington Square Park. Turned off Macy Gray CD. Looked up interview where gonzo journalist Hunter Thompson admitted smoking pot for decades. Acknowledged what a fucked-up mess Hunter Thompson had been for decades. Opened door for Aaron, who asked, "How are you?" Answered, "Great," sobbing in his arms. Ordered Chinese food from Sammy's. Drank more diet soda with chicken and broccoli. Got worse headache from MSG. Took two more extra-strength Tylenol.

11:30 P.M.: Noticed Marijuana Girl snow globe on shelf and immediately threw it in garbage. Decided that one could be straight and have a Marijuana Girl snow globe. Took it out of garbage and put back on shelf. Turned on TV to *That '70s Show* rerun, where cool teenagers sat at table, passing around a joint. Turned off TV. Paced around apartment, hyper from too much caffeine, bloated from Chinese food, and dizzy from MSG. To chill out, took leftover Xanax my brother gave me when I was nervous about getting on a plane. Realized that between the caffeine, Tylenol, and Xanax, I was more doped up now than when I was on dope, and I still wanted some.

CHAPTER 18

APRIL 2003

I kept assuming that quitting would get easier, but it didn't. During my first weird weedless week, I felt horrible. I was constantly coughing and sweating. I couldn't stop eating. Toking every day, I'd been upbeat and energetic. When I refrained, I became bloated, drowsy, and downbeat. I'd morphed into a fat, ugly, alienated, zit-faced twelve-year-old. Not again!

If dope wasn't addictive, why was this worse than kicking nicotine? Out of all my self-medications, marijuana had lasted longest and its effects were strongest. It was my favorite escape. Was I crashing down from a thirty-year high?

I hadn't been conscious that I'd used dope to get over cigarettes. But it was so much easier to resist tobacco while I could inhale something similar. Holding the joint to my lips and sucking in smoke for the last nineteen nicotine-free months had kept me addicted and in denial. I'd been lying to myself. I hadn't really stopped smoking; I'd just found a different way to do it. It was like breaking up with a lover I still slept with.

Not that relying on one drug to get off another was original. I had recently met a man who'd quit a forty-five-year cigarette habit when he'd wound up in the hospital for two weeks for an emergency appendectomy. They'd put him on a Demerol drip, which made him forget to smoke. Though I had never tried it, I started craving Demerol. I hadn't realized that marijuana had solved my lifelong insomnia. Now it was back with a vengeance. I flashed to the image of my friend Roger keeping a bong on his nightstand to get to sleep.

I felt like the staid, sober Roger was the angel on my right shoulder, while the fun but fucked-up Blake was the devil on my left. Self-righteousness dissipated as my anguish increased. Soon I was envious that Blake could soothe himself to sleep, stay peacefully numb and obliterate everything that hurt him with whiskey and cigarettes. I was stuck here, unable to chill out, crawl out of my head, get instant relief.

"How are you feeling?" Dr. Winters asked on Monday, my fifth day without getting high.

"Like death." I sat down on his couch and pulled out my spiral notebook to take notes, as I'd started to do every session.

"Good." He turned his black leather swivel chair to face me directly. "Tell me about it."

I was tired of talking about the minute details of my misery. I stared at him. Who the hell was this guy who knew me better than my relatives and closest friends? I could not stand the idea of rehashing any more of my personal history. I had a strong urge to hear about his family today. "Do you have any brothers and sisters?" I asked. "Were you the oldest kid?"

"Why do you want to know?"

"You said you don't believe in hiding anything from your

patients." He'd already told me about his ex-wife, new wife, young daughter, and the dog. I longed to see the rest of the picture, to reduce him to a cultural stereotype.

"There were four kids in the family. I was the second son. I have an older brother and a younger brother and sister," he said.

I was elated that Dr. Winters was one of four offspring, with three boys and a girl, as in my clan, as if that was why he had automatically understood me. I was especially intrigued that he was child number two. That was why our connection was contentious. I was the oldest. He was just like my brother Brian, the fighter, the second kid who thought he owned the place.

"Where did you live?" I demanded, hungry to learn more. "What did your father do? What religion were your parents?"

"We grew up in Manhattan. My father was a successful businessman. He grew up Protestant. My mother was born Jewish but her family renounced their lineage. Neither had any religious identity."

I jotted down his answers fast, as if I were on deadline for a story. Journalism was a good profession for a snoop; it fit my personality. "Your mother was Jewish? So you're a Jew!" I was almost disappointed. Jewish shrinks were a dime a dozen; I'd hoped he was a WASP just to be different. Well, he was sort of half a WASP. "Did the oldest son go into your dad's business?"

"Why do you want to know that?"

"I want to understand why you've been able to help me so much," I said. "Whether all your perceptiveness has been intellectual or because you had a similar background." I couldn't swear this was my exact motivation for prying. Clearly there was something I was digging around for—I just wasn't sure what it was yet.

He picked up his pen, wrote something in his notebook. Then he put it down, looked at me, and said, "My older brother is a lawyer."

I guessed his brother was the good son, in a more traditional field. Dr. Winters had majored in philosophy, then become a psychoanalyst. He was the black sheep, like me. "You didn't get along with your brother?"

"I am not close with my oldest brother. It's hard to be close to the first child who parents see as perfect."

Aha! Obviously issues with his brother were unresolved. Then again, I'd resolved my sibling issues by moving to a different state. I wondered if my parents first viewed me as perfect and if that alienated my brothers? Did it fuel their desire to surpass me? "In my case the second child was a boy. In a conservative Jewish household, males are god," I said. "Do you get along with your sister?"

"She would say we get along," he slipped in.

I found his domestic angst compelling and wrote down "problems with sister too." He didn't seem to care that I was recording his replies; he was getting used to my obsessive note-taking. It occurred to me that carrying a notebook and pen with me everywhere could be a shield, just like the cigarettes. "Are your parents still together?"

"No," he said. "They divorced when I was twelve."

"Your childhood wasn't happy?"

He shook his head no. "Very damaged."

"You wouldn't use the word dysfunctional?"

"Dysfunctional implies there was some working order or function to it," he said.

Wow. He hated his family's guts. This unexpected divulgence thrilled me. I was used to old-fashioned shrinks who never told patients anything personal. It felt as if I were mining illicit behind-the-scenes territory. Every answer made me want to dig deeper. I was daring him to say "This is none of your business." He wasn't stopping me. He looked a little amused by my curiosity, flattered even.

"Was your mother nurturing?"

He shook his head no, more vehemently this time, leaving no doubt. I wasn't surprised. All the true healers I had ever met had grown up miserable themselves. That was why they were so compassionate.

"My mother was very beautiful. She was a model and an actress," Dr. Winters said, as if this explained everything. "She should have been on stage, where she'd be admired. She should never have had children."

Unable to bear the thought that he had been neglected or abused, I dismissed the notion, picturing his mother as merely vain and preoccupied. Or filled with misguided middle-class notions about propriety, like my mother.

"Have you read George Eliot's last book, *Daniel Deronda*?" I asked. "In the novel, the mother, who is this beautiful actress and singer, gives up her son, Daniel, when he's a baby. She makes sure he's raised by a family who adores him...."

"That was generous of her," Dr. Winters said.

"Are you being sarcastic?"

"No," he said. "The mother made sure her son was loved. That was an unselfish act."

He seemed to mean it. How revealing! I saw it as selfish that the mother wouldn't even attempt to raise her own child. Winters thought it was a good thing to do, as if he wished he'd been similarly spared. I replayed the scene in which the dying actress mother finally summons her now thirty-year-old son to Italy. There she explains her decision to pursue her artistic career and not raise him. She felt that she couldn't do both.

I made a note to buy the book for Dr. Winters. Or I'd make him a copy of the chapter when the son and mother meet, toward the end. I was already feeling a bit better. Focusing on his lousy childhood was a way to avoid my own, but any respite from my latest withdrawal was welcome. I couldn't help but compare our differences, which were striking. My mother was warm and loving. Because she'd been an orphan, she'd always wanted children and adored them. She had too many babies too quickly, but at least I was the firstborn and had her undivided attention for seventeen months. Dr. Winters' early history sounded more dire than I had suspected.

"When did you see your first shrink?"

"In college," he said.

"How long were you in therapy?"

"Including my training, twenty-five years."

I had been on the couch way too long and he had surpassed me. He could have done all that soul-searching in pursuit of his Ph.D. and postdoctorate work. Then again, there were reasons people chose their career. "Did a good shrink save you?" I asked.

"Not really. Ninety-nine percent of the ones I knew missed the boat," he said. "They were terrible. Not intuitive at all. That's why I get so frustrated with my profession. They should help people so much more than they do."

Now I understood. He wished somebody would have come to his rescue when he was young. That was who he had become—the intuitive, heroic healer who could have saved him. This explained his impatience with professional pieties and protocol. I could relate. I'd hated academia and designed my classes to be the kind I wished I could have taken, using the "Instant-Gratification-Takes-Too-Long" method.

"Psychology books had to turn you on." They'd turned me on in high school and I didn't even grow up to be a shrink. "Don't tell me you weren't blown away by *Dream Analysis*?"

"Okay," he agreed. "Freud kept opening doors."

Underneath all the postmodern provocation and swashbuckling, Dr. Winters was a real Freudian after all. No wonder we'd clicked—when we weren't locking horns over everything.

"When did you see your first great shrink?" He had to have emulated somebody.

"My supervisor for my Ph.D. doubled as my therapist," he said. "I saw him for a year."

I was not surprised it was a man. He had a pattern of problems with women. He had a mean mother, wasn't close to his sister, and divorced his first wife. I wanted to know why.

"How old were you when you married the first time?"

He picked up the tiny cell phone on his end table though it hadn't rung. Then he put it down again. "Why do you want to know that?" he asked, his voice deeper. Had I hit a nerve?

"I want to see what mistakes you made," I said. "My students love to hear about my past rejections. Makes them feel less stupid. They identify with the struggle." Knowing he had grown up unhappy made me feel normal, as if everything could be repaired.

"I was twenty-seven," he said.

As long as I kept coming up with different reasons why I was asking, he was satisfied. "Twenty-seven is young. Was your first wife an actress?" I couldn't stop giving him the third degree. I was on a roll, asking him everything I'd been itching to know about him for the last eighteen months.

"No. My mother was an actress." He appeared irked, as if I were mixing up the important points of his biography. Which I wasn't.

"I know your mother was an actress. That's why I asked."

"My first wife was a writer," he said.

Just as bad, maybe worse. The females I knew in both professions were obsessive and ambitious, with huge egos. "What did she write?" I asked. "Did she publish any books?"

"One volume of poetry."

He knew I had published a collection of poems a long time

ago. His first wife must have been whom I'd reminded him of when he'd double-booked my appointments. I bet that was how he'd known what words would give me confidence when my memoir was making the rounds.

"Was she Jewish and forceful?"

"Not Jewish," he said. "Not weak but not forceful."

I threw down the gauntlet. "Your ex-wife is the one I remind you of?"

"No." He picked up his pen and wrote something else down. "Why do you ask that?"

I picked up my own pen and wrote, "I'm not the ex-wife." I was disappointed to be wrong; I'd been going crazy trying to decipher which woman from his life I resembled. "I thought that was why you knew how to encourage me about my book."

"I wrote my thesis on health and creativity," he explained. "How artists don't have to be tortured."

I should have cared about his paper, but I longed to hear more about his former lovers. He knew everything about me, but he'd been fairly hush-hush about his dubious past. I suddenly felt as if I were a spy, hunting for clues to uncover a crime of passion. What was he concealing? "How long were you married the first time?"

He paused for a minute, then said, "Twelve years."

Why the pause? I didn't know if he was debating whether to tell me, or merely counting. It could be significant, what people forgot.

"I know you two have a daughter together, in California. Why did you and your first wife split up?"

He laughed. "Didn't Rilke say you shouldn't get married until your late thirties?"

It was a good avoidance. "Yes, in *Letters to a Young Poet,*" I said. "You remarried somebody more nurturing in 1994, you said, right? How old were you?"

"Why do you want to know?"

It felt like we were playing Truth or Dare.

"I want to write a book about you and the addiction therapy," I threw out, taking the level of honesty one step further.

After my student Stephen's *New York Times* piece about the fight over Kyra's dog, Dr. Winters asked if I thought it was unbiased reporting. I shared Joan Didion's line, "A writer's always selling someone out," and Janet Malcolm's theory that all journalists were murderers. I worried that he'd now put a halt to my intrusive inquiries. Or at least say, "Off the record."

"If you weren't writing about our therapy, would you still want to know?" He looked me right in the eye, as if his intense stare would make me back down.

"Yes." I didn't blink, staring right back. "I'd still be asking." It was completely true. Yet at this point, I might have said anything to keep him answering.

"I was one month shy of forty-two when I remarried," he gave up.

This was beginning to resemble the verbal-sparring scenes in *The Silence of the Lambs,* though it was unclear who was the FBI agent and who was the cannibal.

"You smoked a pack a day of cigarettes from age sixteen to thirty-six?"

He nodded but looked uneasy that I'd memorized so many facts of his existence.

"Did you try pot?"

"Yes," he said.

"Do you smoke it now?" I asked.

"No. Not in a long time."

"You're so thin," I said. "Have you always been able to eat everything you want?"

He shifted in his chair. He was much more comfortable asking his patients intrusive questions than being in the hot seat himself. "No. I have to watch myself."

"Really? How tall are you and how much do you weigh?"

"Why does it matter?" He was squinting, my inquisitiveness getting under his skin.

In the book *The Silence of the Lambs,* and the movie based on it, starring Jodie Foster and Anthony Hopkins, Hannibal was a brilliant psychiatrist who tricked Clarice into telling him too much. If I was trying to manipulate Dr. Winters into spilling his guts, his questions about why I was asking were calculated to make me expose more of myself. I had to go deeper before he would. It was amusing that I was the one with the oral fixation, obsessed with food and eating.

"I told you how much I weigh. You know everything about me. I don't like being the only one vulnerable. I want to even the score," I said. "I don't believe you have to watch what you eat."

"Why not?"

"Because I've put you on a pedestal," I told him. "You're like God, so it's hard to see you with imperfections." I figured he'd like the God part.

"I'm six feet and weigh 165. If I ate whatever I wanted I would weigh a lot more."

"How do you stay so thin?" I asked.

"I diet. I've developed a different relation to hunger."

"Explain," I demanded.

"I decide whether I'm feeling physical hunger or emotional hunger, which can masquerade as a craving for food."

"Do you ever pig out?" I really wanted to know.

"Why do you ask?"

"I need you to help me get my eating under control," I said. Hannibal had found Clarice special because of her unrelenting honesty. There was an unspoken trust between them. He never hurt her.

"Last Saturday night I ate a cheeseburger and french fries, drank a margarita, and ate a whole pint of Häagen-Dazs chocolate-chip ice cream," he confessed.

"Why? Were you upset?"

"No. It was out of physical hunger, because I'd been dieting."

"It wasn't impulsive?" When I lost my willpower with food, I'd buy red licorice and chocolate at the twenty-four-hour Duane Reade at three in the morning, when Aaron was asleep. The way I did it, overeating was hidden and illicit.

"No. I decided a few days in advance that on Saturday night I would eat whatever I wanted," he said.

It figured that he even pigged out rationally. Was that a better way to do it? Let yourself eat a big meal and dessert once in a while in public, taking the badness out of it.

"Have you been addicted to anything else but cigarettes?"

"No."

"Are you depressed?" I asked.

"Nope," he said.

"Underneath every substance problem is a depression that feels unbearable." I paraphrased him to himself.

"That's right. Very good."

"Of course you like it, it's your words." Men were so predictable. "Were you depressed during the twenty years you smoked cigarettes?"

"I wouldn't call it a normal depression," he said. "That's too reductive and conventional."

Heaven forbid anything about him should be called normal or conventional. "What would you call it?"

He thought for a few seconds. "Loss and background despair."

"You're not depressed now?" I repeated, a detective trying to trick a perp into confessing.

He glanced at his cell phone, as if he were waiting for an important call. From his wife? Or a suicidal patient? "I'd say I still feel sadness sometimes," he admitted.

"Someone who had bad early years should incorporate

sadness into their life?" I needed to understand how he did it so I could too.

"You tolerate and accept the dark feelings. You learn to value them." He was choosing his words carefully. "For what they teach you."

"What do they teach you?" I asked.

"Where your moods and feelings of loss come from."

I knew where my moods and loss came from. I was sick of revisiting the same—not even all that dramatic—scene of the crime. "Tell me how to fill in the holes." I still wasn't getting the solution part.

"As an adult, you approximate what was missing from your life."

"If you didn't get enough love, you find good love and that makes up for it?" I asked.

"It doesn't exactly make up for it," he said. "But it helps."

I realized the "you" we were talking about was me. Dr. Winters had found a nice wife more caring than his first wife and his mother; I'd found a sweet, sensitive husband who didn't thwart my ambition. That was why I'd liked the *Daniel Deronda* scene. I related to the female artist who would rather work than have children.

"Is it your mother who I reminded you of?" I asked.

"In some ways," he answered, looking down at the red-patterned rug.

For a minute I couldn't speak, extremely distressed that I could in any way resemble the nonnurturing woman who'd wounded him most. I bet that he'd found my ambition threatening because I had refused to change my schedule to accommodate him. I felt like apologizing, reminding him of my loyalty and adoration, swearing I'd never injure or undermine him.

"If I feel empty without dope, can I let myself eat whatever

I want for a few weeks?" I didn't let on how sad his disclosure had just made me.

"No. Being out of control with food would be dumb. It would only make you feel worse," he reminded me. "You have to be careful or you could sabotage all the hard work you've done."

"Sadness is different than depression?" I was holding back tears.

"I think of depression as emptiness, a vacuum," he said. "Whereas I think of being full of sadness."

"Once you understand, the feelings become manageable?" I asked, avoiding his eyes.

"No. You have to be willing to suffer and let your suffering take you somewhere new," he said. "You don't block out the bad feelings, you let them tell their story."

"Is this like the line from Auden's poem about believing your pain?" It was my fault for demanding the truth when I couldn't handle it.

"Yes, like that," Dr. Winters nodded.

I wondered why I hadn't anticipated the maternal overlap. I was a strong female figure, a Venus vessel. Everybody transferred other relationships onto me. My college beau Brad nicknamed me "Shapiro-Mother," shortening it to "Shap-Mo," the way he still addressed me in e-mails twenty years later. To Claire I was "the sister she never had." My students came to me with their problems, as if I were the school nurse or shrink, tagging me their "Manuscript Doctor." Writing-workshop members called me Priest, Rabbi, Reverend, and/or Guru Sue. My student Jeff insisted I was his "Suru." I shouldn't construe Dr. Winters' admission as an insult. I tried to see it as a compliment that meant I'd affected him and he felt close to me.

He looked at his watch. I looked at mine. Our session was just about over. I closed my notebook and put it back in my briefcase, feeling bruised and rejected, wanting to get away from him quickly.

I stood up and mumbled, "See you Thursday."

"I wrote something about my childhood," he threw out. "It's fifteen pages."

Sensing my intense hurt about the mother connection, he was just offering me a bone. It worked; he'd hooked me again.

"Fiction or nonfiction?"

"I wanted it to be fiction, but it came out completely auto-biographical," he said.

My colleague Kathy was jealous when her shrink mentioned she was writing a book. Not me. I was absolutely enthralled to think that Dr. Winters was also a writer. Everything was turned around tonight!

"I showed it to a well-known critic," he said. "His response was 'Ruthless isn't my style.' "

"I like ruthless. Are you going to let me read it?" I sensed he would.

"Not yet," he said. "It's not finished."

"I didn't know quitting dope would hurt this much. It's worse than getting off nicotine. It's killing me." I lifted the strap of my briefcase over my shoulder.

"Of course it is. It's your last addiction. The final frontier." He stood up and opened the door for me. "You have no crutches left."

That wasn't quite true. I still had him.

Chapter 19

MAY 2003

When I was a teenager and my first boyfriend split up with me after we'd dated four years, it took me four years to really get over him. I deduced that recovering from affairs of the heart took the same number of days you spent together. Since I kept getting stuck in long-term liaisons, Claire made me nix that theory lest I spend my whole young life in mourning. By thirty, if a love connection wasn't working, I'd cut my losses and move on. I developed a breakup ritual: I'd throw on a miniskirt and tight T-shirt to go out dancing all night with my best girl-friends. I began to derive a thrill from dumping disappointing Romeos. I definitely got better and faster at it. Shedding substances resembled getting rid of stale romance.

At first being dopeless made me uncomfortable, anxious, tense, and lonely, as if I had just lost a loyal lover who had been soothing me for decades. Someone who was always there to lull me to sleep, no matter what. Still, like heartbreak, I had to admit that each twenty-four-hour cycle became a bit less horrific. Meanwhile, my dreams became very vivid.

On Saturday my subconscious sent me back to Detroit, where I learned that my old high-school classmate Gayle had died. I went to her house to pay my respects. In real life Gayle was alive and well in Detroit. In fact I'd recently learned that she'd married there and become a minister. Gayle's single sister, Jill, left for Manhattan the same year that I'd moved. Jill was a well-known editor at Random House, the company where my memoir was being published. If I was working out an internal conflict about being in a religious Michigan family or in the New York book world—it was no shock which one involved death. I deduced that the two sisters were two sides of me and I was grieving for my past. Or was I mourning for the years I had been unhappy in a big white house in the Midwest?

On Sunday I cast myself in an action movie set in a huge apartment complex in Florida, during an earthquake. Several former comrades were there. They decided to stay inside and hope the building wouldn't fall down or catch fire. I found this passivity ridiculous and went outside, where everything was crashing and burning around me. I came up with a strategy—I would wait at the side of the high-rise. This way, if it started to tumble, I could run the other way. The most palpable emotion I felt was that no matter what, I was going to survive.

Letting dope put me to sleep for so many years had obscured my reveries, keeping me from either having or recalling them. It was another solid reason for quitting, almost as good as finding that I wrote better clean. Dr. Winters agreed that my substance abuse could have been snuffing out my dreams.

The benefit of sobriety, he added, was that once all of the mood-altering narcotics were out of my system, I would have my own moods back and become more of myself. This wasn't reassuring when that self was moping around and miserable. Yet the next Monday, a month into grieving for grass, I was able to work for ten hours straight. When I checked the clock, which said ten P.M., I felt spent and elated, as if a fever had broken.

The more stuff I quit, the more pages my printer was spitting out daily. To my glee and astonishment, my output kept increasing. I pulled out an old novel and started my new memoir, spilling long, funny first-person rants about Dr. Winters and the addiction therapy. It was an avalanche of fresh material, a tidal wave of creativity bursting from my laptop. The new pages weren't even that rough. Members of my critical Tuesday night workshop, who often told me, "This is throat-clearing. Toss out the first eight pages," were now saying, "Don't stop. You're rocking and rolling." I used to be afraid I couldn't work without cigarettes and weed. Currently without them, I couldn't stop working.

Swept up in this newfound inspiration, I canceled plans to go to parties, readings, dinners with friends. Aaron the misanthrope, a workaholic himself, was always thrilled to avoid any social event. He didn't mind that everything in my realm now paled in comparison to work. Indeed, my turning into a hermit like him made us closer. He'd call me before he came home at night to see if I needed more time or wanted him to pick up an extra ream of paper from Staples or more little bottles of Wite-Out, which I somehow managed to need even with a state-of-the-art computer and printer. When he showed up, he'd rub my neck, kiss my forehead, and marvel at my ever-expanding manuscripts.

Being on the wagon had not weakened my obsessiveness; it merely made me switch obsessions. Mine now included: writing for ten hours at a time, e-mail, and collecting stickers. Lighting scented candles was another growing passion. I arranged seven or eight different-sized and -colored wax circles and squares on a silver tray near my laptop. It looked like a shrine and felt primal to work so close to fire. I obviously missed firing up daily doobies and Capri Menthols, so this quenched my pyromaniac urges a bit. Meanwhile, I didn't care how reclusive or nutty I was becoming as long as my prose kept flowing. I'd never been religious or spiritual, but I felt born-again.

It had taken me nine months to really get over nicotine, a month to fully recover from no gum, and seven weeks to salvage my sanity after I quit smoking pot. Not that I was totally recuperated from being a stoner for thirty years. There were still days that I wanted to reach for a joint in the box above my desk, wishing I could just spark one up and shimmy around my apartment in a smoky haze. Luckily the longing was losing its fervor.

"You might always want to light up, but you'll develop a different relationship to the cravings," Dr. Winters said. "When I was young and single, I would see a beautiful woman and feel I had to have her. Now I can look at a beautiful woman, feel attracted to her, but realize it wouldn't be worth screwing up my marriage."

I hated his analogy. I couldn't relate to wanting beautiful women and I couldn't stand to think of him young, single, and on the prowl. A better comparison was what it felt like to walk by the bakery and smell the aroma of chocolate cake and cannolis on my way to get a chef salad at the diner. It was a challenge but not all that stressful or perilous.

Anyway, I didn't have different feelings about being high, I still felt high. The first time I noticed the fun, dizzy tingling in my chest I was sitting at my regular booth at Cozy's Soup and Burger, on Friday afternoon, reading the paper and sipping my third diet soda. Without anything else to block it, I felt a very distinct caffeine buzz. It was an extreme spaciness mixed with glee, as if I'd become blotto from several bong hits. How cool. At a dollar fifty a soda with free refills, it was the cheapest high yet and I wasn't breaking any of Winters' regulations. This was a surprise perk of sobriety. I could get stoned from diet soda!

"Am I getting tipsy from the caffeine in diet Coke? Or am I crazy?" I asked Dr. Winters.

"Both." He smiled.

"Really? I'm drinking the same amount of diet soda, but I swear it's getting me off. How could that be?"

"With the absence of other substances you are more sensitized to all stimuli," he explained in his science voice. "The effects are greatly exaggerated."

"I don't have to quit caffeine, right? It can't hurt me." I couldn't handle another assignment; I wasn't completely over the bread or dope yet.

"You should cut down," he said. "Caffeine can make you frantic and jumpy. Too much will take away from what you are. Like any substance does."

"It doesn't have the same kind of addictive quality that's in nicotine or alcohol, does it?" I asked.

"Actually, it does," he informed me. "Studies show that caffeine increases the production of dopamine in the brain. It could be mind-altering."

"Mind-altering?" If my mind was being altered, shouldn't I at least get to trip on LSD? Everything I liked was bad for me. Or, with my addictive gene, I had a talent for overusing anything. I'd recently made myself sick eating two pounds of baby carrots.

"Cutting down on caffeine could cause headaches or make you depressed. You could crash. There's even a diagnosable caffeine-related disorder," he said. "That might be the reason you were having trouble sleeping."

There was no way caffeine could create a serious problem, I was positive. Then I recalled that two years before, I had found a lump in my breast. I'd run uptown to see my cool gynecologist, Dr. Cherry. (He and Claire were the only people I would shlep uptown for.) Dr. Cherry gave me a breast exam and said my little lump didn't feel cancerous. Then he asked how much caffeine I was drinking. When I said, "Ten diet sodas a day," he warned that caffeine made cystic breasts more lumpy. With too much caffeine, a problem could arise because it would be harder to decipher whether a lump was anything serious, even on a mammogram. That scared me. The next day I'd stopped all caffeine. Bad idea. I was so groggy and angry I wound up weeping on the subway.

This time I cut down on diet soda slowly. Over the next week I switched to caffeine-free diet Coke at seven P.M., then at six, then at five, so I could sleep easier and not stun my system. It made going out to dinner even more difficult. Local grocery stores sold aislesful of no-caffeine drinks, and everyone had decaf coffee, but restaurants rarely served no-caffeine sodas. My favorite neighborhood Japanese eatery didn't have anything caffeine-free except alcohol, which was off-limits, and water, which was boring. When I asked for uncaffeinated green tea, the waiter looked at me like I was nuts. I bought it at the Japanese market and drank it at home. I don't know why Asian restaurants don't carry it. I was excited to find one local Chinese place that served diet Sprite, which had no caffeine. I tried to develop a taste for it, but it was too bland. I'd given up so much lately, I couldn't compromise on diet soda. I had to put my foot down somewhere.

Like most New York working women, I usually toted a big black purse or briefcase. I began carrying a twist-off twenty-ounce no-caffeine diet Coke with me everywhere. The next time I went into the sushi place for dinner, I hid my secret stash. I ordered a diet soda. When it came, I went into the ladies' room, subtly carting my soda with me. There I poured out the regular diet Coke and poured the caffeine-free version into my glass.

I didn't feel like I was doing anything wrong, since I had paid for the drink that I'd poured into the sink, as well as the liquid that I'd sneaked in. Keeping the leftover caffeine-free soda in my briefcase, I replenished my drink under the table. It seemed as if I were trying to save money by spiking my drink with vodka. But I was doing the opposite—spending double to keep myself from getting high on anything.

"Can I see your ruthless story?" I begged Dr. Winters at our next appointment.

"No. Not yet. I'm still working on it."

He took it from his desk and held it up, pointing to correction marks that he'd made in red pen. The pages were far enough away so I could see the red writing but couldn't read it. What a tease. He'd already told me about her. What more was he hiding?

"It's about your mother?" I sensed gaps in my previous interview with him that his unfinished, ruthless story would fill in.

"Yes," he said.

Too impatient to wait for the rewrite, I couldn't help but launch into follow-up inquiries. "Did she hit you as a kid?"

"Worse than that."

"How much worse?"

"She's been called evil," he said. "A monster."

In a lighthearted mood, all of a sudden I found it comical that I reminded my shrink of a monster. "Is she still alive?"

He nodded.

"Do you ever see her?" I recalled what my brother Michael, the Chicago cardiologist, once said about his patients: "The monsters always live."

"I haven't seen my mother in thirty years," Dr. Winters said calmly. "Since I was twenty."

This fact downright floored me. I'd never known anyone

who hadn't spoken to their mother for thirty years. No wonder he'd given me permission to cancel my trip to Michigan in February! Cutting out crazy family members forever was our control group.

"What happened when you were twenty?"

"Why do you want to know?" he asked.

I heard the *Silence of the Lambs* soundtrack in my head again. "I need the missing puzzle piece to unlock you," I tried.

"I testified against her in a custody trial for my little sister, who didn't want to live with her," he said. "I told the truth about my mother's alcoholism and use of physical violence. I humiliated her in public. She lost the case and never spoke to me again."

There were benefits to being a voyeuristic vulture. If I had minded my own business like a good little girl, I would have missed this melodramatic melee at the heart of who Dr. Winters was and why he'd become that way.

It reminded me of a story that I often made my editor friend Harvey tell my NYU interviewing class. It concerned the time that an acclaimed author took Harvey to lunch to pick his brain for a book on the inner workings of *The New York Times*. Harvey, who had been a high-level editor at the newspaper for almost half a century and was near retirement, was ready to finally reveal everything. But he never wound up giving the author of the book any dirt or juicy tidbits—because the guy was lazy and didn't ask the right questions. That was never going to be my problem. I erred on the side of wildly inappropriate interrogations and overquizzing. I would have made an exceptional FBI agent.

"Do you regret testifying against your mother?" It felt essential to know.

"Yes. It was foolish," Dr. Winters said.

"Why? You stuck up for your sister."

"No, not really. It wasn't about my sister. It was about being angry at my mother," he said. He'd given this a lot of thought. "Nobody should testify against their parents in court."

"I didn't know your mother abused alcohol," I said.

Although he had buried the lead (a journalistic expression Harvey had taught me), I was certain that this was the crucial piece of data I'd been chasing. It solved the enigma of why Dr. Winters—and nobody else I'd ever met—had been able to crawl under my skin and methodically lead me out of the maze of substance abuse I'd been lost in for three decades. I thought my father became an oncologist because he'd felt helpless watching my grandmother die of cancer. Similar motives were at the root of Dr. Winters' ardor for addiction therapy. I would wager that many doctors were fueled by the early desire to save their mothers.

"How old were you when you realized your mom was a drunk?"

"Very young," he said.

"That's the reason why you specialize in substance abuse and addiction!" It was a eureka moment and I could not resist sharing my diagnosis.

"Not true." He shook his head no. "I was originally attracted to treating untreatable conditions."

My analysis was so obviously on the money, it appeared coy that he'd try to deny it. "Come on. Your mother's substance problem ruined your entire childhood," I argued. "No wonder you want to stamp it out."

"I can see why you think so." He relented a tiny bit. "Let's just say I have a certain amount of insight into the horror and havoc that addictions can cause."

"Is there another diagnosis for your mother?"

"Like what?"

I found it hard to believe that a noted shrink, with twenty-five years of experience diagnosing other people's emptiness, had never searched for the medical reason to explain why his mother couldn't really love or take care of him. "Paranoid schizophrenia?" I tried. "Manic depression? Narcissistic personality disorder?"

"She was extremely narcissistic."

"Did it make you hate women?" I wanted to know.

"Why do you ask that?" He wanted to know.

"Aaron had a difficult connection to his mother as a kid." This might be why Dr. Winters had been able to coerce Aaron to commit to me. He knew which wires got crossed by early maternal mistakes and how to delicately uncross them in the male psyche.

"It's not hatred of women. It's terror and confusion," he explained. "Men are much more afraid of the women in their lives than they let on."

It was unclear if he was talking about himself, Aaron, or both of them.

"I remind you of a monster?" I smiled.

He smiled back. "I never said that."

"Why do I remind you of her?" I asked.

"You're unusually forceful and strong for a woman."

I looked at my black jeans, black blazer, and black boots. My mother could usually be found wearing pretty pink or light-purple Armani skirt outfits and high heels. "Because I'm not quiet, sweet, and pastel like I'm supposed to be?"

"You're stylistically staccato," he said. "Tough-talking. Sharp-edged."

He didn't appear to be aware how much he was hurting my feelings. "It sounds like you're saying I'm not feminine."

"There's a difference between character and style," he offered, which didn't make me feel any less insulted.

"My style works for me," I said defensively. "I have almost everything I want in life now."

"Like what?"

"I'm clean, madly in love with my husband. We both

tripled our income last year," I listed. "I adore my agent and editor. Publishing my book has been the biggest thrill of my life."

"Why did you say almost?" he asked. "What else do you want?"

"I want to lose ten pounds before my book tour and sell another book before the first one comes out. I have to be more disciplined and focused. Not sweeter or softer. Just the opposite—I have to get more ruthless." I'd stolen the word the critic had used to describe Dr. Winters' style.

"Be more ruthless, by all means," he said.

"But you're disapproving. You want me to be frilly, shy, and frail," I lamented. "For some stupid reason I still want your approval."

"I wasn't saying you should be shy and frail," he maintained. Then he ruined his point by adding, "Though the more languages one learns, the better."

"Not if speaking a certain language would be lying." I was getting peeved. It felt like he was saying that it was okay for him to be outspoken, out there, and outrageously provocative, but not for me. "I spent my childhood watching my brothers in torn jeans, having a blast wrestling outside in the mud while I was stuck inside, wearing a prim high-collared pink dress and tight pink leather shoes that strangled my feet, helping my mother wash the dishes." I needed him to understand.

"I don't want you to wear pink and do dishes," he corrected himself. "Don't ever be frail and shy. It would bore me to tears. I'd hate it."

"You already hate me because I'm strong and forceful like your mother."

"You don't get it. Those qualities remind me of me. Don't you see that I *am* strong and forceful like my mother?" He cleverly veered himself out of the doghouse.

I was becoming his mirror? He was confusing me. "I want

to dismiss you as a sexist pig with mean-mother issues," I said. "The paradox is that you're the one who's been making me stronger."

"I want you strong, rich, and ruthless," he stated unequivocally. "Really. Be ruthless."

Reassured that he embodied the good father, I switched back to his bad mother. "Do you and your mom call each other or write?"

"I write her letters, but she doesn't answer."

"You two stopped speaking after that trial, when you were twenty years old?" I didn't quite believe it. "She never spoke to you again?" I sensed that he was leaving something out.

"We stopped speaking. Then four years later, when I was in Europe, taking a thousand-mile pilgrimage across France and Spain ..."

It was the kind of physical adventure that would interest Aaron. Stories of people who had traveled around the world, sailing the roughest seas and climbing the highest mountains, tended to bore me.

"I stopped to take a break in northern Spain," he continued. "I walked into an outdoor café. Something grabbed my attention. I turned and there she was."

Aha! I knew it wasn't over. "Did you go up to her?"

"Yes. I had dinner with her." He nodded. "It turned out she had been driving on the same road I'd been walking."

Now, this was gripping. I had always preferred emotional adventures. "How was seeing her?"

"Surreal."

"Was she nice to you?" I asked.

"Yes. She said, 'If you need help, here's how to reach me.' "

"Did you try to reach her?"

"No."

"No? Why not?" Had he been blaming his mother for cutting him off when he hadn't really made the effort?

He hesitated, his face and shoulders tightening. This part of the tale still stuck in his craw, I could tell before he spilled it. "Because right after that I ran into an old friend of my mother's, Phyllis, who knew about our dinner. Phyllis said, 'It must have been horrible for you.' It turned out that what my mother told her about our meeting was filled with contempt...."

"That you were wasting time instead of working?" I felt guilty that I'd thought the same thing. When I was twenty-four, I had finished my master's degree and was freelancing while working full-time at *The New Yorker*.

"Yes." He scrunched his eyes. "That I had been stupidly wandering around, wasting time." The memory of it continued to make him angry and sorrowful, the conflict written on his face.

"That was the last time you saw her? She hasn't answered your letters since then?"

"No," he said. "She hasn't responded to the presents I've sent her either."

"What have you sent her?" I asked.

"Flowers, chocolates, framed pictures," he said quietly. "For Christmas and her birthday."

"Every year?" This was making me really sad.

He nodded.

"And she never responds?"

"Never. But you think she doesn't think about me every day of her life?" he asked, in a vulnerable tone that made me want to cry.

It was not that surprising that I reminded him of his mother; he had a larger-than-life matriarchal figure looming over everything. I did too. Yet I was overconnected to mine, the complete converse of Dr. Winters and his mother's long-term silence. Despite our conflicts, I'd spoken to my mom on the phone almost every night since I had left for college. Lately, if we didn't talk daily, we would at least e-mail each other. Since she bought everyone presents constantly and my father and brothers sucked when it came to remembering important occasions, I overcompensated. This year, since I finally had some money, I had sent her long-stemmed roses for Mother's Day and four different presents for her birthday—a long pink silk scarf, a silver pin, two books, and a fancy black leather photo album. She had responded with a sweet thank-you note and gushed about my gifts over the phone, clearly delighted with them. I suddenly felt so lucky to have her.

Unlike Dr. Winters, I was overmothered. With three younger male siblings, I couldn't help but emulate her. Because she'd grown up as an orphan, I'd sensed our relationship was too important to her. I had to replace her beloved late mother as well as be her only daughter. Sometimes I'd tried to be less involved with her. Other times I'd wondered, without children, what was the point of having all these excessive mothering instincts I'd picked up by osmosis.

In a frenzy of final questions, I extracted a few more intimate details from him. His mother, who now lived in North Carolina, had been married three times. The second husband committed suicide, the next one died of cancer. Of her four kids, she'd only been in touch with her youngest son. When Dr. Winters asked his brother about her, he said she was crazy. I couldn't imagine being deserted by a parent, for any reason.

My father's father was left in Poland by his mother until he was six years old. My dad often repeated the family lore, as if it justified the wretched way Harry had treated his wife, kids, and grandkids, as if nobody could recover from that kind of desertion.

"If you don't have your mother's love, you don't have anything," I heard my father's voice say.

"How did you survive?" I asked Dr. Winters. "Did a nice stepmother help at all? Or an aunt or nanny? A good father?"

"I got an enormous amount from my mother," he said. "She made me resilient and a fighter. I had good instincts. I was lucky."

His success and optimistic outlook was a persuasive argument for analysis. Knowing he'd had to reconstruct his emotional realm from scratch made me respect him more. Instead of becoming bitter and resentful like my grandfather, he had gone the other way. I was grateful that Dr. Winters had become what was missing from his early years: the embodiment of encouragement, kindness, and sanity.

I wasn't really used to supportive men, just women. I recalled how overly empathetic my mother had always been, the Florence Nightingale of West Bloomfield. She fed and took care of her family, friends, and even her friends' families, going to visit her pals' parents in the hospital for hours, flowers and candy in her arms. The reason she'd never made a lot of money from her party-planning business was that she didn't charge enough and gave away too much for free. Once, when a steady customer ordered a pink birthday basket for her little girl, I noticed Mom loading two baskets into her car, one pink and one blue.

"I thought they just ordered one basket," I said.

"Well, how can I bring the girl a present without bringing something for her little brother?" she'd said. "I don't want him to feel left out."

Brian joked that Mom was so emotionally overconnected that if one of her relatives got cancer, it was as if she had cancer too. Another time, when Michael was upset, she couldn't sleep and told me, "If one of my kids is unhappy, how could I be happy?"

I had vowed that I'd never be so dependent on another person. Growing up with rambunctious males whose aggressive traits were overpraised, I wanted to be like them. Soon I was. I smoked like my father, cursed and wrestled with my brothers, pursued a competitive career in the big city like the men I slept with. I loved my mother, but I loathed the insipid feminine caretaker role she'd accepted. In our house, male needs and hunger were given priority. It was the same in Claire's testosterone-filled household. I thought the reason she'd become a well-known architect was to get revenge on her three brothers, who'd hogged all the Lego and Tonka Toys. Lately Claire had been joking that I'd become addicted to quitting things. I worried that next I had to give up my masculine tendencies.

Dr. Winters warned that with no skin, there were no divisions between me and those I cared about. My radar picked up everything, sucked it in. I was feeling too close to everyone, especially him. I preferred to see Dr. Winters as my fantasy boyfriend, or an all-powerful father figure who would save me, or my oldest brother, whom I'd lock horns with eternally. It was still a little upsetting that I'd pressed all his maternal-monster buttons. Ultimately I blamed his issues, not mine.

Yet today, hearing more of his tortured personal history made me want to protect and praise him, cradle him in my arms. Transference was not fair. I was stuck in the least sexy role, the one I had spent all these years avoiding like the plague. With no high to transport me, I couldn't get away from these nurturing feelings that were engulfing me. Sometimes you remeet people at certain crossroads for essential reasons. This was worse than turning into my mother. Ten years younger than the dashing James Bond, I was becoming his missing mom.

Chapter 20

JUNE 2003

Staying clean and writing constantly, I still found time to fight with many of my esteemed cronies. An acclaimed poet pal was peeved that I had missed his last four readings. My writing workshop colleague Kathy accused me of hogging the group with too many of my own book chapters and rewrites, slighting other members. A newspaper editor who'd championed my work for years accused me of biting her head off for being hostile when she wasn't. After tiffs with seven people in a row, I saw that the problem couldn't be all of them.

Twenty months of addiction therapy had changed me. Unfortunately my onetime mentors were not enamored with my supersober self. I couldn't really blame them. Once a voice of support, I'd become critical and intrusive. I kept talking and penning pages about how much better off I was straight. It was obnoxious, but I was brainwashed. Everything was good or evil. Other people's behavior threatened my resolutions. If it was cool for Kathy to toke, it was cool for me. Thus I'd told her that I viewed dope as toxic. I wasn't trashing her, I was protecting myself from a relapse. Rather than being high, I was high-strung. If somebody blew me off, I didn't care. Stopping so many substances, with such sweet results, made it easier to quit people.

I used to joke that I was trying to sell out for years but nobody was buying. Now they were. I usually preferred downtown artists, solo players, partyers, and flamboyant personalities. After selling my sexy memoir and getting free of smoke, alcohol, and drugs, I befriended teetotalers, married couples with kids, rich Upper East Side workaholics, types I once found boring and colorless.

"Don't worry. You're doing incredibly well," said my cousin Miranda. "Becoming sober alters everything. People resent you. Just ignore them." Two years after she'd won her own addiction battles, she had acquired a terrific fiancé, penthouse apartment, and lucrative book deal with Knopf. After rehab, she had switched the crowd she ran with, and was resented for it. Once again somebody in AA had the right words to soothe me, as if they made members memorize a sobriety soundtrack. "You've never been so healthy and together," Miranda said. "Don't feel guilty about being successful."

I didn't feel guilty. I felt mortified by my transfiguration. I had become preachy, prudish, and overly ambitious, hoping to become rich and powerful. I'd turned into the kind of moralistic, single-minded, money-obsessed asshole I had always mercilessly made fun of. Amusingly, one old role model from my past liked my brand-new personality much better.

"You're becoming a Republican, that's fabulous!" said my father over the phone, taunting me gleefully.

Dad's proof was that I'd become more vociferously pro-Israel than he was, which oddly aligned me with the Christian Right. Plus I'd been devouring *The New York Times* Real Estate

Section ever since I'd refinanced our apartment to take advantage of low interest rates. Furthermore, he argued, I was finally earning a decent wage and thus had more to lose. It was a confusing accusation since, politically, I'd been left of left since second grade. A radical in Michigan, I was disappointed that when I'd moved to Greenwich Village in 1981 I was merely considered a mainstream Democrat. Okay, I'd recently told off a tattooed and multiply-pierced NYU student by using Dennis Miller's line, "Can you do anything to become any more unemployable?" But joining the GOP?

My ultraconservative dad did have a point. Yes, I continued to detest the Bush family. But not as much as I hated Arab suicide bombers; thus I wasn't totally against the war in Iraq. I loathed racism and homophobia, advocated social welfare reforms, and taught writing at a local soup kitchen. But when I passed a young healthy-looking white guy on the street begging for money, in front of a "Busboys Wanted" sign on the diner window, I didn't give him any change and actually thought of my dad's unsympathetic line: "Get a job." Courting financial gain with fervor, I could not understand anybody who wasn't hardworking.

"I hate being a lowly assistant at a bank. I wish I could make a living writing, like you do," complained my protégé Jeff, as we shared a chef salad at Cozy's diner. I often met with my students here. Fast and cheap, it was ideal for half-hour lunch/editing/shrink sessions.

Going on a hunch, I asked Jeff, "How much are you drinking?"

"Maybe twice a week," he said. "When I go out with my cousin Pauly. He's been depressed."

"How many drinks do you have?" I asked. Like Dr. Winters, I skipped small talk in favor of the nitty-gritty. "Two beers? Three?"

"Four, maybe," he answered. "Or five. Sometimes whiskey."

"Get rid of Pauly. It's not your job to save him," I muttered, picking at Swiss cheese from the salad while marking up Jeff's latest essay with a black Flair pen.

I had met Jeff, a married twenty-seven-year-old, when he took two of my New School classes the year before. He won me over by chronicling how his wife's elderly Catholic mother caught him jacking off in the bathroom. After selling six first-person essays, he'd taken to calling me "Obi Sue." I tagged him an Italian Philip Roth. Then he got blocked. He was mopier, dressed shleppier, and grew a scraggly goatee. I didn't get the younger generation's penchant for facial hair. He was a tall, sad-eyed teddy bear. I wanted to save him.

"Are you doing drugs?" I continued editing, eating, and intrusively drilling him.

"Coke sometimes," he said sheepishly.

"You're doing cocaine? You could have a heart attack and die!" I admonished. I didn't even know people still did coke. "Be honest. You're probably getting stoned or drunk four or five nights a week," I said. "No wonder you're blocked. If you don't get rid of the drugs and liquor, you can flush your career down the toilet."

"My shrink, Dr. Gold, has been saying the same thing," he said. "I've been seeing him once a week."

I liked the sound of this Dr. Gold. "Why just once?"

Jeff said, "It's expensive."

"Don't you have insurance?" I asked. "How much does it cost you?"

"With the medical coverage, I pay twenty-four dollars a session out of pocket."

"It's that cheap? Are you crazy? Quit wasting money on booze and coke and see Dr. Gold three times a week!" I ordered.

I told Jeff how getting shrunk and straight, like I did, would unlock him, and suggested new rituals to replace the drinking and drugs. I recalled how arrogant Dr. Winters sounded at our first session. I was a pale imitation. Winters had technical jargon, diplomas, decades of experience, and an impressive office, while I was proselytizing like one of those long-robed Hare Krishna space cadets who gave out flowers at the airport. Unlike the cynical Blake, who ignored me, Jeff was enthralled. He pulled a spiral notebook from his backpack and took notes.

"Aside from taking your class again, what other positive things should I try?" Jeff asked.

"Journaling. Exercise. Hang out with sober friends," I listed. "My favorite Dr. Winters edict was getting held every night for an hour without talking."

"So you'll hold me every night for an hour without talking?" he asked, then cracked up.

I wanted to add "and get rid of the facial hair," but held my tongue. Oh no. My father was right: I'd gone right. While losing another addiction, I had once again misplaced my identity. Today I seemed to be morphing into a mix of my Midwest and Manhattan doctor dads.

Early for my Tuesday session, I did *The New York Times* crossword in Dr. Winters' waiting room. He walked out of his office with a messy-haired patient in baggy jeans and sneakers. Winters said something to him, then disappeared. Soon the big lug was staring at me.

"Hi," the oversized guy said, confused, as if he wasn't sure if I was friendly or dangerous.

"Hi," I answered.

He turned around, agitated, then stomped to the bathroom. A second later he was back, pacing the hall. Dr. Winters came out again and said something to him before letting me in.

I sat down on the couch as he closed the door. "Is he okay?" I asked.

"He's high," Dr. Winters said. "I told him to come back in an hour."

What kind of moron did drugs before therapy? Then I recalled that I had shown up here stoned too. I'd been off dope just a few months myself. I had no right to judge him. I took out my pen and notebook, turning to where we'd left off last week.

"What are you always writing?" he asked.

It appeared to irk Winters if I focused more on the page than on him. This, from Dr. Three Cell Phones, double-booker and obsessive vacation-taker, who had the attention span of a teenage boy at the Playboy Mansion.

I looked up and smiled. "I told you. I'm writing a book about you and your addiction therapy, but I need more data." Luckily, unlike Aaron, Winters liked to be quoted and written about. It appealed to his vanity. "How many of your patients who are addicts are straight now?"

"Out of about twenty-five, I think only two are still using," he said. "But they weren't that committed to the therapy."

"Have I been committed to therapy?"

"What do you think?" he asked.

"I want to know if you like me better than your other patients," I admitted.

"You want to think you've distinguished yourself," he said.

"That's right. I'm an overachiever, even in therapy. I had to quit more substances than your other patients." I wrote it down, putting a star next to "overachiever," quite amused by this revelation. "How am I a typical addict?"

"Is this for you or your book?" he asked.

"Both," I said, though I was never sure. I noticed he was more succinct and eloquent if he knew his words were on the record.

"You use substances to rein in your feelings, which seem

big and overwhelming if you can't control them," he sang, as if I were giving him a pop quiz he was acing.

"How am I an atypical addict?" I asked.

"You're out of sequence. You felt too good too soon. For many addicts there's no upside for years, it only gets worse. Or they have a short honeymoon phase. Yours seems to be lasting."

"It was hell for nine months getting off nicotine," I argued. "You even said I suffered too much."

"You should have suffered each time you got off a substance."

"Aren't there addicts who quit and just feel better?" I was sure there were.

"No. There's always ups and downs," he insisted. "Freud rejected the cathartic method of psychoanalysis. Primal scream therapy, where you get a limited quantity of past pain or unhappiness out of your system, doesn't work. Unhappiness regenerates itself. Sustained damage from childhood doesn't disappear."

As I wrote it down, I was disagreeing. "I was never abused. I didn't have the same damage that you had. My mother adored me, told me I could be anything. . . ."

"Then where did all your addictions come from?" he asked, as if it was rhetorical.

"Couldn't they be genetic?"

"A genetic predisposition would lower your tolerance to cigarettes or alcohol. It wouldn't cause you to remain addicted for twenty-seven years."

"You think I'm in denial?" I asked.

"Yes. You can't see darkness. You banish feelings of emptiness, sadness, and hunger. You don't leave enough room for the dark side."

This bullshit again! What happy person didn't banish feelings of emptiness, sadness, and hunger? That was how you got happy. Dwelling on sadness was self-defeating. "What if we split the difference and say I'm having a good year or two?" I threw him a bone.

"Okay, that's a little more realistic." He agreed to the temporary cease-fire.

"Okay, good. I'll get depressed next year. Just for you. I promise."

"So why are you in such a bad mood today?" He swiveled his chair to face me.

I'd forgotten until he reminded me. "All my mentors hate me," I said. "My old friends too. I'm not sure why."

"You have an exposed nervous system and fine-tuned radar. You see through people and they don't like that," he said. "You're highly perceptive and overreactive, a very difficult combination."

I wrote down "highly perceptive and overreactive." It had a good rhythm, like a Gerard Manley Hopkins poem. It seemed the perfect combination for a writer. "I like being psychic," I said. "People used to say that my mother was psychic too. She used to warn me, 'The Goodman women are witches.' "

"Goodman is her maiden name?" he asked.

I nodded yes. "Good witches. How do I stop offending people?"

"Rein yourself in. Don't react to things," he said. "Why just your old friends?"

"Because I don't socialize anymore. All I do is work. I barely go out. I eat dinner every day at five o'clock now; Aaron calls me the 'early-bird special.' I've become boring. I used to be a hedonist. Since I can't have any fun, I resent anyone who can."

"The word hedonist isn't accurate. There is nothing fun about substance abuse. Using isn't pleasure-seeking, it's pain-avoiding," he corrected.

I thought of the anguish on the high guy's face and wondered if he was still out there. What if he destroyed the office? Or hurt himself?

"I'm like Mayor Bloomberg, another former smoker," I said. "If I can't indulge, nobody can. My father is right. I have more money, so I have more to lose."

"Too easy," deemed Dr. Winters.

"It's true. I used to be open-minded. I cared about writing honest poems and helping the poor. Now I want my memoir to sell a ton of copies so I can get rich."

"You were using substances as a defense against what scared you, like desire, competition, and ambition," he said.

"During all the wild mushroom parties, political rallies, and poetry readings, I was just squelching my parents' mid-American values?" I was disappointed at how pedestrian that sounded. "What if I've changed for the worse?"

"You've changed for the better," he said. "When you first came here you were riddled with negatives, a victim of circumstance, very can't-do. Now you're can-do. You look much happier, less oppressed."

For once I didn't want a sycophant, I wanted a harsh mirror to reflect what others were seeing. I shared, in tedious detail, every single tiff and drawn-out argument I had recently engaged in. "In each case I'm sure I'm right but then everybody's getting so mad at me. Why? I must be doing something wrong."

He nodded and took notes before making his judgment. "Nothing you're doing or saying is unreasonable," he said. "But you've learned to take care of yourself first, which is a big change. It's jolting for people who expect you to be more accommodating. You appear selfish and rejecting, but only in contrast to how fawning and pliable you used to be."

"If I'm happier and healthier, why am I coming off cold and abrasive?" I wanted to know.

"You're more impatient, self-righteous, and intolerant of other people's addictions and weaknesses," he offered.

"Good," I nodded, getting it down; that sounded right. "When I'm straight, I'm more difficult to be around?"

"On the surface you're more prickly and irritable. But on a deeper level, can't-dos are always more difficult."

"Am I more difficult than your other patients?" I asked. "Do I tax you more?"

"Yes," he said quickly, but didn't expand on it.

"How?" He was holding back. His going easy on me seemed too superficial. "I need you to tell me what the fuck is going on."

"You have a chronic anxiety level connected to a hyperactive mind that's plugged in to a very analytic level of consciousness," he said. "There's no rest or rhythm. It's all high pitch. There's a continual idiosyncratic intensity that's exhausting."

Like a journalist nabbing the sound bite of the week, I wrote it down fast, half awed by his insight, half mortified and feeling unfairly maligned. "I'm not anxious," I defended myself, suddenly on the verge of tears. "I've been feeling very productive and happy."

"Now you sound like the manic patient who says, 'What's the problem? I feel fantastic. I'm having conversations with God, I'm a genius, I'm discovering the solution of turning salt water into fresh water. Don't take away this great mood.' Then they crash into a black hole."

Dr. Mean was on a roll, having too much fun trashing me. I'd created a monster. What he was saying was hard to hear, but it was my fault, I'd begged him for it. "You're saying that being too confident alienates people?"

"Yes, your confidence can be off-putting and dangerous," he said. "You have to be quieter about it, keep it in check. Realize you're at risk, susceptible to a crash. Any second your extremity could go the other way, for example, toward depression."

"Isn't being successful helping me stay clean?"

"Not using shouldn't be dependent on any one thing, like getting your book published. Because there's always the chance something will go wrong. Even if your memoir is a hit, the excitement will pass and you'll have to go back to yourself. There's a story from the movie *Patton*. After this Roman conquerer has won a great victory, he rides through the streets with a slave beside him whispering, 'Glory is fleeting. Glory is fleeting.' "

"Why?" Aaron liked history metaphors. I abhorred them.

"You should see the movie," Dr. Winters suggested.

"I don't want to see the movie. Why does he have the slave keep whispering 'Glory is fleeting'?" I demanded.

"To remind him to stay humble," Dr. Winters answered quietly.

"How do I stay humble?"

"Stop talking about the multiple books you're writing and how you're going to publish them all and make so much money." He shook his head in disdain. "You've sold one book and you are not rich."

"What if it's a self-fulfilling prophecy?"

"Exaggeration, falsification, magnification, and alteration of the truth are extremely hazardous," he warned.

"Sounds like a rap song." I jotted the line down. "All writers exaggerate. Stanley Kunitz says his job is to transform the mundane events of his life into legend."

"Stanley Kunitz is in his nineties, with twenty award-winning poetry books to his name. He is a legend," Dr. Winters argued. I was impressed he knew so much about him. "When you're famous at ninety you can show off too. In the meantime, stick as close to the truth as possible at all times."

"Why?" I wasn't getting the connection between puffing myself up and puffing on cigarettes and joints.

"You were using substances to get away from what was real because what was real was too painful," he explained. "You have to learn to live in reality, with all its discomfort, disappointment, and chaos. Stop making grandiose pronouncements about the future to avoid the present. You're setting yourself up to get slammed."

"You're saying that I'm insufferable straight?"

"No. You're much better straight," he reassured me. "You're more honest. I find you calmer. Your insights are more astute."

Now that he was being kind and supportive again, I didn't believe a word of it. "I'm actually getting dumber. I used to hate shopping. Now I shop all the time."

"For yourself?"

"No. For other people. I bought expensive stuff for my mother's birthday, and Mother's Day presents for her and Aaron's mom."

"What did you buy them?" he asked.

"Silk shawls, pins, and earrings," I said. "Then I went overboard at Barneys, on birthday presents for Aaron." Before he could grill me, I gave up the specifics: "I got him a black Armani jacket, a raincoat, and two dress shirts. Also I'm paying five thousand dollars for the grand ballroom of the Puck Building for my book party. I just reserved it."

"How much did you spend altogether?" Dr. Winters asked.

"I don't know."

"Count," he said.

I'd spent three thousand dollars on gifts in the last six weeks. Although I planned to write off the book party as a business expense, if you included that, the total was eight thousand. Aside from when we purchased our apartment, it was the most money I'd ever spent.

"This is all since you quit dope," he pointed out.

"I'm not in debt. I can afford it. I still have a lot of money in the bank." I defended myself, inanely, since I could tell he was onto something.

"Stop shopping," he ordered.

"I've already quit everything else," I said. "Why no shopping?"

"It's a bottomless pit. Keep an eye on excitement. It's a drug that medicates against emptiness, a way to act impulsively without thinking." He used his stern-principal voice. "You need to live with who you are, not escape into externals. Shopping takes you out of yourself."

"Not much else does anymore," I complained.

"The problem is you always have to return to yourself," he said. "Any extravagance is a perpetuation of your original pathology."

"You're saying that anything can be addictive?"

"Anything that provides the intensity of gratification that drugs and alcohol do. It's very individualistic. It can be shopping, gambling, overeating, video games, e-mail, pornography, TV, making fast money," he said. "You have to be careful. All excitement is suspect."

"What about sexual excitement with Aaron?" I asked. Aaron and I had been more amorous lately than when we first met. He joked that my kicking the habit was killing him. "I thought hot sex with my husband was kosher."

"That is kosher," Winters decreed, finally granting his blessing for something that brought me pleasure.

I was less liked by the population at large, but my husband, head doctor, and father liked me more. It wasn't a terrible trade-off—especially because I liked myself better too. Being volatile and prickly was a small price to pay for health, a passionate marriage, and career bliss.

Dr. Winters closed his leather book, one of his "it's time to go" gestures. Then he stood up, went to his desk, and gave me a stack of neatly printed pages. "I finally rewrote it," he said.

"Your ruthless story?" I was stunned. I'd assumed he had decided it was too personal to show me, so I'd stopped asking.

"I want to know what you think. What should I do with it. If it's publishable," he said. "Don't show it to anyone, and don't xerox it."

"I promise." I counted nine pages. He'd said it was fifteen pages. Had he cut six pages or spaced it smaller? I ran my fingers over the first one, but held back from reading anything yet. I slipped them into my notebook for safekeeping, feeling honored and important, my dark mood disappearing. "I'll mark notes on it if you want."

"Good. You can e-mail me your opinion before our next appointment," he said. Spoken like an impatient former addict, I thought. Or a real writer.

"Okay," I said. "We'll talk about it when I see you next Tuesday."

"I'm not seeing you for a week?" He paged through his black leather book to check.

"You said you were too booked up," I reminded him.

"I can see you at one-thirty on Thursday afternoon," he said. "If that's not too early for you."

"No, that's okay." It was the earliest time I'd agreed to, but I liked that he was finally acknowledging my body clock. Besides, I found his rush to hear what I thought of his work endearing. When my students brought their assignments to class, I critiqued them the same night so they wouldn't be nervous or scared. I'd stay hours late to finish if I had to. When you handed someone your soul, it was hard to wait a week for their reaction.

Leaving Dr. Winters' office, I saw the stoner guy in the waiting room. He was sitting there calmly, where I'd been sitting forty-five minutes before. He was reading a magazine. I glanced at the cover; it was *Men's Health*. I hoped he would be okay. I guessed what drug he had been coming down from. Cocaine? Heroin? Speed? Or just really high-grade pot, my old drug of choice? As I walked outside, I looked down and noticed that I was cradling my notebook with Dr. Winters' story in my arms, protecting it like I would a baby.

Chapter 21

JUNE 2003

Too hyped up to go home, I went to Cozy's diner. At a booth in the back, I ordered diet soda and began reading the chronicle of Dr. Winters' lonely Dickensian childhood. It was set on Park Avenue, an irony not lost on him. His narrator was a young boy trying to understand the selfish, bitter alcoholic mother who kept hitting him, telling him she wished he was never born.

Before the second page, I was in tears. The images of the abused child were piercing and powerful; I had to take breaks before I could continue. No wonder it had taken him so long to show this to me. I kept it in my briefcase all day and pulled it out to reread fragments, turning pages gently, as if it were sacred text written by an oracle.

What would I have done if I'd hated it? Thankfully I didn't, just the opposite. Yet I had no critical distance or perspective. My only literary instinct was to tell Dr. Winters to expand it, make it much longer. I wasn't sure if that was a response to his actual writing, if I wanted him to confide more to me, or if I had a fantasy that he would become my clone or protégé. I tried to imagine the pages had come from a stranger. But I couldn't separate the words from the author, couldn't stop seeing Dr. Winters as a shocked, hurt, lonely little boy.

That night I spent hours on my e-mail response. I erased "Dr. Winters" and addressed him by his first name, Dan, which I'd recently started using. I typed the letter first, before I put his address on it, to make sure I didn't accidentally send my comments before they were polished. Finally I came up with: "Dan, I've read your story many times. It blew me away, made me cry. It's poignant, gut-wrenching, vivid, and intense, like a novel in nine pages. The rawness and candor reminded me of Sylvia Plath, Ted Hughes, and Robert Lowell. I found it moving and haunting; I can't get it out of my head. I'll give you suggestions on what I would do with it when I see you on Thursday. I feel honored that you trusted me with it. Sue."

When I woke up Wednesday, I found an e-mail that was sent at six A.M.: "Susan—Looking forward to hearing more on Thursday. Yes, it was meant to hit home. DW."

I had been effusive, personal, and emotional. His tone seemed clipped and distanced. I overanalyzed it, finding it weird that he'd used my first name but only his initials. Tuesday he handed me the bitter, naked chronicle of his disturbing background, Wednesday he totally backed off. Male flight behavior? It reminded me of the year Aaron lived in L.A. I'd spent ten wonderful days in bed with him and we'd said "I love you" for the first time. When I flew back to New York, he didn't phone me for ten days.

Lingering sentences from Dan's story kept crossing my mind. Window shopping in Soho that evening, I stopped into the Mont Blanc store. I fell in lust with a sleek five-hundred-dollar silver pen. I tried to justify purchasing it for Dan. I had received a thousand-dollar therapy reimbursement check from the health-insurance company. Originally they were going to pay for part of thirty sessions a year. It turned out that they'd cover sixty annual sessions for treatment of substance abuse. Since Dan had changed my diagnosis, this felt like found money. I counted how much I was saving from not buying cigarettes, dope, alcohol, and gum. The gift seemed to have the ideal meaning, since I wanted him to embark on his own book.

Then I heard his voice ordering me to stop shopping and never trust my instincts, which were always wrong. I took a stab at deciphering my heavier motivations: I hoped to make him happy, shower him with beautiful objects to erase the sterile ugliness of his childhood. I was envisioning myself his savior, the good, generous mother, who would encourage rather than thwart him. My brain intruded, reminding me that I wasn't his mother, his wife, lover, sister, or close friend. I wasn't even his writing teacher. I needed to stop thinking of him as and calling him Dan. He was Dr. Winters! Buying an extravagant present was inappropriate—at least as a reaction to his disclosure. First I needed to talk to him about why his words were haunting me, slipping under the skin he said I no longer had.

I couldn't sleep Wednesday night. I woke up late on Thursday, at twelve-fifteen. I jumped into the shower, relieved I had made the one-thirty session with Dr. Winters so we could discuss his story. Before walking out the door, I checked my voice mail. There was one message. "Susan, it's Dan," the voice said. "I'm going to California and my flight was just switched. I can't see you at one-thirty. I could see you at eleven-thirty today. I know it's too early for you, but can you do it just this once? You don't have to call me back. Just show up."

I immediately phoned his office. Referring to him as "Dr. Winters," I told his machine that I'd heard his message too late and was sorry I couldn't make it. I e-mailed him the same thing, to make sure he got it. I was taken aback by this turn of events. I'd have to wait five more days to see him, which felt excruciating. Unlike the two times that he'd double-booked me, at least I hadn't gone all the way to his office to be turned away. In fact this time, if he was waiting there at eleven-thirty, he was the one stood up by me.

I attempted to work. An hour later, I checked my messages and e-mail. I'd somehow missed Dr. Winters' call back. "Susan, I'm afraid you didn't get my message saying that I can't make our one-thirty session today," he said. "I'm leaving for the airport. Call me to let me know you got this."

Oh no! He hadn't heard my message. Flustered by the miscommunication, I couldn't stand to think of him sitting alone, waiting for someone who wouldn't show. I called again but hung up before leaving another message, which, I worried, would make me seem like a stalker.

I scrutinized the scenario. After he had screwed up those two appointments in the spring, he'd admitted that he found me rigid and inflexible, which is probably why I reminded him of his mean old mother. Tuesday he had handed me his story about how much she'd damaged him. I'd compromised my schedule and agreed to see him at one-thirty Thursday. I had actually been excited to pay him for a session I wanted to spend critiquing his story—and he couldn't even keep the appointment! He did not seem to comprehend that people paid me for my editing advice.

Later that day we swapped another set of messages. I bet he could tell I was flipping out, because he offered to do a phone session on Friday, at midnight New York time. I confirmed on his machine. I used to have phone sessions with my old shrink, Dr. Goode; I loved phone sessions. They reinforced my belief that you could get anything delivered to your home in Manhattan. Plus I felt as if he was doing penance for making me see him on too many early afternoons, acknowledging that I came alive at midnight, the witching hour.

Aaron wasn't thrilled about my late telephone tête-à-tête and went to bed. I sat on the couch, impatiently watching the phone. Midnight came; it didn't ring. At twelve-fifteen, I called Dr. Winters' black-cell-phone number, which he reserved for emergencies.

"I'll call you back in ten minutes," he said, hanging up abruptly.

Ten minutes passed, then twenty, then thirty. What was I doing? While my loyal husband was waiting for me in our big, warm bed, I was in the living room, pacing by the phone, desperate to hear the voice of another man. Damn Winters, he was being the Bad Boyfriend again. By forcing me to wait and by being almost available but not quite, he was pressing all my crazy buttons. I looked at the clock, which now said 12:48. I couldn't believe I was paying this flake a hundred and fifty dollars a session to make me straight and stable. I couldn't believe it was working. "You can do anything as long as it works" was my rule for love and writing. Did it also apply to analysis, getting him out of the penalty box on a technicality?

The longer he took to call, the more antsy, trapped, and sweaty I felt. It was as if I was stuck in the throes of another drug withdrawal. Jesus, I realized the transformation was complete. I was no longer hooked on any substances. I was seriously addicted to Dr. Winters. Craving his comfort and not being able to get it was causing me to jones out.

Before we married, when Aaron acted callous and ambivalent, I'd walked away. I stopped seeing him, did not take his calls, and dated other men. My departure woke him up, motivating him to get into therapy and then propose. Years before the book *The Rules,* I had learned never to chase a man; you let them chase you. This rift with Winters felt more visceral than a garden-variety breakup. Yet wasn't it counterproductive to play hard-to-get with my shrink? He was the man I'd chosen to heal the wounds inflicted by other (flaky and inconsiderate) men.

By one A.M., I was livid. It was time to sleep, not return Dr. Winters' call or show up for any more sessions. After twenty months of dependency, it was over. I had to stop seeing him. The thought made me cry, but that was it. I still loved him, yet this hurt too much. I had to walk away to protect myself. The more I pictured dumping him, the more I knew I would survive. The timing was actually pretty good. No matter how bad leaving him made me feel, I didn't think I would ever smoke, toke, drink, or chew gum again. I dried my eyes. I felt selfish, but I had extracted exactly what I'd needed from him. It would be hard to say goodbye, especially on angry terms. Yet if I could stop cigarettes after twenty-seven years, I could stop anything. Of course, the minute I walked over to turn off the phone, it rang.

"Susan, hi," he said. "How are you?"

"Hello, Dr. Winters," said I, setting a professional tone. "Where are you?"

"San Diego," he said. "Didn't I tell you?"

"You just said California." Was he in a hotel room or staying with friends or relatives? I recalled he had a brother in California. I tried to picture the room he was in.

"What's up?" He sounded groggy and out of it.

I couldn't help but blurt, "I'm feeling very upset now."

"I can hear it in your voice. What's wrong?"

"What's wrong is that you're driving me out of my mind."

"I am?" He sounded quite surprised by this, confused even. "Why?"

"You're an hour late." I sat down at my desk chair.

"I'm sorry. I fell asleep," he explained.

Where was his wife? Asleep in a nearby room, like Aaron

was? "Are you too tired to do this now?" I was very relieved
to hear his voice but felt like I could cry any second.

"No. It's okay. I'm wide awake now," he lied. "What's
wrong? Tell me."

I took a deep breath, wanting to sound calm. "Listen, I
think it was weird the way you canceled me yesterday."

"That was the airline's fault," he argued, too defensively, I
thought.

"Your message could have said, 'I can't make it today.
Sorry. See you next Tuesday.' But you added this bizarre request that I come at eleven-thirty and not call you back to
confirm. What was that about? I never see you in the morning. I always refuse. We've argued about it a hundred times.
You knew I wouldn't come."

"I thought you might," he said softly. "If you got the message in time."

The way he said it made me sad, as if he had this unconscious compulsion to get me to change for him, the way his
mother couldn't. "I left you a praise-filled e-mail about your
story, acting like a good mother," I told him. "You couldn't
handle that. You left me a curt response. Then you set me up
to blow you off, to be the bad mom you really had."

He was quiet for a minute. "You really think so?"

"I think you're punishing me for knowing too much about
you."

"How am I punishing you?"

"You know I'm literal-minded, always on time," I said.
"When I have no skin I am not adaptable. If you act flighty it
makes me nuts."

"You know being off everything makes you extremely emotional, don't you?" he asked.

Blaming me was the wrong tactic. "Yeah, let me tell you
why I'm so emotional now." I raised my voice. "My doctor
told me he would call at midnight, but he didn't. He said he'd

get back to me in ten minutes, but he took an hour." I was enraged and wanted to kill him. "Nobody else does this to me! I feel like I'm sixteen, waiting for a guy who said he's going to call. If some jerk did this to me, even at sixteen, I'd dump him in a second." Holding the receiver between my ear and neck, I reached in the fridge, pulled out a can of caffeine-free diet Coke, and took a sip. "Is that the game here? You want me to blow you off completely like your mother did?"

"It sounds like you want to blow me off," he said.

"Of course I do. My schedule is organized and productive. I write every day, teach three classes a week, have my writing workshop at seven-thirty on Tuesday nights, as I've done for eighteen years, see my husband every night at ten," I said. "You're supposed to be my savior. Instead you're the chaos factor in my life." I took the straw from the soda can and chewed on it.

"Can't I be both?" he asked.

"No! I don't need chaos! I hate chaos! It's not good for me."

"It's not bad that I'm the chaos factor," he said.

"Why not?" He was not really trying to convince me that chaos was good at eight minutes after one in the morning.

"You can't control the world. People cancel all the time. Airlines reschedule," he said. "Life is chaotic."

"Wrong. My life is calm, the opposite of chaotic," I insisted. I'd never been more dependent on anyone. I felt closer to him than my father and my husband. When he went out of town or canceled, it was agonizing; I couldn't bear it. I had to cut my losses.

"Don't regress because of this," he said.

"I'm not regressing," I told him. "I could stop seeing you right now and never smoke, toke, or drink anything again." In fact I was going in the opposite direction of regression. I felt older and more adult than I had ever been.

"I'm sorry. It's easier to need substances than people," he said in his tired, fading voice. I was exhausting him. "Have you ever heard of Jean Piaget's theory of object constancy? It often applies to addicts. If a person isn't visually there, it feels like abandonment."

"This is not theoretical. You did abandon me. You canceled a session last minute to fly out of town and then you said you'd call at a certain time and you didn't call."

"Will you shut up and listen?" He was pissed off himself. "Attachment to people means unpredictability, doubt, feelings of abandonment and chaos. With substances, you have omnipotent control, the way you can always keep a pack of cigarettes in your pocket. They are predictable and present in a way that people can never be."

His anger made him appear more present, so my fury dissipated. It was impossible to stay mad at him, especially because I was still picturing the helpless little boy in his story.

"Have you heard of chaos theory?" he asked. He had mentioned it before; he was big on it.

"The theory that Michael Crichton wrote about in *Jurassic Park*?" I had borrowed the book from Aaron but never finished it. Dinosaurs just didn't do it for me.

"Yes, exactly. Crichton wrote a brilliant summary of it," he said. "Doesn't that help you understand how random the world is?"

"No." I could barely recall it, some obvious warning from the scientist, played by Jeff Goldblum in the movie. It seemed too blatant, an intrusive technique foreshadowing destruction. He might as well have sent up red flares. "It was a math equation about how weather prediction is impossible. It doesn't apply to me," I said dismissively. "It doesn't even work as a metaphor."

Then I thought of Adrienne Rich's poignant poem "Storm Warnings," about how real weather and "weather in the heart" came on "Regardless of prediction." When I had first read the Rich poem in sixth grade, I knew I was like her, one of those sensitive people "who live in troubled regions." Dr. Winters was too, though he didn't like to admit it to himself. The story he'd shown me gave it away.

"It grew out of attempts to make computer models out of weather," he continued. "Did you read the section in *Jurassic Park* about how a complex weather system could have a certain temperature, wind speed, and humidity, but if you repeat it with almost the same temperature, wind speed, and humidity, the second system won't behave the same? It'll wander off and become very different from the first." He'd switched to his male scientist voice. "That's why you'll get thunderstorms instead of sunshine. Do you recall that part?"

"Vaguely," I said, but he'd pretty much lost me. Deep down he was a nerdy science brain, like my father and brothers; that was why I felt so connected to him.

"It's nonlinear dynamics. Weather systems are very sensitive to initial conditions. Tiny differences become amplified." He was pushing it; he really wanted me to understand. "Remember when Crichton mentions the 'butterfly effect.' A butterfly flaps its wings in Peking, and weather in New York changes."

I grabbed a pen and jotted down the butterfly line, which sounded pretty. I liked that he was passionate about Crichton, and Piaget's theories, but I had my own idea of what was going on. "Dan, you're having a bad reaction to letting me read your story."

"No, I really liked your reaction to it."

"It was hard for you to let me see you so vulnerable," I said. "Are you okay?"

"Yeah. I'm fine."

"Are you sure?" I asked. I wasn't his good or his bad mother anymore. I was his shrink.

He paused, as if he had to take his emotional temperature. Constantly checking mine, I recalled Virginia Woolf saying, "I write to find out what I think."

"I'm okay," he decided. "Really."

"Have you shown your story to any other patients?" I wondered how they had reacted.

"No," he said. "Just that critic I told you about. The one who said it was too ruthless."

I was flattered all over again. Then fearful that I'd seen his fragile side before I could handle it. Everything about the story—from me begging him to let me read it, to him showing it to me, to my reaction—was over the deep end.

"That critic was an asshole," I said. "It's not ruthless. It's great. You have to write more." I'd turned into his writing teacher, the same as being his shrink, though it paid less.

"I don't want to write more," he said. "I want to publish it as it is or throw it away."

"It'll be hard to publish now because it's part poetry, part fiction, part nonfiction, and—with all the cutting to different scenes—part play. You've invented your own genre. It's typical of your personality. God forbid your story would fit into somebody else's category."

"But you liked it?" he asked.

He needed a lot of reassurance, like Aaron did. That's what happened if your mother didn't love you enough. "Yes. It's haunting me. I can't get it out of my head."

"Did it overwhelm you?" he asked.

"Can't you tell?" I laughed. "It freaked me out. Made me see you differently."

"As weak?"

"No." I was tired too. He was exhausting me. I hadn't been anywhere but I felt jet-lagged. "It makes me trust you more, and I don't want to. I need you too much. My book on addiction therapy should end with quitting you."

"You can't stop therapy because you want a good ending for your book," he said. "Don't blow me off yet. Please."

I looked at the digital clock on the TV. It was five after two. I couldn't believe I would have to pay him for this session when he was the reason I had needed this session. "Okay, I won't," I promised. "Not yet."

"I was thinking the story could be part of a book on addiction therapy I've been working on," he said.

Did I know he was working on an addiction-therapy book? I puzzled whether I had subconsciously absconded with his idea or if he had stolen mine. He would probably say "Great minds think alike."

"It would be perfect for an addiction book," I told him. "Really good. Poignant."

"Thanks," he said. "I'll see you on Tuesday at four forty-five."

"Please don't screw it up," I whispered before hanging up the phone.

Over a Japanese dinner on Saturday night, I told Aaron the latest minute-by-minute Winters saga. I felt guilty, as if I were asking my husband for advice on how to handle my erratic boyfriend. I was craving Aaron's confirmation that my glorified guru was seriously loco.

"You're both nuts," Aaron decided.

"You don't think it was odd that he canceled on me last minute again?" Aaron was in the black Armani jacket I had bought him for his birthday. It made his shoulders look huge.

"You just quit dope a few months ago. You're still on edge, which is understandable," he said. "I think it's very impressive how you got off everything. I'm really proud of you."

"Come on, he cancels right after he gave me his ruthless

story to read." Did it bother Aaron that I'd never shown it to him?

"I know you can't show me the story without Dan's permission," Aaron added, reading my mind, as he'd been doing a lot lately. "But if you'd offered, I would have said no. I couldn't handle reading it." He shrugged. "I just don't want to know."

It had never occurred to me that I had the option not to read Dan's story. "What about his being an hour late for the phone session?"

"He was trying to accommodate you and overshot," Aaron said. "He's juggling a lot. Family, students, busy practice full of addicts and nuts calling him at all hours with their traumas. Remember, he's in the business of instability."

That calmed me down and seemed to make sense out of everything. Especially when I saw that I was starting to trust Aaron with my raw emotions. Dan's irregular, overbooked behavior had thrown me for a loop. Luckily I had landed right back where I belonged, in my husband's big, strong arms.

Part Three

Chapter 22

JULY 2003

"I'm not a size-two fashion model. I became a writer so I could eat real food, stay home, and wear sweats all day," I told Roger. "I don't think the author's picture on the back of the book makes any difference whatsoever." He edited literary books, on the high-brow side. I was sure he'd say that only the words mattered.

"I disagree," he said. "Sometimes the picture is important."

"Really?" His answer upset me. It was not what I wanted to hear. "Why should the picture matter? It's a book. It's about the words."

We were sitting in a booth at Nobu. I'd insisted on taking him out for his twenty-seventh birthday, but really I wanted to pick his brain about my book-jacket trauma. Although I was still awkward when it came to going out to eat, Roger was a safe person who wouldn't make fun of my myriad restrictions. As a vegan and a recovering alcoholic, he was also a cheap date. He ordered salad, a vegetable roll, a tofu dish, and tea. I picked edamame and the steamed lobster, crab, and shrimp special.

"I can't drink alcohol or caffeine, so I brought my own caffeine-free diet Coke. Can I just get a glass of ice?" I asked the waitress. "You can charge me for a soda."

"No problem." She was unfazed, obviously used to New Yorkers' dietary quirks.

"When's your memoir coming out?" Roger asked.

"Not until Valentine's Day," I said.

"You have plenty of time to take a picture."

"The problem's not the time, it's the clothes," I said. "It turns out that Beth, the vice president of public relations, hates the picture I had taken. She said, 'What's with all the books in the background and the blazer? You look like a college professor.' "

"You are a college professor," Roger said.

"That's what I told her. She thinks I look too studious. She wants me to take a sexier shot. She showed me an author's photo she liked where the woman was wearing red lipstick, a minidress, and stiletto heels. I never wear red lipstick, minidresses, or stilettos anymore." I pointed to my black jeans and black T-shirt, as if he hadn't noticed. "I don't think I ever did." Our appetizer and drinks came. I pulled out my twenty-ounce caffeine-free diet Coke and poured it into my glass of ice under the table.

"Is it Beth Bloomwood?" he asked.

"Have you met her?" I sucked out the insides of several edamame pods. I'd forgotten that everyone in the Manhattan publishing scene knew one another.

"I worked with her at my first job at St. Martin's. She's a very sharp woman, known for being a publicity whiz." He tasted his salad. "I'm sure she's right. Your book is very *Sex and the City*. Look how Candace Bushnell poses."

"She's a size-two blonde," I whined, albeit pleased that he

was comparing my pages to a best-seller that inspired the sizzling HBO series.

"It's fantastic that Beth cares about your book. Extremely impressive. They rarely get someone so high up involved this much before the publication date. You should be flattered."

"I know, but it's a lot of pressure. Look sexy, thin, twenty-five, and smile for the camera next Friday. What if I disappoint her?" I offered him some edamame, but he shook his head no. "My cousin Danny is taking the pictures. His daughter Karin, this hip fashionista, is going to style me."

"You'll look great. Don't worry."

It was an easy thing for a thin, good-looking, twenty-seven-year-old male to say. He looked cute today, strands of his curly hair falling over his silver-rimmed glasses. He'd made the humble choice to be an editor behind-the-scenes while I'd courted the spotlight. I recalled Oscar Wilde's line about the two great tragedies in life. The first was not getting what you wanted, the second was getting it.

"How's your addiction therapy going?" he asked.

"Incredibly well. I'm off dope now too," I bragged. "I feel like I'm completely cured."

"Really?" He seemed skeptical. "In AA they say you're never cured, you're always recovering."

"Well," I backtracked a bit. "I have been irritable lately. Still a little on the vulnerable side."

"Is Aaron helping?"

"He's been great. Though sometimes it's hard for him to understand my oversensitivity. Dr. Winters told him that it was harder to be with an addict in recovery than an addict who's using."

"That's wrong." Roger shook his head. "I totally disagree. When I was using drugs, I didn't pay my rent, never showed up, showered, cleaned, or did laundry. I pissed my pants and vomited in public." He was adamant. "I was completely self-obsessed. When I'm sober I'm reliable, I show up on time. I make every effort to do what I say I'll do."

"I bet he meant during the initial recovery period." I swore by so many of Dr. Winters' doctrines and homilies, I was amazed at the thought that he could be wrong about anything. I tried to reconcile the two schools of thought. "Wasn't it hard when you were in the process of getting clean?"

"Yes." He sipped his tea. "The first ninety days were hell. I was angry, physically ill, totally overwhelmed."

"Ninety days is nothing." I signaled the waitress to bring me another edamame. "Getting off nicotine, I felt like death for nine months." I was so glad all the withdrawal was over.

"Well, four years later I'm still confronting childhood stuff I suppressed," he said, one-upping me.

"Now I'm battling all my food issues," I said. "I want to drop ten pounds. Were you thinner when you were using?"

"Yes. Because I didn't eat. I drank, snorted, and smoked instead."

He excused himself to go to the bathroom. I pulled my notebook from my briefcase and wrote a list of ways to lose weight: try a juice fast, go to a spa, work out three hours a day at my old health club, run on my treadmill daily, get a personal trainer like a Hollywood star who had to get in shape for a movie. I knew I wouldn't do any of them. Roger came back looking pale and said, "Geez, I've been here before."

"When?"

"Five years ago." He seemed spooked. "With a group of friends. When I saw the other room, it came back to me."

"Did you like it?" I was disappointed; I'd wanted to be the one to turn him on to the chichi eatery.

"I don't think we ordered any food, we just drank. I was totally fucked up." He shook his head. "This happens to me all the time. I feel like I've lost years of my life."

"I'm sorry." I touched his hand.

I'd heard former addicts say things like that, but I couldn't relate. I'd been upbeat and more productive than ever, teaching three classes, working on two book projects. Earlier that week I'd handed drafts of the manuscripts to Lilly, who said to give her a few weeks to read them.

The day before, Dr. Winters had warned that letting go of both book projects, "my babies," could lead to postpartum depression. He asked how I was going to fill the hours I'd spent writing. I had no idea why he was bugging me about my future plans when I felt content with what I'd just accomplished. I recited the line from the poem I liked, about achievement being redemption. He insisted, for the tenth time, that it wasn't.

"You're doing so well. You're only twenty-seven years old and you have a great job you're really good at and a sweet girlfriend you love," I assured Roger. "Not to mention all this self-knowledge and wisdom."

"Thanks." He smiled. "Getting clean has given me the life of my dreams."

This I could relate to. "Me too." I clinked my diet soda against his cup of green tea.

Sure that everything was under control, I ordered rice pudding for dessert, thinking that a tiny bit of bread product wouldn't kill me. The pudding came in two little chocolate cookies. Who ordered chocolate cookies? I only had eight days to get in better shape for my close-up. That didn't stop me from scarfing down the entire dessert. Rome wasn't built in a day, I told myself, fearing it could be destroyed in one.

To repent, I decided to walk the mile home to burn off the calories. I paid the hundred-dollar bill. It was the cheapest I'd ever gotten away with at Nobu. As we walked outside, Roger insisted I share a cab with him.

"Are you going to buy something new to wear for your sexy photo shoot?" He waved down a taxi at the corner of Houston Street.

"I have this short, low-cut black dress I bought a while ago." I hopped in the backseat with him. "But it seems so stupid. Smart people don't buy books because of an author's looks." I certainly never did.

"Sometimes they do," Roger countered.

"I have three words for you: Philip Roth. John Updike. Salman Rushdie."

"That's six words," he said.

"Not that I'm comparing my work to theirs," I clarified. "But none of them is a bathing beauty."

"Naomi Wolf, Dani Shapiro, Elizabeth Wurtzel." He threw out contemporary female nonfiction writers who looked like bathing beauties in their book photographs.

"You don't think their books were best-sellers because they looked dishy on their dust jackets, do you?" I asked, as the driver stopped in front of my building.

"Of course I do," he said. "Thanks for the great dinner."

"Fuck you." I kissed him goodbye, hoping he wasn't right.

The minute I opened the door to my apartment, I marched to my closet. Buried under jeans and sweaters, I uncovered my infamous slinky black minidress. I'd bought it when I was single, thirty-four, and a buff 127 pounds. It was the month Aaron and I had split up because he'd refused to tie the knot. I'd joined a health club to get meaner and leaner. Then I'd forced myself to go uptown to Bergdorfs for something hot to wear on the prowl to replace him.

I'd pulled the black size-six number from a sales rack. Slithering into the glamorous garment, it was lust at first sight. It exaggerated my breasts and minimized my waist and hips. Usually a size eight, I wasn't sure if my body had changed or the designer was lying, but I didn't care. I couldn't believe this bit of luscious material, on a satin hanger, was on sale for $150. It was a lot of money for a struggling freelance tomboy who preferred the Gap. Still, it was so flattering, feminine, and slenderizing, I had to have it.

I wore the minidress the next night, for my first post-Aaron date, with a shrink named Joshua. It worked its magic and he promptly fell for me. Six weeks later I wore it for my first post-Joshua date, with Aaron, who refell for me and proposed. After we were pronounced husband and wife, I hung the minidress in my closet, returning to my trusty sweats and T-shirt. Periodically Aaron asked: "Hey, whatever happened to your low-cut black dress?" The last time it saw the light of day was when I had put it on—and let him take it off—for our fifth anniversary.

Although I was overjoyed that instead of the seven-year itch, Aaron and I were tighter than ever—so was the minidress. I could still zip up the back, but just barely. It was dumb to try it on after a big meal, not to mention the unneeded dessert. I stood in front of the full-length mirror, held in my stomach, and practiced posing for my new provocative photo. I put my hands on my hips to make my waist look smaller. Then I crossed my arms, trying to show attitude, as well as my diamond wedding ring.

I looked fine for my age. Futhermore, I was too intelligent and busy to obsess about the size of my body, I told myself. A fiercely feminist workaholic, I was certain that I had outgrown the diet dilemma years ago. Yet suddenly, choosing every meal and snack became a conundrum. Weight issues kept looming larger, until they became the forefront and focus of my therapy.

Smoking and toking had stemmed my lifelong eating disorders, according to Dr. Winters. With no barrier to fence in my appetite, it felt voracious and all-engulfing. When I ate from emotional (and not physical) hunger, he said, I was using certain foods in the same irrational way I had used other addictive substances. Before I could conquer all my food insanity, he insisted I rehash my entire eating history.

I was positive that I was overfed as a baby. Pictures proved I was chubby in elementary school. I was big-boned and by fourth grade had reached my current five-foot-seven-inch height. Although I felt like an obese outcast, I was in reality only ten pounds overweight. At age ten I begged my mom to send me to an all-female fat camp in Upstate New York, where my friend Hillary was spending the summer. My mother, who was beautiful, vain, and svelte herself, agreed. Weighing 137 in my "before" picture, I was the thinnest girl there. I was 127 pounds in my "after" picture a month later. Back home in my mother's kitchen, I soon packed on the lost ten pounds. I went back to the fat camp and repeated the pattern for two more years. Until, at thirteen, I discovered Europe, cigarettes, alcohol, dope, confessional poetry, and boys (not necessarily in that order).

In high school and college my weight fluctuated. Once, in my twenties, I got down to 107 pounds and a size two. I didn't think it was anorexia. It seemed to be a reaction to being dumped by Richard, a gourmet cook who fed me more than my mother. After our breakup, I couldn't stand food for six months. I thought I looked great so small. Claire said I looked too bony. Luckily my desire—for food and love—soon returned. After the short-lived Richard-starvation-shiva, I'd never been able to fit into a size two again. A few years later I experimented with bulimia, but found it too gross. I must not have been doing it right, because I never lost weight that way. When I'd extracted information about it from my father, he'd listed medical complications that could result from making oneself vomit: "ruptured esophagus, aspiration, pneumonia, and death." That put an end to that.

The most I ever weighed was four months after I married, the time I gained twenty pounds when Aaron had insisted I give up cigarettes. When I quit quitting, the extra weight fell off. I thought I would feel content with my current status as a 137-pound nonsmoker.

Now, posing in front of the mirror, I tried on high heels with the dress, which made my legs look longer. I debated how to push myself into rejoining my old health club. During those spite-Aaron months in 1995, when I'd bought the mini, I exercised six days a week. I was never an athlete. However, as a neurotic Jewish pseudointellectual, I was a good student. Thus I became the teacher's pet of Matt, a gorgeous gay former Broadway dancer who taught aerobics, step, and body-conditioning classes.

I stayed a Matt-groupie until Aaron became my husband. In fact, they overlapped. I was slated to wed at a Soho loft at nine P.M. one Saturday night in July. I didn't know what to do until nine, so I showed up at Matt's six o'clock Funky Low Impact. When a classmate asked, "Hey, Sue, what are you doing later?" I'd answered, "Getting married." She assumed I was kidding. I never went back.

At various stages since then I had swum, speed-walked, lifted weights, and bought a treadmill I used to run a mile in nine minutes to get an endorphin buzz. But it was all halfhearted. My daily choice always came down to: work or work out. I would always rather be reading or writing. Hanging the minidress back up, I listed important women I admired: Golda Meir, Eleanor Roosevelt, Virginia Woolf, A. S. Byatt, Lucille Clifton, Katha Pollitt, Julia Alvarez, Gloria Steinem, Judi Dench, Aretha Franklin, Hillary Clinton, Margaret Thatcher, Katharine Graham, and Oprah Winfrey. None of my female role models was a fashion model. I revered their minds, work, talent, and/or political commitment. That was what counted! I rallied myself into a feministic frenzy. Yet since I wasn't changing the world, creating masterpieces, or running for office, I hoped this wasn't just a way to justify my laziness.

I was never going to make my mark on the world as a bathing beauty. My body of writing was more important to me than the body on my book jacket. High-energy and excited lately, I was looking better. Everyone said so. My line was: "Instead of liposuction, try happiness." But then why the hell did I have an urge to use the leftover Adderall to starve myself for eight days? (Maybe I wasn't a hypocrite, but a poor predictor of my mood swings.) "Don't trust your instincts, they are always wrong," I heard Dr. Winters' warning, playing hourly in my brain between sessions.

After stopping so many self-destructive substances, what I ate was now determining how I felt every day. To outsmart my overeating, Dr. Winters had a plan. I had to learn the difference between emotional and physical hunger. He insisted that my eating habits revolve around tedious rules and routines, when he wasn't slamming me for being too rigid and inflexible.

I was getting used to my boring food regimen of protein and fat with no bread products. Every day I would eat three meals—fruit in the morning, chef salad in the afternoon, frozen yogurt at night. That was all, no snacks. I figured the big portions added up to a healthy daily 1,500 calories. If I wanted more, I had to write down what else I wanted to eat. Next I figured out exactly what feeling was motivating this urge. Then, following Dr. Winters' annoying instructions, I had to wait one hour. If I still wanted the extra food, I could have it. Though I rarely still wanted it, all the scrawling and overthinking about what I could be consuming felt anal and ridiculous.

Once a week I was allowed to switch my chef salad for an Asian dinner, but variations addled me. After my mini-screwup at Nobu, I knew that eating out was risky. But when my friend Irene asked me to have dinner the next night, I agreed. I hadn't seen her in months and assumed I would be okay at Evergreen, which had an extensive Chinese and Japanese menu.

They served caffeine-free diet Sprite, which I was training my-self to tolerate.

"You're looking terrific," she said, hugging me hello.

"You're looking terrific too," I told her. "Really thin."

"Thanks. Yeah, I finally dropped some weight after the miscarriage," she said.

"Are you feeling okay?"

She nodded yes and picked up the menu. I recited my latest dietary regimen and ordered no-caffeine diet Sprite, edamame, and steamed shrimp and vegetables. She ordered tea, the spareribs appetizer, and a few pieces of sashimi in sympathy.

"I'm going light on the bread too," she said.

"No diet Sprite," the waiter came back to inform me. "We're out."

"Okay. I'll take a diet Coke," I said. It was past seven o'clock, but one late diet soda with a little caffeine in it couldn't cause much harm.

"Are you still seeing Dr. Winters?" Irene asked.

"I'm going twice a week now," I said. "You too?" I as-sumed she was, although she hadn't mentioned anything about him since he'd gotten her off painkillers last year.

"No, I stopped three months ago." She avoided my eyes. Uh-oh, I'd touched a nerve.

"Why?" It was unrealistic to expect everyone to be as en-amored with him as I was.

"He was too sexist," she said.

I didn't disagree. Neither did Dr. Winters. He'd admitted it last time I had accused him of trying to make me quieter, sweeter, and less threatening. I finished the edamame, notic-ing a correlation between my anxiety level and how fast I shoved them in my mouth, the way I used to chain-smoke when I was stressed out. "Did anything specific happen?" I asked, knowing I was being intrusive. Yet if you hooked a friend up with your shrink, I rationalized, you were allowed to inquire how it was going.

"He kept focusing on my marriage, as if that was the main thing in my life that needed to be fixed. I didn't agree. I was more intent on getting my career together." She poured tea. "I kept telling him that you have to make yourself happy."

"I agree with you." I chewed on the leftover pods.

I was jealous when Irene was seeing Dr. Winters, but this news made me feel let down, less connected to her. Irene and I went way back. Our mothers were best friends growing up on the Lower East Side. It seemed poetic four years ago, when Irene married John, a lawyer I'd fixed her up with. The poetry didn't last long. After her miscarriage and an illness last year, she had developed the painkiller problem, which was why Winters had to come to the rescue in the first place.

"He was always ten or fifteen minutes late for our sessions, which was rude," she added.

"He's late with me too." After I mentioned his double bookings and the recent phone-session debacle, I felt disloyal and added, "But I'm completely done with cigarettes, alcohol, dope, and gum forever. He's gotten me off everything." I didn't feel entitled to include bread since my cookie-relapse forty-eight hours earlier.

"I know. I'm still clean. He is smart about addictions," she conceded. "John and I had one session with him. Since then we've been seeing a couples' therapist he recommended."

"That's good."

"I just couldn't bear Winters insisting that the biggest problem in my life was my disappointing marriage," she continued, as if she owed me further explanation.

"That is odd." I was miffed by his remarks too, maybe since I was responsible for the match. She'd somehow misinterpreted Winters' meaning, I guessed. Or she'd taken one of his casual remarks too seriously.

"It hurt my feelings." She poured more tea.

"I'm sorry," I said, as if I'd somehow hurt her feelings in tandem.

"It was so hard to ignore what he said, you know?" She was pretty, with shoulder-length dark hair and bright blue eyes, but she seemed tired and sad today.

It was also hard for me to ignore Dr. Winters. I took everything he said too seriously. Sometimes I would reject his far-fetched ideas out of hand and have a delayed reaction when his words came back to haunt me. The fact that Aaron had been his patient, and that Winters made him marry me, made him invested in our union. I talked so much about my work and addictions, it luckily left little time for Dr. Winters' left-over-from-the-fifties rules for romance. Then again, Aaron's ring might not have been around my finger had the chauvinist pig not intervened.

Later that night I went into Aaron's den. He was sitting at his desk, reading his e-mail. I told him about my dinner with Irene.

"I bet when Winters met John, they didn't click," he guessed. "Maybe he blames John for not making Irene happy. You know Winters is always honest. He couldn't lie if he wanted to."

"John's a good guy." I defended him, since I had picked him for Irene. "He's honest, hardworking, and he loves her."

"That doesn't necessarily mean Irene and John are a good couple. When I first saw Winters he told me that Lori and I were a bad match."

"He did?" Since Winters had been Lori's thesis adviser at Columbia, this surprised me.

Aaron nodded yes. "He thought Lori and I were too cerebral together and your visceral sensibility balanced me better."

I had no idea what this meant but liked the way it sounded, largely because I'd won.

"Do you remember our first Winters session together?" he asked wistfully. Most couples reminisced about their first date, first vacation, or first child. We were nostalgic about our first shared analysis.

"Of course I do." That lively, ludicrous fifty minutes had altered everything. How could I forget?

"When you went to the waiting room and I was paying him, he told me his opinion of you," Aaron said. "I didn't even ask, he just offered." He shut off his computer.

I turned his black swivel chair around to face me. "Are you going to tell me or what?" I just noticed that Aaron and Dr. Winters had the same black leather office chair. When I'd bought it for Aaron, had I subconsciously picked out Dr. Winters' exact model by accident?

"He said you were a woman of substance and that I'd never do better."

"After one session, he said that?" I sensed there was more. "What else did he say? I've waited seven years. You have to tell me."

"Winters told me, 'You're forty-five, moody, out of shape, and frustrated with your career. Who the hell are you waiting for?' "

I cracked up, trying to decipher if Aaron was joking or serious, falling in love with both of them all over again. "He really told you that?"

I kissed Aaron's neck. He kissed me back. I sat on his lap, facing him, wrapping my arms around him. He unwrapped them and pushed me off.

"I have to get to sleep." He stood up and walked to the bedroom. "I have an eight o'clock meeting tomorrow morning. I've been going to bed too late. I have to get off your *meshuggeneh* schedule."

We had been clicking so well—and so often—in bed recently that this rejection really threw me. I also felt devastated by his insult—in Yiddish yet—about my night owl-hood. When we met, Aaron used to stay up late every night with me. I went into the living room. Usually I would go back to work, but I'd already finished both of my book projects. I glanced at the copies of the new manuscripts I had given Lilly. Rereading them now might be bad luck; surely I would find typos I hadn't caught before. Hungry and horny, I turned on the TV. Nothing was on. I paced, then painted my nails with clear polish. When they were dry, I started reading an article in this week's *New Yorker*, but I was too hyper to concentrate. I told myself I should just go to sleep. But I was wide awake, getting edgy. I'd been sleeping so well lately. What was wrong?

At two-thirty, I zeroed in on the culprit. It had to be the last caffeine-laden diet soda I drank later than I was supposed to. Bizarre how something so small could push me off balance. I recalled Dr. Winters' dumb theory about systems that were sensitive to tiny differences. Some cliché about a butterfly in China changing New York weather. I reread the poem "Storm Warnings," about the people who lived in troubled regions. That didn't help either.

I checked my e-mail, no new messages. Why hadn't Lilly read my manuscripts yet? Oh yeah, it had only been two days. I turned on the TV again. Winters said I was too reactive, but the intense feelings were hard to stop, they were flooding me. I couldn't be that upset because Aaron was too tired to make love, could I? Was I just insecure about my upcoming photo shoot? I had to stop being so uptight. I had always been pho-togenic. But in a quiet, natural way. If I'd written an ambitious literary novel, they would expect a smart, literary-looking photo. It was my own fault for selling out and writing a sex book. I'd set myself up.

I went to the shelf and pulled down my red photo album. Paging through, I stared at my photographs from book events, readings, and parties over the years. My eyes went right to the drinks, cigarettes, and joints in my hand. How stupid I'd been, letting people snap pictures of me while I was using. Did I think it made me look cool? It seemed pathetic.

Scrutinizing my younger images, a deep dismay hit. All I could see were the decades I'd wasted. Instead of facing my problems, I was weak, allowing my predisposition toward addictions to take over. I wasted years being wasted, chain-smoking, and partying, cutting corners to avoid depression and discomfort. That was why I hadn't published a big book years before, when I should have. Then the photograph would have shown a younger, prettier, less wrinkled author. I was en-raged that I hadn't gotten it together until I was forty. I felt blindsided, ambushed by emptiness and regret. I couldn't bear the intensity of emotions; I just wanted them to go away.

I went into the kitchen. I had intentionally left only carrots, celery, and apples in the refrigerator so I wouldn't be tempted. On impulse I picked up the phone and called the twenty-four-hour deli across the street. Screw the stupid minidress. A book wasn't about visuals. It was about words. I was too old to wear a minidress! I ordered three Hershey's chocolate bars and three Twizzlers red licorice. I went to the intercom and told the doorman not to buzz, so the order wouldn't wake up Aaron. I was ashamed and didn't want him to see me like this.

I waited by the door until I heard the elevator. The young delivery guy brought my bag of junk food at 4:49 A.M. I was wired and impatient, as if I were waiting for a cocaine or heroin fix. It seemed funny that it was only a five-dollar secret candy stash. I handed him a ten and said, "Keep it," thankful that he'd hurried. The second he was gone I scarfed it all down. Afterward I was satisfied and filled up. For a few min-utes. Then I wanted more. I realized, with horror, that I had not been cured of anything. I felt sick, after all this time and therapy, to find myself in serious danger. The sugar rush left me intensely craving both a joint and a cigarette.

Chapter 23

JULY 2003

"Don't worry if you relapse. It's how you respond to a relapse that counts," Dr. Winters had written on the back of one of his business cards. By now I had a whole deck.

After my late-night pig-out, I went back to normal eating the next day, as if nothing had happened. Thankful that I had never relapsed on cigarettes, dope, alcohol, or gum, I saw that my whole eating enigma remained unresolved. It wasn't as black and white as stopping the other substances; I couldn't just quit food. I fretted that I would gain tons of weight from the junk food, but decided to be nice to myself and not get on the scale. By the time my cousin Danny came over to take my new photographs a week later, I was 137 pounds, back to normal.

Danny was my father's first cousin. By day he was a real estate lawyer who had helped Aaron and me purchase our apartment. By night he was a photographer. There was definitely a family resemblance between all the men on the Shapiro side. It felt comforting, as if Danny were an artsy father substitute supporting my book. (The real one, in Michigan, kept threatening to move to Alaska whenever I brought up my memoir.)

Danny's young daughter, Karin, my stylist, approved of my black minidress and the stiletto heels I'd bought on Eighth Street for twenty-two dollars. I put on red lipstick and black eyeliner, more makeup than I'd worn in years. I wore flipflops, carrying the stilettos, as we took the elevator up to the top floor of my building. It was the tallest and least charming high-rise in Greenwich Village, but it had a lovely paved roof. I sat on the steps and put the shoes on. Karin posed me on a metal stairway with the New York skyline in the background.

"Put your hands on the railing," she said, showing me how to lean to my left side, with my right foot forward.

"Okay." I looked down. It was the perfect scenic backdrop for my book, which took place in Manhattan and had a tough and raunchy urban tone. "No black-and-whites or close-ups, right?"

"I promise," Danny said.

"Are you sure I look okay?"

"Smile." Danny pointed his Contax at me.

"Do I look fat?" I asked.

"No. You look really good," Karin reassured.

"You look like you need a drink," Danny said. "To chill you out."

"I don't drink anymore," I reminded him. It was interesting that you had to tell people ten times before it sunk in. Only recovering addicts remembered.

"Not even a glass of wine?" he asked.

"I quit drinking." I raised my voice, always surprised when people pushed the subject.

"Can't you smoke a joint?" Karin whispered.

"No," I told her. "I quit toking too."

"Okay. Don't worry about it. You look fine," Danny lied. "Just try to smile."

While he snapped away, I kept thinking that even a cigarette would have helped. That was the problem with sobriety. I was too uptight and no longer had any quick trick to mellow me out. I had never felt so awkward and uncomfortable. I could barely stand in the ludicrously high heels and I was sure I looked dumb in the dress. I held my stomach in and pushed out my breasts while keeping the wind from blowing my hair in my face. It was too windy. Danny went through six rolls of film, but it seemed pointless. I already knew this photo shoot was an unmitigated disaster.

"I should have just worn jeans. Why did I listen to Beth Bloomwood? She's not standing on a roof in a tight dress with heels she can't walk in. She wears pants to work, with flats," I complained to Aaron when he came home that night. "I don't wear dresses anymore. I have to look like myself."

"I love how you look in that dress. You never wear it for me anymore," he said. "Why don't you model it for me with those new high heels you bought?"

He meant it as foreplay, but I was so worried over the photographs, I desperately wanted another opinion on how I'd looked. I didn't believe Karin or Danny. "Okay," I said, putting the dress back on.

"You look gorgeous." He kissed me. "I'm sure Danny's photographs will turn out great. When do you get them back?"

"He said to give him two weeks." I felt very unsexy and impatient to see the terrible end result, wanting to get the disappointment over with. I had an idea. "Will you do me a favor?" I asked, looking out the window. It was eight o'clock, but the sky was still light.

"What?" Aaron looked worried.

"Will you take a few pictures of me in the same pose on the roof?" I asked. "Just so I can get a sense of how I looked."

"Do we have to?"

"Please?"

"Are you sure this is a good idea?" He definitely did not want to be dragged into this. "I don't take very good pictures. Why don't you just wait to see how Danny's come out?"

"Please, please, please," I cajoled. "It will just take a few minutes."

I repainted my lipstick and eyeliner and we took the elevator to the roof. Again I wore flip-flops and carried the heels, putting them on upstairs. I stood in the same corner, arms leaning on the railing, the way Karin had posed me. Aaron took the ten frames left on my roll.

When he was done I insisted that we go out to dinner at Sammy's, on Sixth Avenue and Tenth Street, across the street from One Hour Photo. When I picked up the photos, it was my worst nightmare. I looked fat, phony, awkward, and uncomfortable. I had envisioned Susan Sontag's famous old photograph, when she was a raven-haired beauty in her twenties. I resembled the picture on her latest book jacket, taken forty years later, when she was heavier, wrinkled, and recovering from cancer. How brave of her to use it.

"I can't believe how old I look." I was crying, contrasting her bravery with my superficiality, even while I was in the throes of it.

"I told you, it's just a cheap camera," Aaron said, getting pissed off. "I'm not a photographer. I was probably standing at the wrong angle. There was no flash or light meter or anything. I think you look pretty, but I'm sure Danny's will be a lot better."

"I hate them. I look like hell," I mumbled all the way home, feeling despondent. "I'm throwing them away."

"Don't. I like them. I'll keep them," he said.

"No, you won't." When we got home, I tore up all the

pictures. I rushed to throw them down the incinerator where I had thrown the stoned images of myself I'd loathed ten months before. How tragic that I also hated how I looked straight.

"I'm sure I'm going to hate my new pictures," I told Dr. Winters, crossing my legs. Did he notice that I was in a skirt? I'd been wearing skirts and dresses more lately. Not because he said he liked women better flowing and flowery. I always wore more skirts in the summer; it was cooler. I liked not wearing socks. "I made Aaron take pictures of me in the same pose so I could get a preview."

"Why the hell did you do that?" he asked in a pissy voice.

"I didn't want to wait two weeks to see how they came out."

"That was stupid," he said.

"Because it was impatient?" I asked.

"Yes. Because you lack tolerance if you don't get what you want when you want it. You have to delay gratification and learn how to suffer."

"I did suffer. The pictures Aaron took were horrible," I said. "I can't believe how old I looked."

"Sometimes recovering addicts experience a time gap," he said. "There's a disparity between your image of yourself and what you really look like that's jarring. Part of you feels like you're the age when you started using."

"I wish I looked thirteen again. I looked great at thirteen."

In the trick photograph of me holding up the Leaning Tower of Pisa, I was trying hard to look older. Now I was desperate to look younger. The goal was to like how I appeared when I was sober and looked like my age and myself, but it seemed unattainable.

"In some ways you are still thirteen," he said. "It's as if the intervening years didn't happen. Your psyche has been in cold storage."

"It's not bad to feel young," I argued. "I want to feel younger. Why is that bad?"

"You were smoking and getting high as a substitute for learning how to deal with anything uncomfortable or stressful. Instead of developing coping mechanisms, you relied on substances to take you away from your feelings."

"This again?" Did he intentionally repeat his theories over and over, the way you taught little kids to memorize the alphabet? It was annoying. Yet I did the same thing in my classes, reiterating my rules ("Err on the side of formality," "Never take no for an answer") until they became second nature. "You sound like a broken record."

"What didn't you like about the photographs Aaron took?" He ignored my insult.

"I already told you."

"Tell me again," he said.

"I looked old, wrinkled, and fat in the photographs," I said. "I want to lose weight. I stay on my diet for a few weeks, then I screw up and pig out on chocolate and licorice. I feel like I'll never solve this eating insanity."

"Food might be the hardest addiction to figure out." He looked at me with sympathy.

"I thought nicotine was the hardest, then dope." It wasn't fair. "Why is food harder?"

"You can't just quit eating. Picture if you had to smoke three cigarettes a day to stay alive while trying to stem your nicotine addiction."

"Some people figure out the food maze," I argued. "They learn to eat moderately. Or exercise."

"Not so many," he said. "Look at the failure rate of dieting."

"My sister-in-law works out twenty hours a week. Aaron

sticks to his no-bread diet and hasn't gained any weight back." Dr. Winters was thin. If he could learn to keep his hunger in check, why didn't he think I could?

"How do you think you look?" he asked.

"I look like a healthy forty-two-year-old woman," I answered.

"You could learn to accept that."

"What if I want to be thinner?"

"Learn to live with more hunger," he said matter-of-factly.

I stuck carefully to my food schedule. I was busy, so it was easier. My three summer night classes went well. Aaron and I were both working round the clock. We didn't have the time or inclination to go on a trip, but we spent a romantic seventh anniversary at an uptown hotel. Lilly loved both of my manuscripts and passed them on to Dina. I swam every day, settling into a nice nonsmoking, nondrinking, nontoking routine. Dumb as it seemed, I diligently recorded my minor emotional ebbs and flows in my journal. On days when I only ate two meals I felt hungrier, but the tiny pangs in my stomach no longer scared me.

When I lost two pounds, I decided that Dr. Winters' hypothesis on the difference between emotional and physical hunger was quite intelligent and innovative. Then I read five memoirs in a row about food addiction, along with Dr. Phil's new best-selling diet book. Turned out they all said the exact same thing: Stop eating for emotional reasons. It seemed there wasn't anything about my recovery that was original except that it was the first time it was happening to me.

Dr. Winters went out of town for a long weekend and rescheduled our Friday session. (He gave me three days' notice, which was allowed.) When he was out of town, I had a dream about him. We were having a therapy session outside, in front of a big highway. He looked thin and gaunt. Suddenly he said he was hungry. He stood up and ran across the street to get something to eat. Right in the middle of our appointment.

I analyzed potential meanings. Ever since Dr. Winters had shown me the story about his childhood, I saw him as vulnerable and fragile. I felt that I fed him. My subconscious was afraid he would fade away without me. I hated that he went out of town so often, and my reverie illustrated my fear of abandonment. He had the nerve to just get up and leave while I was trying to solve my food problems; it was like coitus interruptus. The highway implied there was danger involved, or I was at a crossroads. Interestingly my subconscious had transferred the hunger I was feeling onto him.

Back in New York, where he belonged, Dr. Winters was amused by my dream and all the ensuing interpretations. I bet he was flattered that I'd obviously missed him.

My cousin Danny finally dropped off the yellow envelope filled with my new book photographs. I ripped it open. I could already tell I was going to hate the images. I pulled them out quickly. I don't know if it was the dimming light from the sun going down, the angle, Danny's generous eye, his fancy camera, or my distance from it. But I absolutely loved them! It was amazing! I looked really thin and sexy. What a pleasant shock. After all the turmoil, worry, and agony I'd put myself through, I had come out just fine.

Aaron loved them. My cousin Miranda loved them. Claire loved them. I ran over to show my agent Lilly, who loved them too. What a relief. Comparing the old "studious" photograph to Danny's *Sex and the City* shots, everybody I showed them to agreed that the new roof shots were way better. I ran the pictures by Dr. Winters. Not to get his opinion, just to show off how fantastic they were.

"They look too posed," he said.

"What?"

"These pictures seem too staged. Phony." He shook his head. "They don't look like you."

"Are you joking?" He knew every ounce of the emotional upheaval I had gone through over the photographs; he had to be ribbing me. He wasn't. Since I'd already made the decision, didn't he have the good sense to lie?

"No joke." He wore his earnest expression. "I like the other ones better."

He probably liked the book-and-blazer images of me better because I looked cutesier and more easygoing. The black dress and spiky heels scared him. The look was too hard. He preferred his women sweet, light, and less threatening. Or was he just getting off on being Dr. Chaos?

"Go fuck yourself," I said.

It turned out that my editor, Dina, and Beth Bloomwood also thought the pictures looked too posed. They wondered if I could take them one more time. Wasn't Winters ever wrong about anything?

"You do look very thin and sexy in these shots," Dina, the sweet diplomat, explained. "But you seem uncomfortable in the high heels."

"I was uncomfortable." I tried to stay calm. "I couldn't walk in them."

"How about just a picture in the black dress from the waist up? That way you can wear flip-flops," Dina suggested. "You need to smile. We want you to look really happy and comfortable with yourself."

"Sure," I told her. "No problem."

Chapter 24

AUGUST 2003

"Susan, I have to cancel today. Call me on my cell phone," Dr. Winters' voice told my answering machine.

It was late afternoon Friday, and I was about to walk out the door for our four-fifteen session. I had only checked my messages at the last minute because I was waiting for a callback from Lilly. I called him right back. "It's me," I said. "I just got your message."

"I'm sorry. My daughter is sick at camp," he said. "I have to go pick her up."

Where was his wife? Though I knew she worked, I doubted she was getting $150 to help addicted crazy patients be less addicted and crazy. Hadn't Dr. and Mrs. Winters heard of child care? They should invest in a full-time nanny instead of jetting off on twelve vacations a year.

"Susan, are you still there?" he asked.

"I'm trying to do what you recommended and not react

right away," I said, not sure whether I wanted to cry or scream. I had two meetings I'd postponed twice because he kept switching my sessions around. I could handle it when he gave me a few days' notice. How many times was this guy allowed to cancel on me last minute? Three strikes and you're out, and this was his fourth.

"This is chaos theory at work," he added.

It was Winters' chaos alone, and it wasn't good for me anymore.

"We can reschedule for Monday at four-fifteen," he said. "Okay? I'll see you then."

Without saying anything, I hung up the phone.

Unlike most Manhattan shrinks, Dr. Winters wasn't going away in August, but I was. I had made reservations to fly to the Midwest to see my family on August 10. Fuming at yet another last-minute cancellation, I decided that he was doing me a favor. Since I was planning on spending three weeks in Michigan anyway, it was the perfect time to get rid of him. I envisioned simply blowing him off on Monday, not showing up and not calling, letting him sit there and wait for me. Losing the $15,000 a year I was paying him for two sessions a week, not to mention the recommendations and free press I provided, would make him regret mistreating me. But that was just the price he would have to pay for screwing me up again.

"What's that?" I asked Aaron when he walked in that night, pointing to the manila envelope under his arm.

"Your student Naomi's applying to *Saturday Night Live*. She wants me to critique some sketches she wrote," he said casually, putting the envelope on his desk.

"What? Why did you say yes to her?"

Aaron, who was juggling four overdue TV scripts of his

own, constantly bitched about all the leeches who thought professional writers should be on twenty-four-hour call to help wannabes for free. He said no to his NYU TV/film students, who hounded him to read their rewrites over the summer. When I asked him if he wanted to read my new addiction memoir, he'd said he didn't have time. So then why would he make time to read the work of one of *my* students? After taking two journalism classes with me, Naomi had taken a job working at the magazine that used to be run by my colleague Blake, who'd become her mentor and lover. I'd never taught her to sleep with people in positions of power. Now it felt like she was deserting me and journalism for TV, flagrantly soliciting my husband to help her.

"Are you saying you don't want me to read her work?" Aaron asked.

"No. I don't want you to read her work," I admitted, pissed off and very hungry. I felt like ordering in a pepperoni pizza, but I would settle for Chinese chicken and broccoli, which was on my diet. Not a great idea, since it was eleven P.M. Definitely emotional hunger. It would be better to write down my anger at Aaron, as well as my fury at the asinine, unreliable Dr. Winters, rather than eat away the rage. I took a breath and went to the living room, where I scribbled exactly what was upsetting me. The words flew from my pen, the way I used to write an angry op-ed essay on deadline. But instead of fighting for world peace, or making an articulate antiwar argument, the topic on hand was my own current, inane War of the Roses.

Naomi had met Aaron twice. The first time was last term when I'd coerced him to speak to my New School class about how he'd gone from penning humor pieces for the *National Lampoon* and *Village Voice* in the 1980s to selling scripts for TV/film. After his lecture Naomi asked me if she could show Aaron her prose sometime. I said no, he was too busy. Then he had bumped into her in June, when she was interning at a downtown animation studio where he'd been writing and producing a new pilot. She'd asked him to read her work. He'd said no, he was on deadline for his own work, he'd reported. I thought it was rude that she'd persisted, after I'd already told her he didn't have time.

A few weeks later, I'd received an odd "new address" card from Naomi, announcing her move from Brooklyn to Manhattan. On the front was a provocative picture of her wearing a low-cut T-shirt and tight jeans. Inside was a cryptic rhyming poem about lawn chairs. Miffed, I'd shown it to Aaron. He guessed she was trying to be a quirky comedy writer, while showing off her breasts at the same time. Guess it worked on Blake.

I was upset, but I didn't sweep my anger under the rug by smoking, toking, or overeating, like I would have in the past. I pictured ordering in baby shrimp with hot pepper and peanuts, realizing I hadn't finished my salad today, so it could have been physical hunger. Then I decided against it. Neither did I let it go and pretend everything was fine. What I did was march into Aaron's den and tell him what I was thinking, edited down to the shorter, calmer version. "You're too busy to read your students' rewrites over the summer. You're too busy to read your wife's book. So why are you offering to read Naomi's work?" I asked.

"Because you like her," he said.

I didn't believe him. I didn't think he was doing it for me. I thought he was doing it because she was a cute girl fawning all over him. The more I thought about it, the more it riled me. I tried to not overreact, but I felt betrayed, as if Naomi, Blake, and my husband had all somehow stabbed me in the back. I decided to order in sliced turkey from the deli. Even if it was Aaron hunger, it was less calories than Chinese food.

"You don't need to help a cute twenty-two-year-old ex-student of mine you barely know," I said.

"I don't know her at all," he said. "I never met her."

"Yes, you did. You met her twice," I said. "Once in my class and once when she bumped into you at the animation studio. You also saw a picture of her on that card I showed you."

"I did?" he asked. "When?"

He looked confused. Ever since we'd been together I'd trusted Aaron implicitly. But all of a sudden *Up the Down Staircase* was turning into *All About Eve* in my head. My discomfort had to do with Naomi's sexy photograph. It was the shot of a good-looking twenty-two-year-old, while I had felt very forty-two in my recent attempt at a provocative pose.

"I'll e-mail her no," Aaron said.

"You already said yes. What reason will you give?"

"I'll say it turns out I'm too busy." He went to his computer and turned it on.

"Really?" I usually went out of my way to help students. I hated how petty I was being, but I couldn't help it. I was glad he was making my paranoia go away by telling her to go away.

"No problem." I watched him type in a few lines and send it. Then he turned off AOL. The friendly male voice said "Goodbye." Aaron came and sat down on the couch next to me.

"I was only doing it for you." He nuzzled my neck.

I pushed him away. "I'm in a bad mood today."

"Why? I'm sorry about Naomi, I thought I was doing you a favor. I'll read your new manuscript, I didn't realize you'd finished it already. Don't be mad at me."

"I'm mad at you and I hate Dr. Winters' guts," I said. "He canceled last minute again."

"He doesn't mean to be a flake." Aaron rubbed my back. "He really cares about you."

It was an interesting role reversal. At our first couples' session, I had been going on the assumption that Aaron's insensitivity was an insurmountable obstacle. Then Winters insisted that Aaron was still there for me. Seven years later, Aaron was reassuring me that Dr. Winters cared about me. I tried to deduce what this male duet denoted. That Aaron and Dan were twin father figures I'd forever be forgiving? That they were switching off being the star and understudy of our psychodramatic revival of *Cyrano de Bergerac*? That it took a Village to keep me happy and clean? Greenwich Village?

"I'm hungry. I'm ordering in turkey from the deli," I declared.

"You're taking your anger at Dan out on me," he said. "Don't order food now. It's stupid to eat this late and it'll only put you in a bad mood."

That was a big change. He sounded like Dr. Winters. In the past, when I wanted to order in food late at night, Aaron was passive. Sometimes he'd offer to go out and get it for me.

"I can order in turkey and take out my rage on you if I feel like it." I leaned over and bit his ear.

"Listen, you bitch. I'm getting sick of this," he said playfully, grabbing and lifting me up.

"Hey! What are you doing?" I screamed as he carried me into the bedroom, Rhett Butler-like. He dropped me on the bed and ripped off my clothes.

For years I had been after him to act out my fantasies of being taken. His newfound machismo wildly turned me on while scaring me at the same time. I pretended to fight him off, but he held my hands behind my head and overpowered me. I was no longer pining for Chinese food, or sliced turkey. I actually felt hungry for my husband. After I came three times, crying and sweating, Aaron fell right to sleep. I put my arms around his waist, astounded that after seven years of marriage, he'd become Tarzan. He'd been way more aggressive since he'd been back in therapy. Whatever verbal testosterone Winters was pumping him with, I prayed he wouldn't stop.

I was not known for being friendly or docile early in the day, but the next morning Aaron and I held each other for an hour before he went to work. After he left, in a mellow daze, I went to take a shower. I hadn't weighed myself in weeks and I stepped on the scale. When it said 127 pounds, I didn't believe it and stepped on the scale again. I put in new batteries, but I was still 127. I looked in the mirror. I really did look thinner. When had I lost ten pounds? My first thought was that I must be dying of cancer. My second thought was, damn Dr. Winters! How could he be mending me when I was still so mad at him? His stupid and not even original strategy about delineating between emotional and physical hunger worked liked a charm. I'd been eating less. Come to think of it, that was why I'd been emoting all over the place.

I attempted to rein in my feelings and act rational. I made a plan to show up for my Monday session to end it nicely with him, in person. I would explain that I needed the kind of time and attention that he obviously couldn't offer. On my way out of the building, I noticed an envelope with Naomi's name on it at the concierge desk. My heart pounded. I feared that Aaron changed his mind and read her sketches. He'd lied to me, placating me with mean hot sex but commenting on her work though he'd told me he wouldn't. I opened the envelope. Inside were three of Naomi's sketches. Nothing was marked on them. No comments, no critique. She'd dropped them off, but my husband hadn't read a word.

Feeling madly in love and lust with my husband, I turned my hostility back toward my head doctor. "Do you know that was the fourth appointment with me you screwed up last minute? Where was your wife on Friday? Why couldn't she go pick up your daughter from camp?" I launched my tirade as soon as I walked in.

"She was on Long Island. I'm sorry for canceling our appointment," Dr. Winters said. "When you have children, you can't control things like that."

"Don't give me that bullshit. Ever hear of backup child care?" I said, my voice agitated. "For all the money you charge, you can't afford to keep a babysitter on retainer? I mean, you're not an ear doctor or plumber. You're a busy shrink, for Christ sakes. Why do you keep telling your patients to be dependent on you?"

"I tell addicts that I will be far less reliable than your substance but it's still much better to rely on me," he said.

"Don't you think that's an odd paradox when you're so ambivalent about being depended on?" I asked.

"How so?" He was wearing blue jeans today. I hated when he wore blue jeans. I wanted him to look—and act—older and more professional.

"Of all the fields in the world, you chose psychotherapy. Then you develop an addiction theory based on having unstable clients transfer all of their intense emotional needs onto you, one to five times a week." I crossed my legs; I was wearing blue jeans too. "Then you take twelve vacations a year, teach too many classes and overbook, so you're switching sessions around constantly. You're courting chaos."

"I see your point," he nodded, trying to suppress the half smile he showed whenever I was outshrinking him.

I was about to cite his horrible relationship with his mother as the cause of his confusion about closeness. But then I chose another tactic, one more likely to elicit sympathy. "When you cancel last minute it hurts," I wailed.

"Just because it hurts doesn't mean it's bad," he answered in a quieter voice.

"What if one of your patients overdosed?" I asked. "Unless I'm the only one whose sessions you keep screwing up."

"You're not the only one. I had to cancel five appointments on Friday," he reported.

"What if you can't reschedule? Don't you lose a lot of money?" I attempted to add it up in my head. I figured he was down between $750 and $1,000 for all of those Friday cancellations.

"I am never motivated by money," he said.

"I don't believe you," I said. "If you do this for fun, why are you charging me so much?"

"Do you want to know more about my financial situation?"

"No, I don't." I actually wished he would stop revealing so much. Aaron had the same problem, being too honest. He often shared all kinds of personal details I did not need to hear, about sex with old girlfriends, his past credit card debt, stomach ailments. It was as if he had never learned how to monitor himself. I was sure it came from not having a good mother who listened as a kid. The minute he had an attentive, warm female audience, he spilled every single thought he had, trying to make up for lost time.

"Why don't you want to know?" Dr. Winters looked confused and hurt, as if I was supposed to be flattered that he wanted to confide in me. "If I'm not motivated by money, it means I'm here because I want to be."

"It means I have no power over you at all," I admitted. "You can be as flaky as you damn well please and there are no consequences for you."

"There are more important consequences than money," he argued.

"Is your daughter okay?" I couldn't help but ask.

"Yes. She's okay."

I almost wished her illness was more serious, to justify his cancellation. "When you cancel on me last minute, it makes me feel unimportant. It ruins my day." I crossed my arms, uncrossed them, then scowled at him. "What would you say if I didn't show up today and never came back?"

"I would be distressed," he said.

"No, you wouldn't. You would blame me, compartmentalize, and say I was being inflexible."

"I know you're inflexible," he said. "So it would be my fault."

"I feel like you're being flippant." I uncrossed my legs. I was wearing black ankle boots with black socks. "It seems like this is funny to you."

"It's not." He lifted his left knee over his right leg. He was wearing brown penny loafers with brown socks. "You're misreading my emotions. I feel uncomfortable."

I was glad he was uncomfortable, but I was sure I felt worse. "Because you don't like me to call you a flake?" I asked.

"I don't like to see myself as irresponsible or careless. I should be more careful." He put his right elbow on the chair's armrest, then leaned his chin on his palm. One of his fingers covered part of his eye. Like Aaron, he couldn't take criticism from a woman. When I said anything negative, his body cringed or hid, as if he feared he was going to get hit. "I am sorry."

That sounded too general to me, not contrite or personal enough. "You don't seem sorry," I said, feeling tears coming on.

He put his hand down, as if to see me more clearly. He could handle my pain better than my anger. Sensing the extent of my dejection, he added, "If you quit now, I would feel like a failure."

Good, failure was more emotional. "Why?" I tested.

"Because I give you something you need and I want to live up to that."

"Like a business contract?"

"More like a marriage contract, based on trust, dedication, hard work, and emotional investment," he came up with.

That sounded earnest and rueful, much better.

"Does it bother you when patients quit therapy?" His marriage metaphor was a little too intimate and I now needed to get general.

"It depends on the reason someone leaves."

"Has anyone left in anger?" I sensed someone had. Was it a man or a woman?

"There was someone who left because I was too impatient and confrontational."

"Did that upset you?"

"Yes. I was regretful because it was a missed opportunity."

"Did it bother you when Irene stopped seeing you?" I asked.

"No. She was never that committed to the therapy."

"She thinks you're sexist." I was using her anger at him to fuel my own.

"I am sexist," he said. "Does that bother you?"

"I don't think your sexism matters as long as she stays off the painkillers."

"She's still off them?" he asked, looking concerned.

"Yes. And she and her husband are seeing the couples' therapist you recommended."

"That's good to hear. Perhaps she'll come back some-time...."

He always wanted everybody to come back. I didn't. I'd told students who had already taken my class twice to study with another professor the next term. Then again, it was easier to stay friends with former students than former patients. "Do you ever advise your patients to end therapy?"

"I don't think it should be extreme, all or nothing. Some

patients come to see me once a year. I don't like the word termination," he said. "Sometimes important relationships continue forever. Even after death."

That was an extreme thing to say. Who had died? I immediately focused on who was sort of dead to him. "Is your never wanting to end relationships connected to your mother cutting you off?"

"No," he said, too fast. "My mother tried to get rid of me, but she couldn't." He sounded annoyed. I wasn't sure if he was angry at me or her.

" 'Cause you bumped into her in Spain by accident when you were twenty-four?" I asked.

He nodded, seemingly pleased that I'd recalled the details. How could I not?

"Talk about the chaos theory," he mused.

That was why he liked the chaos theory so much. If his mother couldn't control the ending, then it didn't have to be so negative and etched in stone. You never knew, maybe they would accidentally cross paths again on his next trip. Could that have something to do with all his traveling?

"She hasn't answered your letters in almost thirty years, right?"

"That doesn't mean she doesn't think about me every day." He'd said this before. It made him feel better to think it. I found the sentiment touching.

"When a former patient calls or writes, I bet you make a point of returning their call."

"Always." He nodded.

"Because you know how much it hurts when somebody doesn't?"

"How important it is," he said.

"You'll always call me back?" I asked, my anger now mixing with need and vulnerability. "No matter what?"

"Yes." He didn't hesitate, nodding again.

"Last night, when I was really upset with you, Aaron took care of me," I said.

"Good." He sat up taller, pleased. "How did he take care of you?"

"Sexually," I said. Looking down at the red rug, I added, "It was the hottest sex I've ever had," feeling myself blush.

"How does that feel?"

"It's confusing. He offered to help Naomi, this cute little student of mine, and I freaked out. I don't know why. It seemed like there was something inappropriate about the way she was pursuing him. She'd sent this sexy photograph. . . ."

"You were jealous?"

I nodded. "I usually don't get jealous of Aaron." It was odd, I had felt more jealousy toward Dr. Winters than I had felt toward my husband.

"You've never been so intimately connected to Aaron before," he told me.

"I told him not to help her. Does it sound like my imagination?" I asked. "Or that I overreacted?"

"It's never your imagination, but you always overreact."

I liked how that sounded and wrote it down. "Why did I feel like that?"

"You just did your own provocative photograph," he said. "You recognized the instinct."

"It felt dangerous."

"Passion is always dangerous," he warned.

"In the past, if a lover was screwing around on me, I knew. I had good radar." I shook my lower leg a little, it was falling asleep. My boots only had a one-inch heel; I no longer bothered to wear my high heels for him. I was wearing my small wedding band too; I hadn't been showing off my diamond lately. I was a writer with a book coming out, which, in the hierarchy of my head, trumped being a wife. "Why would I pick up bad vibes when he was completely innocent?"

"Your radar is wrong now because it's mixed up with feelings that weren't there before."

"Why don't I trust my husband?" Aaron had been to see Dr. Winters early that morning. I wondered what they'd talked about, knowing it was me. Claire thought it was weird to share a shrink with your husband, that it was some kind of conflict of interest. But I was starting to like it. Knowing Aaron had been here earlier made me feel protected, as if the two of them were strategizing on how to better bodyguard me.

"Because you never really needed Aaron before," he surmised.

He was right. When we were married seven years ago, I loved my husband, but I didn't need him. "Did I tell you that Aaron's been paying all the mortgage and maintenance bills?"

"Really?" Dr. Winters looked pleased.

"He makes so much more money than I do, I told him he should pay. I want him to take care of me. I like feeling gratitude, that's why our marriage is so much better."

"Aren't you sexist?" he asked with a smile.

Oh boy, I was. I recalled that he had encouraged Aaron to pay most of our bills. Come to think of it, hadn't it been Dr. Winters' idea? If traditional roles were what had improved our sex life, I was all for it. "Well, if my book makes a million dollars, I'm paying off the mortgage," I added. I wasn't a total Barbie doll bimbo. "Did I tell you Aaron's coming with me to Michigan? I'm afraid to fly alone."

"Since when?"

"Since the World Trade Center attacks. I keep thinking I'm going to die in a plane crash. I might fly back to New York with him instead of staying in the Midwest for three weeks," I said. "I'm getting too dependent on him."

"You say the word dependent with disdain. You should have a flourishing dependency on each other that you both enjoy."

Is that what Dr. Winters and his wife had? "I'm too dependent on you," I threw out.

"No, you're not. If you remained like this ten years from now, maybe. But it's been an extreme period of transferring your need for continual substances onto a few people."

"I get too upset when you cancel," I disagreed. "I need you too much."

"Even if you were pathologically dependent for a certain period, with addicts, that's normal. I have one patient whose addiction is ruining every area of her existence. I told her, 'You have to listen to everything I say and let me run your life.'"

"You did that to me. You changed the way I live, work, eat, act, speak to my family, friends, and husband. . . ."

"I'm talking about almost an infant–parent dependency with this patient—"

I cut him off. "That's what I felt like with you. Why did I feel that way?"

"There's something called a core pillar," he explained.

I liked the phrase, which seemed to turn a high-school infatuation into a scientific equation. "But I still feel like that," I admitted.

"That's merely how you feel, it's not an accurate depiction." He wrote something down on the back of a business card and handed it to me, two words in all capital letters: FEELINGS MISINFORM.

He hadn't given me one of his adages in a while; I'd missed them. I put it in the pocket of my briefcase. "Bad things can happen when you're too reliant on others."

"Things can go wrong. There's more opportunity for disappointment," he conceded. "You can't control people the way you controlled substances; the world gets more complicated. What does Aaron think of the changes?"

"He loves when I need him more," I said. "Here's the wild card. My father called last night. When I told him I might not stay in Michigan for the three weeks I'd planned, he got offended. He wants me to stay the whole time."

"Why?"

"I haven't seen him in a year," I said. "He hasn't been feeling well."

"Your father needs you more because he's feeling vulnerable?" he asked.

I nodded yes. "All my life I've desperately wanted my father to open up to me. Now that he's finally getting emotional, I can't handle the Jewish guilt."

I realized that I was nervous to leave my fantasy father to connect with my real father, while needing my husband next to me so I wouldn't die on my way to fight with my three brothers. Male dependency was going haywire.

"Are you sure you can handle seeing your family now?" he asked.

"I'm only scared about the plane flight," I said. "Once we land in Michigan, I'll be fine."

Chapter 25

AUGUST 2003

Sunday was my father's seventieth birthday. By the time we arrived at my parents' Michigan house at seven o'clock that night, my brothers, their wives, and their kids were already gathered in the kitchen. We kissed everyone hello. All Shapiros of all sizes were eating and talking at once. My mother said, "Say hi to Aunt Susie and Uncle Aaron," to my squealing nieces and nephews, who offered waves and hugs. Brian and Eric congratulated me on my upcoming book. I beamed, pulling out the galley from my briefcase. Michael, in from Chicago, sat next to Aaron and launched into a story about taking care of Studs Terkel, a heart patient of his. It was nice to be home. What had I been so worried about?

Then I surveyed the pasta, chicken, lamb chops, hamburgers, deli meats, fish, garlic bread, pizza, vegetables, salad, cheese, seafood, and six different kinds of potatoes spread buffetlike on the table and the marble island in the center of the room. Wall-to-wall food. I noticed beer cans and an open bottle of red wine on the table and spied a pack of smokes in my sister-in-law Jill's open purse on one counter, three birthday cakes on the other. I immediately longed to smoke, toke, drink, and shove ten pieces of gum into my mouth, along with the three cakes.

Leaving Aaron with the food, alcohol, cigarettes, and relatives, I rushed upstairs with our bags, mumbling that I had to find everyone's presents. Really I needed to take a few breaths and leave an emergency message for Dr. Winters. Alone in my pink childhood bedroom, I found the toys, books, and clothes I had packed. I was just a little flustered, that's all. I put away my clothes, telling myself to calm down, everything was okay, I'd be fine.

Back downstairs, I handed out my carefully chosen gifts, which didn't seem to interest my father or brothers. I held up the Spider-Man, Superman, and Hulk pool toys for my nephews, Sammy, Benny, and Abe, explaining that they would look better blown up. The boys ignored me, tossing the superheros under the kitchen table. At least my adorable and perceptive nieces, Dara and Andrea, were paying attention. They threw off their clothes and ran to the living room to try on the black dresses I'd brought.

"It's so pretty, Aunt Susie," cooed Dara, a blond bombshell at five.

"Way cool," declared Andrea, a gorgeous four-and-a-half-year-old, who had long chestnut hair, like mine.

"Come model your new outfits for Grandma," my mother called, handing me and Aaron plates and silverware. "Only in New York would they make little kids' clothes in all black."

"I want Gampa's birthday cake," said Benny, already a sugar addict at three.

"We'll light the candles after dinner," said Grandpa, the birthday boy, who was now holding baby Abe on his lap and wearing a paper party hat.

Amid the alcohol, cigarettes, and kaleidoscope of fattening carbs, I spotted something I could eat: a plate of jumbo grilled shrimp. Thank the Lord. Pure protein, not many calories. My mother knew I loved shrimp and that I was watching my weight. She'd obviously gotten it for me. I was relieved and filled my plate.

"Hey, save some shrimp for me," said my sister-in-law Jill.

Of the entire smorgasbord, she desired the one dish that fit my diet. It figured. But my sisters-in-law came over with their kids to eat my mother's food twice a week. I visited once a year, had been here twenty minutes; Jill was already being competitive. Or was I? I replayed Dr. Winters' warning that I should not respond to any anger or discomfort I felt right away. I should think about it first, keeping my mouth shut.

I realized she was probably just kidding around and my response to her comment was too extreme. I liked Jill, a scientist and fellow food-and-nicotine addict, the only other serious career woman in the clan. She had recently lost her laboratory job, so I could see how the attention I was getting for my book could be hard for her. Giving her the benefit of the doubt, I complimented her sweater and told her how pretty her daughter Andrea looked. It annoyed me that Aaron had already broken his no-bread diet by eating my mother's pasta and pig-in-a-blanket hors d'oeuvres. I ignored that too and went back to the counter. I took a piece of plain chicken and green beans, proud of myself for finally being able to resist all my mother's fattening temptations.

"Boy, you're hungry today," Jill said, staring at my plate.

I looked at her plate, filled with spaghetti, garlic bread, salad, and fried chicken. Was she joking? She didn't seem to be, but it didn't make sense. Since she'd last seen me, I had lost ten pounds and had quit smoking, toking, and drinking. She had gained weight and still smoked. What was going on? She felt I was taking something from her. Attention? My brothers' time? My parents' love? All the colleagues who were angry at me were substance abusers who couldn't yet conquer their own demons. Was I the poster girl for clean living or a dartboard?

Instead of answering Jill, I turned to my father. "Daddy, aren't you going to open your birthday presents?" I pointed to the special photo book of his life I'd made him.

"I'll look at it later, honey," he said, handing baby Abe to my mother and picking up Benny. "Come here, Benny, come to Grandpa."

"Are you coming to New York for my book party?" I asked. My father's plate was also filled with pasta, bread, and fried chicken. I tried to stop noticing what everyone was eating and drinking.

"It's hard for me to fly," he said, tickling Benny, who giggled and put a cookie in his mouth.

"I might be able to fly in for it," said Michael. "I'll cook for you guys again."

Last time he had come to town, Michael had made Aaron and me an elaborate, delicious Indian meal. "We loved your chicken tikka," I said, wondering if the stereotype that all Jewish people communicated with food and drink was true, or if it was all families, or just my family.

"My new specialty is chicken marsala with mushrooms and wine sauce," Michael said.

"Chicken sounds great, but I can't eat food cooked with wine anymore," I told him.

"The alcohol burns off when you cook it," Michael said, as if it was stupid of me not to know this.

"You're going to fly to New York? Scum city?" My father looked surprised that anybody would want to fly to visit me.

"Yes, we all know how much you love your old city." I made a goofy face, suddenly four years old again, competing with my nieces and nephews.

"What? Why would anybody want to go to that dirty, loud, disgusting place?"

My father continued his anti-Manhattan harangue, which he'd been expanding since the day I moved there. I looked at him. He didn't look so good. He was kind of pale and his stomach was bigger, hanging over his pants. He'd found the ten pounds I'd lost. Had all my relatives put on weight, or was it my imagination? I was seeing the world through addictions, as if I had X-ray eyes that zoomed in on everyone's oral intake.

My father, Jill, and I were nicotine fiends. Brian, who'd had two beers, and Mike, who had finished the bottle of wine, now seemed overindulgent to me. Monica, who used to get high with me, had addicts in her family. Her father, a well-known writer, was a notorious smoker and drinker. Benny and Andrea were already junk-food freaks. We all overate. My mother was eating too much bread, as well as overfeeding everyone, including my husband, who looked over at me and smiled, totally oblivious to my disdain. I pictured my mother stuffing the faces of her own four little kids. It appeared obvious where my instinct to self-medicate came from.

"You're really not going to come to my book party?" I asked my father. He had flown to Chicago to see Michael a few weeks before. Why couldn't he fly to New York?

"Benny's my bruiser," he said, ignoring my question. "Aren't you, Benjamin?"

Lost in a swirl of hurt and confusion, I stood up to get more food. I wanted pasta, but reached for a piece of fish. Though I hadn't forgiven Dr. Winters for his flakiness, calling up his voice was comforting. I recalled his instructions to stay hyperconscious of my feelings, to rein them in so I wouldn't wind up overreacting or using again.

Okay, I felt annoyed at Michael, weirded out by Jill, jealous of the affection my parents showed their grandchildren, and rejected by my father. I was also worried about him. After his recent hip replacement, Mom said he'd been using too much pain medication. A week before, he had simply quit taking all painkillers. It was good that he'd stopped, but cold turkey was too sudden. He'd gone from cigarettes to pills to carbs. It was none of my business; I didn't mention it, noting that I'd crossed over from physical to emotional hunger. Still, protein wasn't going to do much damage.

"That's the third time you've filled your plate," Jill commented loudly.

"I weigh 127 and I'm off cigarettes and alcohol," I shot back. "What about you?"

Huge mistake. She stood up, her eyes tearing, and ran right out of the kitchen. My brother Eric followed her.

"You had to start," my mother said, glaring at me.

"I didn't start anything." I defended myself while the room turned quiet.

Michael finally broke the silence with, "Most food is cooked with alcohol."

"I told you I don't drink anymore. I don't want food cooked with alcohol in it!" I raised my voice. "You're a cardiologist, for Pete's sake! Most heart problems are caused by too much smoking, eating, and drinking. Don't you know anything about addiction?"

"If alcohol is burned off in cooking, it doesn't matter," he said in his doctor voice, playing the maven to overcompensate for being the youngest, as he always did.

This time he was wrong. I'd interviewed several drug and alcohol counselors, as well as Dr. Winters. In AA they maintained that there was such a fine line between drinking and not drinking that you never tempted fate. You didn't walk by a bar, you walked around the block. You didn't drink alcohol-free beer or eat food cooked with alcohol because any taste or association could make you go off the wagon. I'd had almost two years of addiction therapy, was almost finished researching and writing a book on the subject. Couldn't anybody in my family ever allow me to be an expert on anything?

Eric came back to the kitchen, scooped up Andrea, said, "I think we're gonna leave," and left. I looked out the window to the driveway, where Jill was packing up their car.

"You didn't mean to upset her," Monica said.

"No, of course I didn't." I was glad somebody was defending me, though maybe it had more to do with her rivalry with Jill than my innocence.

"Watching Jill bug you was like seeing a kid smash a stick against a bee's nest," Brian offered. "Then she cried when she got stung."

Was he defending or trashing me?

"But we didn't have Gampa's birthday cake!" Sammy wailed.

"Yeah, Andrea needs cake too," Dara said, staring longingly at Andrea from the window, clearly upset that her favorite cousin was leaving so abruptly.

"You're not in AA and you were never an alcoholic," Michael was still arguing.

"Look, drinking lowered my resistance to other substances," I said. "In my addiction therapy—"

"We don't want to hear about it," my mother cut me off with a horrified look on her face. She hated when I talked about being in any kind of therapy, as if it was a direct insult to her.

"Mom, I'm proud of my addiction therapy. Everybody knows I'm doing it. I'm writing a book about it. What's the big secret? You look like I just announced I've been giving blow jobs to strangers."

"No, that's your other book!!!" my mom shrieked and ran out of the room.

Monica, Brian, and Michael cracked up. My father shook his head, put Benny down, and stood up. He picked up his cane and wobbled upstairs after my mother. I looked at Aaron.

"Well, that *is* your other book," Aaron said.

"I know it is." I couldn't help but laugh too. Welcome home.

After my brothers and their kids went back to their respective homes, I apologized to my parents. The rest of the week was quiet and uneventful until Thursday, when all our electricity went out. When I heard, on a battery-operated radio, that New York's power was out too, I was afraid it was terrorism. Mayor Bloomberg came on the air, swearing it was just a big electrical snafu. I didn't miss the air-conditioning or television, but it was hard to not check my e-mail. (Was that my latest addiction?) Aaron and I slept in the basement, where it was coolest.

Friday afternoon, the power was still off and I was feeling claustrophobic in my mother's muggy house. I went out to take a walk around the block. Before I could leave the driveway, it started to rain. Well, I could still swim in the rain. I ran to my room and changed into my bathing suit. Outside in the backyard, I jumped into the pool. While swimming my first lap, I congratulated myself on solving that problem. I would avoid being stuck in my mother's big white suburban food-laden house, stay cool, and exercise all at once. Then I heard thunder. Looking up, I saw lightning. The pool was surrounded by trees. Leave it to me to survive death by plane crash only to be hit by lightning. I ran inside.

I found my mother in the kitchen with my father and Aaron. On the table were six flashlights, two lit candles, and a battery-powered lantern. She was standing at the refrigerator, shaking her head and pulling out food.

"You have to eat the rest of the lamb chops and hamburger; it'll spoil," she yelled at my father, in disaster mode, as if it were World War III. She handed him the plate and he dug in.

"Here's the corned beef and pastrami." She gave it to Aaron, with a fork and the mustard.

"You should finish the chicken, cheese, and salami." She handed me two trays.

I wasn't the least bit hungry. Yet I stood near the marble island and, by candlelight, ate my mother's wilty cheddar, chicken, and lukewarm salami. I didn't even like salami. Two slices, three, four, five. As if the electricity wasn't going to ever come back on. As if this was the last food on the planet. As if we would all be better off obese and sick to our stomachs than, heaven forbid, throwing any unwanted food away. After physical, emotional, and Aaron hunger, here was another category to explain why I was eating: pleasing-my-mother hunger. It was my worst nightmare. I was once again trapped in her oversized kitchen with food that I couldn't stop guzzling. Fat was my fate.

I had to fight it. When the lights and phone came back on an hour later, I went upstairs and called Northwest Airlines to change my plane reservation. I had to get back to New York, where I could starve. Then I e-mailed my sister-in-law. "Jill— I'm sorry if I hurt your feelings," I wrote. "After giving up cigarettes, I've had a rough time with food issues. I've been very sensitive. I didn't mean to overreact. I'm heading back to Manhattan early and don't want to leave on bad terms."

I was relieved when she answered right away. "I'm sorry too," she said. "I'm probably just jealous that you sold your book."

"Well, I'm jealous of your beautiful daughter," I told her.

Thus my August vacation lasted eight days. I was surprised I'd made it that long without smoking, toking, drinking, or chewing gum. I ate no bread, pasta, cake, or cookies, but still managed to gain six pounds and piss off every member of my family in the process. My last phone and e-mail messages in Michigan were to Dr. Winters, saying I would be back in town Monday. Did he have any open appointments left in August? I offered to take all of them.

Chapter 26

SEPTEMBER 2003

I woke up in New York on September first thinking that, for twenty years, I'd always spent Labor Day in Michigan. I felt guilty, as if I'd flunked my summer vacation. Then something weird happened. I went to put my wedding ring in my jewelry box and I realized that the second glass box, where I kept a few special jewels my mother had given me, was missing. I'd been back two weeks but hadn't noticed it. I'd left the key for some workmen, who'd been in the apartment to fix the air-conditioning. I feared they'd stolen it. I tried picturing what I'd left in the glass box. There was a long white pearl necklace, diamond earrings, and a gold pin. All day I looked for it. Finally I called Aaron at work to ask if he'd seen it.

"You had your writing workshop party the night before we went out of town," he said. "Didn't you hide your jewelry in the front drawer?"

He was right. I recalled putting the glass box in my front sock drawer for safekeeping. When I opened it, the jewelry box was right there, with my mother's expensive presents inside. What was that about? It seemed connected to my disappointing Midwest jaunt and/or the blackout food episode, but how?

On Tuesday, I told Dr. Winters my fear that I'd misplaced my mother's jewelry.

"You externalized the loss you were feeling," he guessed.

I was still pissed off at him, but at the same time I felt gratitude that he'd nailed it so quickly. "Part of me wanted to lose her presents?"

"Are you asking or telling me?" he asked. I wasn't sure. "What kind of jewelry was it?" He wanted to know.

"I didn't misplace anything Aaron gave me or anything I bought myself. It wasn't even jewelry she'd bought for me," I said. "It was three of her own pieces—a necklace, earrings, and a gold pin—that she passed on to me. Pretty and high-priced, but not really my style."

"Why not your style?"

"Too fancy for me."

"You wanted to lose it because it was all about her, not you," he said.

"I don't know what happened to me in Michigan." For weeks I'd been trying to deconstruct it. "I used to love hanging out with my family in August. I'd have a great time."

"Yes, people doing drugs together can get along so well," he said.

I laughed. "When I was drinking, smoking, and overeating, I was medicating myself?"

"Right," he said. "Everything was just fine when you were anesthetized."

"My mom always overfeeds, that's part of her shtick. She

grew up a poor orphan. To her, food equals love. Why did I get so upset this time?" I asked. "Because I still have no skin?"

"Because her way of love is narcissistic and self-centered. If you don't buy into it, you can't connect with her. There was a failure to recognize and respond to your needs." He sounded confident and matter-of-fact. But was he talking about my mother, or his?

"Well, she's not recognizing my father's needs. After hip-replacement surgeries, the last thing he needs is to stuff himself on carbs and gain weight," I said. "Why can't she change?"

"She doesn't want to," he said. "There's too much in it for her to stay the same. It's her way of getting affection and attention."

"Her grandkids want to visit her all the time. They love the birthday ritual so much that sometimes she puts out cake, ice cream, and party hats when it's not even anybody's birthday. They adore her."

"Little kids are easy to control," he said. "It would be very uncomfortable for her to stop overfeeding. When you changed, it seemed aggressive. Being thin and eating moderately is being different from them, which caused all the rifts."

Although I liked his compassion, this seemed off base. My family had been the same way for decades. I was the one whose perception of everything had been dramatically altered. "I'm too old to blame my parents for my problems," I told him. "Tell me what I did wrong."

"You superimposed your new personal agenda on the people around you, which is also narcissistic." He didn't miss a beat. "It's unrealistic to expect others to change to accommodate you. You're intolerant of anyone who's not on the same mission you are."

That felt more accurate. "It seems I can only stay clean, thin, and happy in my little ten-block radius. Aaron's in the den. You're two blocks away. My agent and editor are close by. My local diner makes my exact chef salad. But I'm not transferrable. Is this an addict thing?"

"Yes." He nodded. "You can micromanage everything here. You're in total control."

"I feel like I'll never be able to travel anywhere again," I said.

He looked sympathetic. "You will, don't worry. It's like you've just spent time in the detox ward of a hospital or a rehab center with comprehensive treatment around the clock. The variables are controlled. When you leave, the outside world is full of perils."

"It gets easier?" I asked.

"Yes. Within time you'll become less rigid. When an alcoholic first gets sober they can't even be in the same room with people drinking. After a while it's no longer threatening."

I noticed something different about him—his skin was tan. "Hey, didn't you tell me you once had skin cancer and can't sit in the sun?" I asked. He looked cute with a tan. As if his normal good looks weren't distracting enough.

"Yes. We went to the beach on Fire Island over the weekend," he admitted sheepishly.

Somebody who'd had skin cancer obviously shouldn't be baking in the sun. I assumed the "we" was his wife and daughter. I was glad he hadn't insisted I give up sunbathing. I'd given up enough pleasures. Though he wouldn't call them pleasures; he'd call them pain-avoiders.

"Did you wear sunscreen at least?"

"Yes," he said. As if we both didn't know how vain and dumb it was to sunbathe. I decided not to analyze it further, lest he make me give up the sun too.

In an episode of the claustrophobic comedy *Curb Your Enthusiasm,* the nutty hero saw his shrink at the beach in a thong bathing suit and could no longer be his patient. Aaron said Dr. Winters mentioned that he liked to Rollerblade and ride his bike. I tried not to think about my shrink at the beach, Rollerblading, or bike riding, which creeped me out. I wanted to think he had been sitting in the office while I was gone, seeing patients in a jacket and tie, missing me.

"Okay, I see why my mom kept overfeeding me, that's her compulsion. But I still can't figure out why Jill was watching what I ate. And why did Michael insist on cooking for me with alcohol?" I asked. "Was that as mean as it felt?"

"No, none of it was hostile or directed at you," he said. "It was self-protective. If your addictions are a serious disease that requires far-reaching treatment, then your relatives might have the disease too. It hit too close to home. They weren't angry, they were unnerved."

I felt bad that I'd gotten so angry at my family. At the same time I was thrilled to be back in New York. In two weeks I'd lost the weight I'd gained. When people overate in front of me, I overate. Dr. Winters was so thin, I bet his influence kept me from eating, as if I was such a Zelig that I took on the habits of the people nearest to me.

"I feel like all my addictions are connected to my mother. Do you think I started smoking, toking, and chewing gum to avoid her overfeeding me?" I asked.

"It's more complicated than that," he said. "You know how people in AA talk about reaching for the bottle as if it's a baby's bottle of milk and they *nurse* a drink. . . ."

"My mom always said that when my father smoked, it was like he was sucking on a tit."

Dr. Winters nodded, launching into a discussion of Melanie Klein's theory about an infant's grandiosity. It involved a baby's belief that it was omnipotent and controlled the mother to get its needs filled. If the mother wasn't there or was unresponsive, the baby felt anxiety and dread. Later in life that individual tried to re-create the soothing sensation of nursing by using substances. Thus, he explained, smoking and drinking compensated for an infant's feelings of deprivation and ruptures in their first primal attachment.

Though he sounded overly academic, like a Psych 101 text, this philosophy intrigued me. "What percentage of addicts have an early disconnection from their mothers?" I asked.

"One hundred percent of them," he answered.

"You chose to work in a population defined by their mother traumas!" I laughed.

"Not necessarily." He seemed defensive. "The same could be said of psychotics."

"That's not true," I argued. "Psychosis could be genetic. Or caused by birth defects or physical trauma. You gravitated toward people with the mother rift because what's familiar fascinated you."

"Well, I'll admit the territory resonates deeply and personally," he said, smiling.

Did this principle apply to my own background? If, as an addict, I was like a nursing infant, then smoking had taken the place of my mother, who was supposed to fill me with a sense of well-being, warmth, and peace. I knew Freud acolytes who believed that was where all depression originated, from early maternal discord. Even my father, who was antipsychology, often said, "If you don't have your mother's love, you have nothing."

The problem was, I was convinced I had my mother's unconditional love. Klein's hypothesis only worked when I plugged my father into the paradigm. Although he'd supported me financially and loved me, in a vague, distant way, my early deprivation was my missing dad. He was the one who wasn't really there. He was always at work. What little free time was left he divided between my three brothers. They didn't smoke because they had him. Maybe I emulated my father by chain-smoking because I was hungry for him. I wanted to taste and smell like him, which kept him closer to me at all times.

This might be the reason why I'd responded so well to Dr. Winters' care and counsel, why I couldn't bear it if he'd cancel or a cell call took away his attention for even a second. I entertained the notion that paternal nurturing was all I'd needed. How ironic if the addiction part of my therapy had actually been secondary, an unconscious excuse, a smoke screen.

"Doesn't the classic therapist–patient relationship re-create infancy?" I asked.

He explained that a Freudian therapist stayed silent and anonymous to create the same narcissistic illusion that an infant had, that only their needs counted and the other person in the intimate primal relationship didn't have needs of their own.

"Normally the therapist doesn't intrude on that illusion," he told me.

"But you did."

"With addiction therapy I eventually try to be who I am and disturb the illusion."

"Why?" I asked. "To drive me insane?"

"Instead of controlling a substance, an addict needs to connect with a person to get what they need. People are unpredictable and chaotic, so the transition can be painful."

"This could be a rationalization for your flakiness," I said, skeptical.

"What do you mean?"

"You're saying that you screwed me over for four sessions to test me?" I folded my arms.

"No. But when I brought something personal into our treatment, it seemed only fair to tell you the real reason. That I was preoccupied with that lawsuit about the dog, that my daughter got sick at camp," he said. "I don't think it does you a favor to protect you from things you're going to have to deal with anyway."

He sounded cold and detached, making lame excuses for a pattern of disregard I couldn't forgive. "Stop telling me personal details about you. I don't want to know anything else." I looked at my watch. "It's time to end."

I kept thinking that I had been in therapy almost two years; it was time for me to end my relationship with him altogether. I just wanted to make sure I was in control of my food addictions and that I could handle all the excitement from the upcoming publication of my book. I felt like a long-suffering wife, biding my time before filing for divorce.

That night I received three e-mails in a row from the Midwest. Jill sent a message that she'd cut down on cigarettes and had lost eight pounds on her first two weeks of Weight Watchers. My father said that, by following my "*farchadat* diet" and not eating bread for a week, he'd lost six and a half pounds. Michael wrote that he'd stopped drinking but still thought it was okay to prepare food with alcohol since it all burned off during cooking anyway.

Chapter 27

SEPTEMBER 2003

I decided that I would definitely quit therapy in the beginning of October, on the day of my two-year anniversary with Dr. Winters. Yet because he'd helped me so much, I didn't want to make the decision based on unresolved rage. While I kept seeing him twice a week, I found myself constantly debating and disputing him. No matter how much I argued with him in my journal, trying to understand his flightiness and scheduling mistakes, I just couldn't get over it. I needed a shrink to figure out what to do about my shrink.

Breaking down what was bothering me, I put the blame on his overly busy schedule, the cause of most of our disputes. It was impossible for him to juggle all of his students, colleagues, and patients while keeping up with his family obligations. That must have reminded me of someone. My father? My workaholic husband? My mother, who had too many kids too fast? Dr. Winters overbooked his life, trying to fill a huge internal void. Who the hell liked to have a hundred different people dependent on them at all times? Oh my God, I did. It occurred to me that *I* was the one he was reminding me of. I had tons of people coming out of my ears. I was a people collector—with colleagues, protégés, editors, writing-work-shop members, needy strangers, friends, and family members calling, faxing, e-mailing, stopping by daily.

When I was freelancing, I worked with as many as twenty or thirty editors at the same time. I'd turned down a bunch of editing and staff-writing jobs because I never wanted to be stuck with one editor, in one office, from nine to five. It was more interesting to stay diverse during the day. By night I'd juggled a hundred students for the last dozen years. One course with twelve students wasn't satisfying enough. I taught three to six classes every semester and gave the heads of my departments permission for my enrollments to exceed the usual limits. I was famous at NYU and New School registrations because my crowded courses filled up so quickly. (It didn't hurt that I'd helped so many of my students publish thousand-dollar pieces, thus covering at least part of their tuition.) I was an award-winning writing teacher; I dug the distinction. Though I didn't have any official appointments or a high salary, being sought after by students made me feel special.

Still, there was a downside to playing the Pied Piper. I recalled a pupil two terms ago who requested office hours and complained when I said I didn't have time. I corrected his rewrites and met with him after class twice but, as an adjunct, I just didn't feel obligated to give him the entire hour during the day that he'd requested. I had my own writing to do. Hell, I had another journalism major the year before who was shattered when—after a ten-week class—I couldn't remember her name.

When I was on deadline for my own writing, I didn't return calls for five days at a time. I'd blown off former protégés who

e-mailed timely essays they expected me to edit. I'd said no to
meeting several kids' parents, and often turned down requests
to write graduate-school recommendations, not to mention
dinner and drink invitations. Staying overloaded, simultaneously engaged in too many areas, I'd inadvertently stepped on
many of my students' feelings. I thought my sharp criticism,
insight, and help made up for my idiosyncrasies and busy
schedule. In reality, I was as arrrogantly overbooked as Dr.
Winters.

"Do you know I have ninety-eight students this term? I was
thinking about why I teach so many crowded classes," I told
him during our Monday afternoon session. "I overbook for
the same reasons you do. To feed some kind of emotional
hole. You know what helps? I know that when I'm insensitive
or hurt them it's not because I'm mean or callous. My inten-
tions are honorable. I'm a kind person, but sometimes I get in
my own way. If I let you be human, I'm letting myself be im-
perfect too."

"So you're going to stop being mad at me?" he asked.

"You're never allowed to cancel on me again," I said, of
course knowing he would. He couldn't help it. He'd be forever overextended; it made him feel important. That's who he
was. Thus it seemed essential to set up a contingency plan. "If
you double-book me, send the other person away, not me. If
it's an emergency, you should offer me the first phone appointment you can, preferably the same day."

"Okay. I'll protect our sessions more," he agreed.

He might have been a chaotic flake, but he was *my* chaotic
flake. Despite his flaws, he'd proven himself worthy of my
trust, fixing things I didn't even know were broken. It amused
me to think that the person saving my life was semiwacko. Yet

shrinks were supposed to have unstable personal lives. That's why they'd become shrinks.

Dr. Winters was the one thing I couldn't quit.

When I left his office, I walked to the Mont Blanc store in Soho and found the sleek silver pen I had picked out for him a few months ago. I'd already endlessly scrutinized all the potential analogies. I wanted to help him finish his addiction book, to teach him the way he'd taught me, to take care of him, to liberate him. Or, since he'd turned me into him, I wanted to turn him into me. Was a pen phallic? Or pregnant?

I asked the saleswoman if they could have it sent to his office the next day. When she agreed, I wrote a card that said, "I don't know how to thank you for everything." Reaching for my American Express, one of his business cards I didn't even know I still had tumbled out and fell to the floor, back side up. Staring at me, in his handwriting, was FEELINGS MISINFORM. Sometimes feelings didn't misinform. It was fall. Elated to be back in my glorious city, I'd sent my mother and father forty-nine white roses for their forty-ninth anniversary. I'd reconciled with several of the colleagues who'd been angry at me. I'd taken a group of former students—including Naomi—out to dinner. After two turbulent years I wanted to be at peace with the world, especially with Dr. Winters. It felt important that I give him the present so he'd know I'd forgiven him.

"I have something to talk to you about" was how he began on Thursday.

"Uh-oh." Did he think my gift was inappropriate? Too expensive? Did he hate it?

"I'm raising your price to one seventy-five a session," he said. You could tell he'd rehearsed the way he'd said it.

"I thought you didn't care about money."

"I didn't say that."

"You want to get rich, like everyone else?" I asked.

"Yes."

I was a nouveau almost-riche capitalist myself. Still, this really bugged me. First, I'd just given him a very overpriced pen and now I felt stupid about it. I knew he'd received it, but he didn't mention it or seem to have any idea how much it meant to me. Beginning our session by raising his price was especially galling because it was September 11. I had all these feelings about being downtown on such an eerie second anniversary. I'd spent the morning and early afternoon commemorating the day my own way, playing melancholy Marvin Gaye music and lighting scented candles. I didn't want to think about his greedy financial agenda. It made it seem like he didn't care about me, that he needed to get paid more to tolerate me.

"Are you raising all of your patients' fees?" I asked. I knew money usually meant something more than money, but I wasn't sure what this time. "Everyone who sees you can afford that much?"

"Most of them already pay more than that," he said.

"Really?" He'd said it before; I still didn't believe him.

"It's a fair price. I've been doing this twenty-five years."

"I didn't say it wasn't a fair price. I just don't think I can afford that much now," I told him. "I got paid for my book last year. I don't think I'll get any more money until it comes out in February."

"I always think therapy should pay for itself," he offered.

"What does that mean?"

"If it's working right, you ask your boss for a raise, get a better job, rearrange your life."

"Well, you're the one who keeps telling me to be realistic and not spend money I don't yet have. I've only grossed fifteen thousand dollars teaching this year. If I see you twice a week I will be spending every cent I make on therapy. Not that you're not worth it. You're worth way more than that," I told him. "Can't you wait to see if I wind up selling a second book?"

"Okay." He let it go. "Let's wait until October."

I wouldn't be able to afford it in October either. Though I'd completed and handed in two more book projects, Dina and Lilly had told me nothing was going to happen soon, that I should sit still and wait until the publication of my memoir in February. Everything would be determined by whether it sold well or garnered good reviews. Everything was so crazy in the publishing world there was a chance that if the book tanked, I might be out in the cold. Whenever I argued that my addiction book was finished, funny, and timely, Dr. Winters told me to shut up, be patient, and listen to Dina and Lilly.

When it was time to go, I stood up. Then he stood up.

"I wanted to thank you for the pen you gave me," he said. "I've never had such a beautiful pen." He looked straight at me when he said it, but he seemed embarrassed. It was difficult for him to accept presents; he was like Aaron that way.

"Seemed like the perfect metaphor," I told him. "From one writer to another."

He smiled. "You're big on metaphors," he said.

On my way home I pondered only seeing Dr. Winters once a week. After all, I was clean, thin, happily married, excited for my book to come out, absolutely fine. Finer than I'd ever been. How much more could one expect from life?

A few blocks from my apartment I stopped at a pay phone to check my messages. There was one from Lilly, letting me know that my editor, Dina, had just made an offer on my addiction book. I was stunned. Then I was proud of myself for rushing to get it done. Perhaps impatience could also be a virtue. I screamed "Yes!" and jumped up and down in the middle of the street. I couldn't believe Dina bought my second book before the first one was even out yet. What a vote of confidence. I wasn't a fluke! The timing seemed fascinating. I could now afford to keep seeing Dr. Winters twice a week. Talk about therapy paying for itself.

Lilly and Dina had transformed the anniversary of the saddest day in the history of New York into the most amazing day I'd ever had. I thought of what my parents would say and how much fun it would be to break the good news to Aaron, Claire, Roger, and all my friends.

I looked in my briefcase, scrounging around for more coins, past my credit cards, FEELINGS MISINFORM, my NYU and New School I.D.s. I only had one quarter left. Who would I call with my last change? It was a no-brainer. I quickly dialed Dr. Winters and left a message for him. I just realized I knew his number by heart.

Back at my apartment, I sat at my desk to make more phone calls. I noticed that one tiny candle on the silver tray was still burning. I was sure I'd blown all of them out when I left, but I hadn't checked a second time to make sure all the little flames were snuffed. I'd been gone for hours. I knew that smokers mindlessly caused a lot of fires, but I'd always been careful to fully put out my cigarettes. Besides, I was a non-smoker now. My aromatherapy candles were supposed to be a healthy replacement for the cigarettes. Maybe Freud was wrong and there was such thing as an accident. On the best day of my life, I had almost burned my apartment down.

Aaron phoned to congratulate me on selling the book; I was looking forward to celebrating in person. That night I put on the black silk teddy he'd given me a few anniversaries before. I usually didn't care what time he worked until, but this time I was annoyed, turning the TV on and off, checking the clock, pacing. I didn't feel physically or emotionally hungry for food. I only wanted my husband. He didn't show up until almost one A.M.

"Why the hell are you so late?" I yelled at him the second he walked in the door.

"I was getting my computer fixed." He put his briefcase down. "Sorry it took so long. That's incredible about your book. We'll have to go out and celebrate. Over the weekend." He looked at me. "Didn't I buy you that nightgown? It looks so good on you."

"Getting your computer fixed until one in the morning? That's the dumbest thing I ever heard."

"It was the only time the techie could come. He works full time. You must have had a great day. I want to hear all about it."

I sat down on the couch and flicked the TV back on. Crossing my arms in front of my chest, I ignored him, deciding not to mention my little mishap with the scented candle that could have destroyed our whole building.

"Can I have a hug?" he asked.

"No. I'm mad at you." I turned off the television and lights, then marched into the bedroom, slipping under the white down covers.

A few minutes later he came in, shut the lights, and crawled into bed next to me. We lay there in silence.

"Dan said I love you more every day," Aaron offered.

I cracked up and rolled on top of him, unable to stop laughing. Or let go.

Chapter 28

OCTOBER 2003

In the dream I knew I'd been off cigarettes for two years. I was waiting at a cheap Italian restaurant; I hated waiting. On my way downstairs to the ladies' room, I saw the cigarette machine. Packs were eighty-five cents. I pulled exact change from my pocket. Though they didn't have my brand, I pushed the latch for Marlboro. When it came out I held the hard red pack in my hands. Instead of ripping off the plastic wrapper and lighting one up like I wanted to, I stopped and realized I couldn't do it. I'd quit smoking. I didn't open them.

I woke up and marveled at how appropriate and timely my dream was. It was October 6, exactly two years of being smoke-free. In the last twenty-four months I'd often lit up in my dreams, but now even my subconscious was insisting I remain smokeless. I looked at the clock. I'd overslept; it was already eleven o'clock. Aaron was gone. He'd taken one of Dr. Winters' hideously early morning sessions.

I went to the living room, where I called in for the news-papers and diet soda, as I usually did. My doorman buzzed when the deli guy arrived twenty minutes later. Though my tab was seven dollars, I gave him a ten and told him to keep the change. After all, it was a special day. I put the soda in the fridge, then turned on my laptop. While waiting, I pulled out all the newspapers. Oddly there was something extra in the brown paper bag the deli guy had delivered. A pack of red Marlboros in a box, just like the ones in my dream. Was it a test from God? It was too odd, like a scene from a David Lynch movie where somebody would wind up murdered and the mistaken cigarette pack would provide the only clue to uncover the crime.

My impulse was to run to the trash compactor in the hall and throw it away. I would have been totally justified. Then I decided that cigarettes were almost six dollars a pack and the delivery guy, who'd probably made the mistake, would get docked for the money. I jumped up, realizing that our eleva-tors were slow and I might be able to catch him. I buzzed my doorman six times.

"What?" he said. It was Gene, the morning guy.

"Gene, did the deli delivery boy leave yet?" I yelled into the intercom.

"Just leaving now."

"Stop him!" I yelled. I was holding the pack in my hands. I wanted it gone. "He gave me the wrong order. There's a pack of cigarettes here."

"He's coming right back up to get them," Gene said.

I waited at the door. As soon as he showed up, I handed him back the pack.

"Thanks. I mixed up the orders." He put them in his pocket. "Sorry for the mistake."

"I didn't want these!" I said. "I quit two years ago!"

I couldn't believe, even after my great dream, that it seemed

like a close call. For a second, holding the box in my hands, I'd
wanted to open them and smoke one. It felt like I'd accidentally bumped into an old lover who remained sexy and allur-
ing. No, I wasn't going for it. Yes, it still hurt a little.

When I arrived at my four o'clock session at ten minutes
after four, Dr. Winters' door was open. Usually it was shut and
I sat in the waiting room until he was ready. This time I just
walked in.

"Don't tell me you've taken over my bad habit of being
late," he said.

"Don't tell me you were actually on time today." It figured
the one day I'd had an important lunch meeting that went a
little longer than expected would be the one time he was
ready for me when he was supposed to be.

"I hate to admit I was," he said.

"Sorry," I said, but I wasn't really. I was glad for once I'd
kept him waiting. I finally had a life. "It's my second anniversary. Today it's two years since I've had a cigarette." I told him
about my dream, the deli mistake, and my new theory about
why I'd almost burned down my apartment right after I sold
my addiction book.

None of it surprised him in the least.

"So how are you feeling now?" he asked.

"Happy. Hyper. A little discombobulated. I can't believe
I'm completely off alcohol, dope, gum, and bread too. Aren't
you surprised I didn't relapse on any of them?"

"Haven't yet relapsed," he said. "You have to stop using
the past tense if you want to stay clean."

"I know I'll stay clean forever." I took out my notebook
and turned to today's page.

"Stop saying forever," he admonished. "If you're one hundred percent sure, you'll start using again. Ninety-nine percent
sure is better."

I thought of my close call that morning, caused by a delivery guy's minor mix-up. "Why is ninety-nine percent sure better? Tell me again."

"Because it shows you understand that you can't have power over everything," he said sternly. "Remember it's a day-to-day challenge."

"Yeah, yeah, yeah, I know. It's just that the equation seems so simple. I'm sure that quitting five substances led to selling two books, losing weight, fixing my marriage, and feeling reborn. On one side are stupid habits. On the other side dreams come true," I said, smiling, light, disheveled, and giddy. "I feel like I've reached all my goals. What's next?"

"Think about what you're beginning," he said.

I flashed to the famous ending of my favorite novel, *Portnoy's Complaint,* when the shrink turns to the antihero and says, "Now vee may perhaps to begin. Yes?"

It felt like I was starting life over happy and clean. How extraordinary that at age forty-two, I was lucky enough to get a chance to begin everything again.

"What do *you* think I'm beginning?" I asked him.

"Character change. Confusion. Uncertainty. Chaos," he answered. "Finding out how the new you fits or doesn't fit into your old life."

"You're a ball of laughs today," I said. "But I think I get what you mean. A lot of things aren't as black and white to me anymore."

"It's all gray now," he confirmed.

"I know. I hate it. It's still hard to go to social events or make plans or go out to dinner. It's hard to be with my friends and family. I'm wishy-washy and can barely make decisions. What's that about?"

"Selflessness versus selfishness," he said. "You feel guilty being selfish."

"When I say no to people and take care of myself first?" I asked.

"Exactly. Keep taking care of yourself first."

"I tell myself that when I'm whole and successful, I have so much more to give everyone."

"I believe that," he said. "I have a metaphor for you. If there's a problem with air pressure on a plane, the flight attendants tell you to put the mask over your own head first, before you help your child. If you put the mask on your child's face first, you could lose consciousness. Then what good would you be?"

"That could just be a rationalization for selfishness," I suggested.

"Could be," he admitted. "But it's a pretty good one."

The image of the plane reminded me of something I'd been meaning to tell him. "Oh, I think I figured out why you travel so much."

"Why?" He sat up and stared at me, looking intrigued.

"You're running away because your work isn't thrilling enough. You're stuck in a rut. You have this innovative, explosive addiction therapy you've developed for decades. It's like you've discovered how to cure cancer, and it works on your patients, but you can't tell the world about it. You're blocked. You helped me finish my book on the subject, but you can't finish your own."

"That sounds right." He looked surprised he hadn't thought of it.

"I used to help everyone get books published, except myself," I said. "I can tell you how to do it."

"How?" he asked.

"Quit traveling and do everything I say," I instructed. "At the end of one year, you'll be over your wanderlust and your book will get published."

He caught that I was imitating him and laughed, though we both knew I wasn't really joking.

"You're right." He picked up his cell phone on the table, looked at it, then put it down again.

"Or I just don't want you to ever leave town," I added.

"I'm going to show you some pages soon. I'm using my ruthless story for the introduction."

No wonder he couldn't finish. "I wouldn't tackle that part now. Why don't you do the scientific section first?"

"Why?" He crossed his legs, then uncrossed them. Why was he so antsy today?

"You told me you regretted going to court when you were twenty, when you went public about your mother's abuse." I turned back through my notebook. I found the exact passage, which I'd underlined. "Your exact words were 'Nobody should testify against their mother,' " I said. "Writing about your mother's alcoholism would be like testifying against her again. I bet that's why you're stuck."

"I have to include that part in my book," he said, disappointed.

"But you still have a fantasy that you and your mother will reconcile, and you're afraid writing about her will ruin it."

He stared at me for a minute, then nodded, looking a little pale. "Something happened."

Aha! I knew I was right. "What?"

"I'd sent my mother chocolates for her birthday, in this beautiful painted box, which had a picture of the New York skyline on it." He was speaking slowly, as if he had to get all the details right. "For the first time in twenty-eight years, she responded. She wrote me a note that said, 'Thank you for the chocolates and the box.' She sent it to my name, in care of my father, who sent it to me. Even though she has my address."

He stood up, went to his desk, and handed me the postcard. On one side was the picture of a garden. The postmark said North Carolina. I turned it around and read the eight words his mother had written, shakily, in black ballpoint pen. No date, no dear, no love, no signature. My mind jumped all over it, like Sherlock Holmes inspecting the clues of a suspicious crime scene. I wondered why she'd sent it to his father. I guessed that she wanted her ex-husband to know that her son had sent her chocolates. Or was there something emasculating in not sending the postcard directly to her fifty-two-year-old son's home, as if he was still a dependent child? More important, how could Dr. Winters have kept this important new development from me?

"When did this happen?" I demanded to know.

"The postcard came three days ago," he said.

"You've been sending her presents for years. What changed this time?" I asked.

"She's eighty-three and sick."

I prayed she'd be like the mother character in *Daniel Deronda*, who felt compelled to make peace with her estranged son before she died. He needed the closure. Hell, at this point, I was so overinvolved with him, *I* needed the closure.

"How did you feel to hear from her?" I handed it back to him.

He gently tucked the postcard into the middle of his leather appointment book and closed it, as if it were a treasured bookmark. "Like a glacier has moved." He was trying to be restrained, but he suddenly seemed younger, boyish, his eyes barely containing his glee and hope.

"Don't fly to see her yet," I warned him.

"Why not?" he asked. "Don't I have to try?"

"What if she slams the door in your face? You can't be a masochist." I recalled a theory he'd told me about how, if given the choice, a child abused by their mother or father would first run to their abuser rather than the good parent.

"I'm going slow," he assured me, as if the matter was already under careful advisement. "I decided on my next move. I'm going to send her a present for Thanksgiving."

"Good, go slow. And you should do the scientific part of

your book first," I told him. "You can write the introduction another time."

"But that's the part of the book I want to write most," he argued inanely.

"You can get to that part later," I said. What a joke, me telling him to be patient, the blind leading the blind.

Before I left, I handed him a check for $175, our new amount. He wrote a note down on the back of yet another business card and handed it to me. It said, "Stay vigilant or you'll get ambushed." I slipped it in the pocket of my brief-case. Compared to his recent emotional upheaval, his giving me another cute little saying seemed quaint, silly even.

On my way home I stopped at Smoochies, the new low-cal ice cream shop on Eighth Street that I'd begun going to a few weeks before. I'd switched the regular frozen yogurt I ate at night for a medium mixed chocolate and vanilla Smoochies, which was only 250 calories. It seemed ingenious, trading twice the amount of food for less calories. I'd checked my weight every day just to make sure that, like the scene in the funny novel *Sheila Levine Is Dead and Living in New York,* they weren't lying about the calories. Nope, I was still 127 pounds. After ordering my regular, I noticed that the special flavor of the day was roasted almond.

"Want to taste?" said the cute, perky young guy behind the counter.

"Sure," I said.

He handed me a tiny spoonful. It was great. "I bet my hus-band would like it," I said. "I'll take a roasted almond too." Aaron usually told me not to bring him home any frozen yo-gurt, because he didn't like to eat anything before bed, so I just got him a small one to taste the new flavor. I had the cheerful counter guy punch my Smoochies card twice. I patted myself on the back for being such a nice wife, worried I was becoming an overfeeder like my mother.

When I had to run out for a chore later that afternoon, I passed by Smoochies one more time. On a whim I decided I liked the roasted almond better than the chocolate and vanilla swirl and worried they might not have that special flavor of the day again. I stopped in and got myself a medium roasted almond to leave in the freezer. When I went to pay, I reached back in my purse to pull out the free-Smoochie card for the guy to punch. (After eight punches you got a free one.) I accidentally pulled out my "Stay vigilant or you'll get ambushed" card instead. Like I needed a reminder of Dr. Winters' adages, which were eternally etched in my brain. I tossed his note in the trash can.

Later that night, watching *Law & Order,* I finished my chocolate and vanilla swirl while Aaron ate his small one.

"It's good, but I'm not that hungry," he said.

He put the leftover half-melted frozen yogurt on the end table. I finished his, then wanted more. At the commercial I snuck to the freezer. Standing there with the door open, I ate the other I'd bought. Aaron walked into the kitchen and caught me.

"You have to quit Smoochies," he yelled. "You're getting addicted."

Oh my God, I was. Damn Dr. Winters and his ambush. Quickly devouring the medium toasted almond, I swore to myself that I'd stop Smoochies cold turkey tomorrow. I'll nip it right in the bud.

ACKNOWLEDGMENTS

I would like to express my deepest gratitude to ...

My fantastic, amazingly perceptive, inspiring editor, Danielle Perez, who once again said "Yes!"

My brilliant, understated agent, Elizabeth Kaplan, who once again e-mailed "this one's not bad."

My colleagues whom I drove crazy daily, including webmaster Eric Shapiro, great P.R. gurus Barb Burg and Susan Corcoran, agents John Ufland and Judy Heiblum, and assistants Shannon Jamieson and Courtney Kenney, who lied daily by saying, "Sure, it's no problem."

My long-term supportive Manhattan friends and mentors Sandy Frazier, Elizabeth Maxwell, Harvey Shapiro, Hugh Seidman, Red Garrison, Judy Manelis, Larry Bergreen, Rina Drucker Root, Matthew Flamm, Karen Salmansohn, Miriam

Chaikin, Ruth Gruber, Harriet and Bill Walden, Helen Stark, Jane and Eliot Wald, and Howard Fast, who for years said, "You can do it."

My eternally loyal gang from Michigan: Karen Sosnick, Cindy Frenkel, Lisa Applebaum, Arlene Cohen, Andrea Miller, Caren Emmer, Timmy, Mike Schwartz, TCBIII, Jody Podolsky, Laura Berman, Amy Nederlander, Gary Rubin, Ronit Pinto, Lynne Schreiber, E. J. Levy, Scott Grant, Judy Burdick, Jack Zucker, and my guardian angel SG, who loved me even when I couldn't do it.

My understanding employers Robert Polito, Michael Zam, Mary Quigley, Laurel Touby, and Taffey Akner, for letting me teach classes as late in the day as possible, downtown, where I'm in total control.

My encouraging fellow writers and editors Julie Just, Margo Hammond, Ivy Landsman, Ryan Harbage, John Strausbaugh, Molly Jong-Fast, Diana Schwabble, Judy D'Mello, Seth Kugel, Leslie Feller, Jake Cooney, Stacey Kramer, Rob Bates, Kristen Kemp, Diane Spear, Harold James, Devan Sipher, Kathryn Stern, Norm Green, Gary Kordan, Alice Phillips, Nicole Bokat, Amy Koppelman, Suzy Hansen, Karen Siplin, Chrissy Perciso, Gerry Cornez, Roberta Bernstein, Jill Hamburg-Coplan, Kate Walter, and Wendy Shanker, who once again read millions of pages.

My magic head shrinker and (not so) secret weapon Dr. W., who once again said, "Don't trust any instinct, you're always wrong."

My sweet, nurturing, long-suffering Midwest *mishpocheh,* who said, "Go ahead, tell the whole world you're still in therapy."

My warm, loving extended family the Kahns, the Zippers, the Brownsteins, and the Greenwalds, who don't care if I'm still in therapy.

My handsome, wise, hysterically funny, perfect husband, CR, who (mistakenly) said "Thank god, you finally wrote a book that I'm not in!"

About the Author

Susan Shapiro has written for the *New York Times,*
Washington Post, Los Angeles Times, Village Voice,
Cosmopolitan, Glamour, Jane, People, and Salon.com.
She's the author of the memoir *Five Men Who Broke*
My Heart, which has been optioned for a movie by
Paramount Pictures, and co-editor of the anthology
Food for the Soul. She lives in Manhattan, where she
teaches at N.Y.U., the New School, and Mediabistro.

Visit her at www.susanshapiro.net.

Susan Shapiro has written for the *New York Times, Washington Post, Los Angeles Times, Village Voice, Cosmopolitan, Glamour, Jane, People,* and Salon.com. She's the author of the memoir *Five Men Who Broke My Heart,* which was optioned for a movie by Paramount Pictures, and coeditor of the anthology *Food for the Soul.* She lives in Manhattan, where she teaches at N.Y.U., the New School, and Mediabistro. Visit her at www

ALSO BY SUSAN SHAPIRO

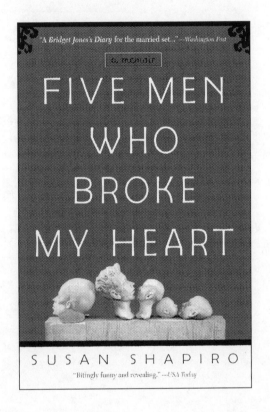

"A *Bridget Jones's Diary* for the married set..." —*Washington Post*

a memoir

FIVE MEN WHO BROKE MY HEART

SUSAN SHAPIRO

"Bitingly funny and revealing." —*USA Today*

Available from Delta

Printed in the United States
by Baker & Taylor Publisher Services